CHILTON'S REPAIR & TUNE-UP GUIDE
SATELLITE ROAD RUNNER 1968-73

Road Runner • Satellite • Belvedere • GTX

Vice President and General Manager JOHN P. KUSHNERICK
Managing Editor KERRY A. FREEMAN, S.A.E.
Senior Editor RICHARD J. RIVELE, S.A.E.
Editor IVER T. ROSENLUND JR.

CHILTON BOOK COMPANY
Radnor, Pennsylvania
19089

SAFETY NOTICE

Proper service and repair procedures are vital to the safe, reliable operation of all motor vehicles, as well as the personal safety of those performing repairs. This book outlines procedures for servicing and repairing vehicles using safe, effective methods. The procedures contain many NOTES, CAUTIONS and WARNINGS which should be followed along with standard safety procedures to eliminate the possibility of personal injury or improper service which could damage the vehicle or compromise its safety.

It is important to note that repair procedures and techniques, tools and parts for servicing motor vehicles, as well as the skill and experience of the individual performing the work vary widely. It is not possible to anticipate all of the conceivable ways or conditions under which vehicles may be serviced, or to provide cautions as to all of the possible hazards that may result. Standard and accepted safety precautions and equipment should be used when handling toxic or flammable fluids, and safety goggles or other protection should be used during cutting, grinding, chiseling, prying, or any other process that can cause material removal or projectiles.

Some procedures require the use of tools specially designed for a specific purpose. Before substituting another tool or procedure, you must be completely satisfied that neither your personal safety, nor the performance of the vehicle will be endangered.

Although the information in this guide is based on industry sources and is as complete as possible at the time of publication, the possibility exists that the manufacturer made later changes which could not be included here. While striving for total accuracy, Chilton Book Company cannot assume responsibility for any errors, changes, or omissions that may occur in the compilation of this data.

PART NUMBERS

Part numbers listed in this reference are not recommendations by Chilton for any product by brand name. They are references that can be used with interchange manuals and aftermarket supplier catalogs to locate each brand supplier's discrete part number.

ACKNOWLEDGMENTS

The Chilton Book Company expresses its appreciation to the Plymouth Division, Chrysler Motors Corporation, Detroit, Michigan, for their generous assistance.

Manufactured in the United States of America
Ninth Printing, June 1983

Chilton's Repair & Tune-Up Guide: Road Runner and Satellite 1968–73
ISBN 0-8019-5821-0 pbk.
Library of Congress Catalog Card No. 73-4347

Contents

1 · General Information and Maintenance

Introduction

In recent years, the growing complexity and expense of maintaining an automobile has created a need for an inclusive guide outlining repair and maintenance operations which may be performed by the do-it-yourselfer. This book, covering the Road Runner since its introduction, and Satellite, Belvedere, and GTX models from 1968, answers the home mechanic's needs.

Road Runner represented Detroit's first entry into the economy supercar market, consisting of a light two-door body with a high-performance 383 cu in. engine coupled to a four-speed manual transmission. Frills and chrome were notable by their absence; the car's objective was maximal performance for minimal cash. For those wanting even more performance, the 426 cu in. Hemi was available as an option. Over the years, Road Runner has evolved from its original all go, no frills concept; however, it still reigns as the standard bearer of Plymouth's performance line.

All post-1967 models of the Satellite are covered. Representing the consumer and family approach to the automotive marketplace, this sporty intermediate offers two-door, four-door, and station wagon body styles.

Car Serial Numbers

1968–73 SERIAL NUMBER LOCATION

The serial number identification plate is located at the top of the instrument panel and is visible through the windshield, between the left windshield wiper pivot and the "A" post.

SERIAL NUMBER INTERPRETATION

All Plymouth serial numbers contain 13 digits. They are interpreted as follows:

1968–69

The first digit designates the car line.
    P—119 in. wheelbase
    R—116 in. wheelbase

The second digit indicates the price class.
    E—Economy
    L—Low
    H—High
    P—Premium
    K—Police
    T—Taxi
    S—Special
    O—Superstock
    X—Fast Top

Model Identification

1968

1969

1970

1971

1972 Satellite

1972 Road Runner

1973 Satellite

1973 Road Runner

The third and fourth digits indicate the body type.

21—two-door sedan
23—two-door hardtop
27—convertible
29—two-door sports hardtop
41—four-door sedan
43—four-door hardtop
45—two-seat station wagon
46—three-seat station wagon

The fifth digit indicates the engine size in cubic inches.

B—225 six
C—Special six
D—273 V8
F—318 V8
G—383 V8
H—383 High-Performance V8
J—426 Hemi V8
K—440 V8
L—440 High-Performance V8
M—Special V8 and/or 1969 440 Six Pack V8

The sixth digit indicates the model year.
8—1968

The seventh digit indicates the assembly plant.

A—Lynch Road
B—Hamtramck
C—Jefferson
D—Belvedere
E—Los Angeles
F—Newark
G—St. Louis
P—Wyoming (Export)
R—Windsor

The remaining digits indicate the vehicle sequential serial number.

1970–71

The first digit indicates the car line.
R—Satellite/Road Runner

The second digit indicates the price class.
E—Economy
L—Low

M—Medium
H—High
P—Premium
K—Police
T—Taxi
S—Special
O—Superstock
N—New York Taxi

The third and fourth digits indicate the body type.
21—two-door sedan
23—two-door hardtop
27—convertible
29—two-door sports hardtop
41—four-door sedan
43—four-door hardtop
45—two-seat station wagon
46—three-seat station wagon

The fifth digit indicates the engine displacement in cubic inches.
C—225 six
E—Special order six
G—318 V8
H—340 V8
L—383 V8
N—383 High-Performance V8
R—426 Hemi V8
T—440 V8
U—440 High-Performance V8
V—440 Six Pack V8
Z—Special order V8

The sixth digit indicates the model year.
1—1971

The seventh digit indicates the assembly plant. These codes and information are the same as for 1968–69 models. The last six digits indicate the vehicle's sequential serial number.

1972-73

The first digit indicates the car line.
R—Satellite/Road Runner

The second digit indicates the price class. No identification is provided by the factory for the following digits: G, H, K, L, M, P, S, T.

The third and fourth digits indicate the body type.
21—two-door sedan
23—two-door hardtop
29—two-door special
41—four-door sedan
43—four-door hardtop

45—two-seat station wagon
46—three-seat station wagon

The fifth digit indicates the engine displacement in cubic inches.
C—225 six
E—Special order six
G—318 V8
H—340 V8
M—400 two-barrel carburetor V8
P—400 four-barrel carburetor V8
T—440 V8
U—440 High-Performance V8
V—440 SixPak V8
Z—Special order V8

The sixth digit indicates the model year.
2—1972

The seventh digit indicates the assembly plant. These codes and information are the same as for 1968–69 models. The last six digits indicate the vehicle's sequential serial number.

ENGINE SERIAL NUMBERS

The serial numbers for all six-cylinder engines are stamped on the joint face of the engine block, next to the no. one cylinder. On 273, 318, and 340 cu in. V8 engines, the numbers are stamped on the front of the engine block, just below the left cylinder head. Serial numbers for the 383, 426, and 440 V8s are stamped on the oil pan rail, below the starter motor opening, at the left rear corner of the engine block. All vehicles equipped with the 400 V8 engine have their serial numbers stamped on the right bank joint face, just ahead of the location of the no. two cylinder.

Until 1972, the engine serial number consisted of fourteen digits. They are interpreted as follows: power train (first and second digits), cubic inch displacement (third, fourth, and fifth digits), whether or not the engine has a low compression ratio (sixth digit), manufacturing date code (seventh through the tenth digits), and production sequence number (eleventh through the fourteenth digits).

The engine coding interpretation was changed in 1972. It is possible that the engine code may contain either 14 or 15 digits. The new coding is read as follows: On six-cylinder engines, and 400 and 440 cu in. V8s, the first letter will designate the model year (series), the next three (the second, third, and fourth digits) will show the engine displacement in cubic inches, the next one or two letters (depending on the engine type) identify the model, the next four numerals give the factory building date code, and the next number shows on which shift the engine was assembled.

On 318 and 340 V8s, the first letter designates the model year, the second the manufacturing plant, the following three (third, fourth, and fifth) the cubic inch displacement, the next one or two (depending on the engine type) designates the model, the next four numerals identify the factory building date code, and the last four mark the engine sequence number.

Special Engine Markings

Oversize and undersize engine components are identified by various marks. These marks may be located on the top, right front engine pads or on the crankshaft counterweights. Moreover, some 383, 400, 426, or 440 cu in. engines may have oversize valve stem markings stamped on the ends of the cylinder head on the untapped boss. For an explanation of the meanings of the various marks, consult your local Plymouth dealership.

TRANSMISSION SERIAL NUMBERS

Manual Transmission

The serial numbers for all manual transmissions are stamped on a pad on the right side of the transmission case. Using PP 833 1861 0275 as an example, the serial number is interpreted as follows: manufacturing plant (first and second letters), transmission model number (third, fourth, and fifth digits), manufacturing date code (sixth through the ninth digits), and production sequence number (tenth through the thirteenth digits).

Manual Transmissions

Type	Model Number	Application
3 speed	A-903	6 cylinder models, 1968–73
3 speed	A-745	8 cylinder models, 1968–69
3 speed	A-230	8 cylinder models, 1970–73
4 speed	A-833	8 cylinder models, 1968–73

Automatic Transmissions

The automatic transmission identification code and serial number are cast in raised letters on the lower left side of the bellhousing.

Automatic Transmissions

Torqueflite Model Number	Application
A-904-G	6 cylinder models, 1968–72
A-904-LA	318 cu in. models (see note)
A-904-A	273 cu in. models, 1968–69
A-727-A	318 and 340 cu in. models
A-727-B	383, 400, 426, and 440 cu in. models

NOTE: 318 cu in. models may be fitted with either A-904-LA or A-727-A transmissions.

Lubrication

The oil in a modern internal-combustion engine serves three basic purposes. Chief among these is the reduction of friction between moving parts. The second purpose is to clean and hold in suspension the various undesirable by-products of the combustion process. In addition, it must trap and hold the particles of dirt that enter the engine accidentally. The third purpose of the lubricant is as a secondary means of cooling. By carrying heat to the oil pan, where this heat is dissipated, the lubricant acts as a secondary cooling system.

FUEL RECOMMENDATIONS

In recent years, Chrysler Corporation has been gradually reducing the compression ratio of all of their engines to enable them to run on unleaded or low-lead regular-grade gasoline in order to reduce vehicle emissions. As all engines and gasolines vary in actual compression ratio and octane rating, follow the recommendations in the factory owners' manual. If the manual is not available, use the rule of thumb that engines with a compression ratio of 9.0:1 (consult the "General Engine Specifications" chart) or higher require premium gasoline; however, if one is using regular gasoline, and the engine performs properly, no advantage will be gained by the use of a higher-octane fuel. Conversely, if the engine is heard to knock or ping, switching to the next higher grade of fuel is called for. If one has been using a regular grade of fuel, and the engine suddenly begins to knock or ping, it is most likely that the engine requires a mechanical adjustment, even though the use of a higher grade of gasoline may temporarily cure the offending noise.

The uninterrupted use of unleaded gasoline in Chrysler Corporation vehicles is not recommended. It is necessary to use one tank in four of leaded gasoline, as valve seat wear may result if this precaution is not taken. All post-1971 Chrysler Corporation vehicles are designed to operate on regular grade gasoline. However, as mentioned above, because gasolines vary in antiknock properties, it may be necessary to change fuels or adjust the engine to enable the vehicle to operate on regular grade gasoline.

ENGINE OIL RECOMMENDATIONS

Engine Oil Selection

For best performance and maximum engine protection, only those lubricants should be used that meet the requirements of the API classification "For Service SD-SE or DG-MS" and are of the proper SAE grade number for the expected ambient temperature range.

Continuous high-speed operation or rapid acceleration requires heavier-than-normal lubricating oil. For best protection under these conditions, the heaviest oil that will permit satisfactory cold-weather starting should be used. SAE 30 and 40 are recommended. Multigrade SAE 20W-40 and 20W-50 oils may also be used.

In normal usage, oil additives are not necessary.

For high-performance engines equipped with one or two four-barrel carburetors or three two-barrel carburetors, it is recommended that one pint of Chrysler Hi-Performance Oil Additive (Sulfurized Ester) be added at every oil change. This additive will provide optimum engine component protection under all operating conditions.

Ambient Temperature	SAE Multigrade
Where temperatures are consistently above 32° F	SAE 20W-40, SAE 10W-40, or SAE 10W-30
For year long operation where temperatures occasionally drop to −10° F	SAE 10W-30 or SAE 10W-40
Single Grades	
Where temperatures are consistently above 32° F	SAE 30
Where temperatures range between +32° F and −10° F	SAE 10W

Oil Changes

Change the engine oil at intervals of three months or 4,000 miles. To accomplish this, run the engine until it reaches operating temperature. Jack the car and place suitable stands beneath the vehicle. Crawl under the car and locate the oil drain plug in the rear of the oil pan. With the aid of either a socket wrench or an open-end/box wrench combination of $\frac{7}{8}$ in., loosen the oil drain plug and allow the oil to drain into a container large enough to hold the entire contents of the crankcase. (See the "Capacities and Pressures" chart.) After the initial surge of oil, wait at least five minutes to allow as much oil as possible to drain from the engine. This slowly dribbling oil contains much of the dirt held in suspension by the lubricant.

Removing the oil filter (Courtesy of Chrysler Corp.)

Replace the drain plug in the pan. Lower the vehicle to the ground. Fill the crankcase with lubricant of the proper viscosity through the oil filler tube on the engine top and start the engine. Check for leaks and turn off the engine. Recheck the oil level and fill as required.

Oil Filter

The engine oil filter should be replaced at every second oil change. Follow the procedures for oil changing and, after the oil has drained from the engine, place an oil filter wrench around the filter as close to the base as possible. Remove the filter. When replacing the filter, be sure to lubricate the oil filter gasket with a small amount of engine oil.

CAUTION: *Hand-tighten the filter. Do not overtighten it.*

Replace the drain plug in the pan and lower the vehicle to the ground. Fill the crankcase with lubricant of the proper viscosity through the oil filler tube on the top of the engine, start the engine, and check for leaks. Turn off the engine, check the oil level, and fill as required.

Oil Checking

After stopping, allow 3–5 minutes to pass to allow oil to drain from the engine down into the crankcase. Pull the dipstick from the engine and wipe the lubricant from the dipstick with a clean, dry rag. Insert the dipstick again. Remove the dipstick once more and observe the level of the oil indicated. If additional oil is necessary, add the appropriate amount through the oil filler tube on top of the engine and check again.

CAUTION: *Be sure not to overfill. Too much lubricant is as troublesome as not enough.*

Routine Maintenance

Proper maintenance is designed to stop trouble before it begins. Following the manufacturer's routine maintenance recommendations to the letter will be rewarded by many miles of trouble-free driving.

AIR CLEANER

The paper element of the air cleaner should be inspected and cleaned every six months and replaced every two years, except on cars fitted with the Fresh Air Induction System. On models so equipped, the filter should be inspected and cleaned at every engine oil change and replaced every year. If the vehicle is driven frequently in dusty or sandy areas, more frequent filter inspections and replacements are recommended.

To remove the air cleaner, disconnect the air cleaner hose at the air cleaner and remove the cleaner from the carburetor. Remove the filter element.

Inspect the filter element. If the filter element is saturated with oil for more than one-half of its circumference, replace the

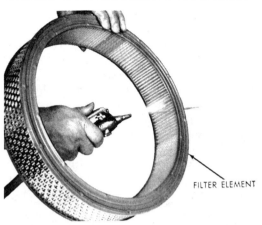

FILTER ELEMENT

Cleaning the air filter element (Courtesy of Chrysler Corp.)

element and check the rest of the crankcase ventilating system for proper functioning.

Clean the filter element with compressed air. Hold the air nozzle at least 2 in. from the inside screen, allowing the air to pass through the filter from the inside. *Do not use compressed air on the outside surface of the element.*

After cleaning, examine the element for punctures and discard it if it shows any pin holes.

Reassemble the air cleaner and install it on the carburetor. Refit the air cleaner hose.

PCV SYSTEM

All vehicles are equipped with a Positive Crankcase Ventilation (PCV) system. An explanation of this system's operation will be found in the "Emission Control" section; for normal maintenance information, adhere to the following procedures at yearly intervals.

1. Warm the engine to operating temperature; be sure the choke is off and the vehicle is at curb idle.

2. Pull the PCV valve from the rocker cover and place a finger over the valve inlet. If it is operating properly, a strong vacuum will be felt.

3. If no vacuum is felt, replace the PCV valve. Remove the crankcase inlet air cleaner from the opposite side of the engine. Hold a piece of stiff paper over the opening in the rocker cover. Wait one minute. If the system is operating properly, the paper should be drawn by the vacuum against the rocker cover opening.

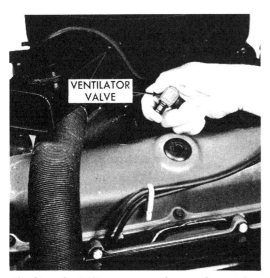

Checking the PCV vacuum at the ventilator valve (Courtesy of Chrysler Corp.)

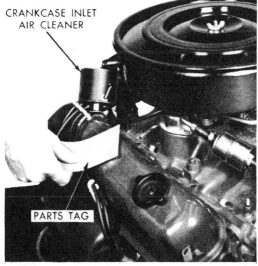

Checking the PCV vacuum at the crankcase inlet air cleaner opening (Courtesy of Chrysler Corp.)

4. Turn off the engine. Remove the PCV valve from the rocker cover as described above. Shake it back and forth; a clicking noise should be heard. If it is not, the PCV valve is inoperable.

5. If any of the tests above are not satisfactory, replace the PCV valve and proceed to the following steps. If the above tests were passed, no further service is required of the PCV system.

6. With a new PCV valve installed, repeat step three above. If the paper is not drawn against the rocker cover, the ventilator hose and the passage in the lower part of the carburetor must be cleaned.

7. Remove the carburetor PCV hose and soak it in a noncorrosive solvent for 15 minutes. It is recommended that it be thoroughly dried with compressed air.

8. Remove the carburetor. (Refer to the carburetor removal procedure in the "Emission Controls and Fuel System" section of this book.)

9. Turn a ¼ in. drill, *by hand only*, through the carburetor PCV passage. It is not necessary to disassemble the carburetor; it may be necessary, however, to use a slightly smaller drill bit to prevent the enlargement of the carburetor PCV passage.

10. Disconnect the crankcase inlet air cleaner hose. Inspect the hose and clean it in the same manner as previously described. Remove the crankcase inlet air cleaner. Thoroughly wash it in a solvent, then wet it slightly with SAE 30 engine oil. Position the air cleaner so that any excess oil will drain through the vent opening.

11. Assemble the components in the reverse order of removal and again test the operation of the PCV system.

EVAPORATIVE CONTROL CANISTER

All 1972 and some earlier vehicles are equipped with an evaporative control canister. For its purpose and operation, refer to the "Emission Control" section; for normal maintenance, see below.

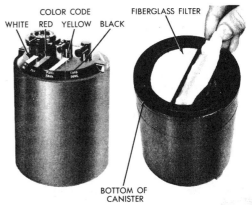

Servicing the evaporative emission control canister (Courtesy of Chrysler Corp.)

The evaporative control canister requires service at intervals of 12 months or 12,000 miles. If the vehicle is driven in dusty areas, the canister may require replacement more often. To service the canister (located in the engine compartment) simply unscrew the bottom and replace the fiberglass filter element.

HEAT RISER SERVICE

A heat riser is a thermostatically controlled valve located below the exhaust manifold, in front of the exhaust pipe inlet. When the engine is cold, the valve closes, directing the exhaust gases upward into the intake manifold. The hot exhaust gases warm a stove in the intake manifold. The intake gases are warmed as they pass over the stove on the way to the combustion chamber. As the engine warms up, the valve opens and allows the exhaust gases to exit out the tailpipe without first passing through the intake manifold.

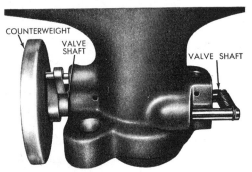

Typical heat riser valve (Courtesy of Chrysler Corp.)

If difficulty is noticed in the warm-up period, or if the car runs lean after it is warmed up, check the heat riser to make sure it turns freely on its axle.

Heat Riser Operation Check

1. Locate the heat riser counterweight.
2. If the valve is operating correctly the weight will rotate freely.
3. If the weight is stuck, soak the axle with penetrating oil and tap it sharply on the end. Do not try to make the weight rotate by tapping it. Do not force the weight; this will only shear the axle.
4. If the weight will still not turn, heat the heat riser with a torch, being very careful not to start a fire. If the weight will not rotate, remove the valve and replace it.

DRIVE BELT SERVICE

Various engine accessories are driven by belts. For proper operation of these accessories, it is necessary that their belts be properly adjusted. Adjustment may be

considered correct when a 5 lb push or pull applied to the point on the belt midway between two accessories results in a ¼ in. deflection. To obtain this value, loosen the accessories' mounting bolts and tighten the belt until the above ¼ in. deflection is obtained.

The condition of the belt is also important. If the belt is glazed or frayed it must be replaced. When checking the condition of a belt, check the entire surface as a belt will often wear badly in only a small section.

FUEL FILTER

All cars are equipped with a fuel filter in the fuel line near the carburetor. These must be replaced every two years or 24,000 miles. To replace the fuel filter, remove the clips holding the filter and rubber tubing in place. Position the new filter and be sure the arrow on the filter points in the direction of fuel flow to the carburetor. Start the engine and check for leaks.

Fuel filter location (Courtesy of Chrysler Corp.)

FLUID LEVEL CHECKS

Manual Transmissions

The manufacturer recommends Dexron type automatic transmission fluid as the proper lubricant in all three-speed and four-speeed manual transmissions. In warm climates, however, the fluid may be drained from the three-speed manual transmissions and the transmission refilled with multipurpose gear lubricant SAE 90.

If excessive gear rattle occurs at idle speed in the A-833 four-speed transmission, the automatic transmission fluid may be drained and the transmission refilled with multipurpose gear lubricant SAE 140.

Automatic Transmissions

Only Dexron type automatic transmission fluid is recommended by the manufacturer for use in all Torqueflite automatic transmissions.

Manual Transmission Lubricant Checking

The lubricant level should normally be checked every six months. If the car is used for towing, or if the transmission is otherwise highly stressed, however, the lubricant level should be checked at intervals of three months or 4,000 miles (every engine oil change).

To check the lubricant level, raise the car on a hoist or other suitable support, crawl under the vehicle, and locate two square-headed screw-in plugs on the side of the transmission. The top plug is the filler plug; the bottom is the drain. Unscrew the top plug and fill the transmission as required until the lubricant level is at the bottom of the filler plug hole. Replace the plug and lower the vehicle.

Capacities

Year	ENGINE No. Cyl. Displacement (Cu In.)	Engine Crankcase Add 1 Qt for New Filter	TRANSMISSION Pts to Refill After Draining			Drive Axle (pts)	Gasoline Tank (gals)	COOLING SYSTEM (qts)	
			Manual 3-Speed	4-Speed	Automatic			With Heater	With A/C
'68	6-225	4	6.5	——	15.5	2	19	13	14
	8-273	4	6	——	15.5	4	19	19	20
	8-318	4	6	——	19.5	4	19	18	19
	8-383	4	6	9	15.5	4	19	17	18
	8-426	6	——	9	15.5	4	19	18	——
	8-440	4	——	9	15.5	4	19	17④	18④
'69	6-225	4	6.5	——	15.5	2	19	13	15
	8-318	4	6	——	15.5	4	19	16	'19
	8-383	4	6	7	18.5	4	19	16	17
	8-383	4	——	7.5	15.5	4	19	16	17
	8-426	6	——	7.5	16	4	19	18	——
	8-440	4	——	7.5	18.5	4	19	17	18
'70	6-225	4	4.75	——	17	2	19	13	15
	8-318	4	4.75	——	16	4	19	16	19
	8-383	4	4.75	——	19	4	19	16	17
	8-383	4	4.75	7.5	16	4	19	16	17

Capacities (cont.)

Year	ENGINE No. Cyl. Displacement (Cu In.)	Engine Crankcase Add 1 Qt for New Filter	TRANSMISSION Pts to Refill After Draining			Drive Axle (pts)	Gasoline Tank (gals)	COOLING SYSTEM (qts)	
			Manual 3-Speed	4-Speed	Automatic			With Heater	With A/C
'70	8-426	6	—	7.5	17	5.5	19	18	—
	8-440	4①	—	7.5	19	5.5	19	17	18
'71	6-225	4	6.5	—	17	4	21	13	13
	8-318	4	4.75	—	17	4	21	16	16.5
	8-340	4	4.75	7.5	16.3	4	21	15	15
	8-383	4	4.75	7.5	16③	4	21	14.5	15
	8-426	6	—	7.5	17	5.5	21	15.5	—
	8-440	4①	—	7.5	19	5.5	21	15.5	17
'72	6-225	4	6.5	—	17	4.5	21	13	14
	8-318	4	4.75	—	17	4.5	21	16	17.5
	8-340	4	—	7.5	16.3	4.5	21	15	15.5
	8-400	4	—	—	19	4.5	21	14.5	15
	8-440	4	4.75	7.5	16.3	4.5	21	14.5	14.5
'73	6-225	4	4.75	—	17	4.5	19.5	13	13
	8-318	4	4.75	7.5	17	4.5	19.5⑥	16	17.5
	8-340	4	—	7.5	16.3	4.5	19.5	15	15.5
	8-400	4	—	7.5	19⑤	4.5	19.5⑥	16	17
	8-440	4	—	—	16.3	4.5	19.5	16.5	16.5

① 3-2 bbl—6 qts
② N.A.
③ 2 bbl—19 pts
④ Hi-Performance option—18 qts; A/C—19 qts
⑤ Satellite w/4 bbl—16.3 pts
⑥ Station wagons—21 gals
— Not Applicable

Automatic Transmission Fluid Checking

Although the fluid level should be checked at regular, six-month intervals in normal service, it is advisable to check the fluid level more frequently, especially if the car is used in competition or for trailer towing.

The fluid level check should be made only when the engine and transmission are at their normal operating temperature. Engage the parking brake and place the selector lever in the neutral position. After the engine has idled for about two minutes, move the selector lever slowly through all the gear positions, pausing momentarily in each and ending with the lever in the neutral position. Open the hood and find the transmission dipstick at the left rear of the engine compartment. Before removing the transmission dipstick, wipe off the cap and the top of the filler tube to prevent dirt from dropping into the filler tube. When the fluid is hot, the fluid level should be at the "full" mark, or slightly below. Add any necessary fluid through the transmission dipstick tube.

Brake Master Cylinder Checking

The brake master cylinder fluid level should be checked every six months. Locate the master cylinder on the driver's side of the firewall in the engine compartment. Before removing the master cylinder cover, wipe it clean to prevent foreign matter from dropping into the master cylinder.

To remove the cover from 1968–70 models, unscrew the retaining bolt, remove the securing clamp, and lift off the cover. For 1971–73 models, move the cover securing clamp to one side and lift off the cover.

If necessary, add brake fluid to within 1/4 in. of the top of the cylinder reservoir. Only brake fluid conforming to SAE requirement J1703 (70R3 type) should be used. Refit the master cylinder cover.

NOTE: *If the car is equipped with front disc brakes, the fluid level can be expected to fall as the brake pads wear. No noticeable drop in fluid level should occur in a car fitted with front drum brakes. A low fluid level may have been caused by a leak and the entire hydraulic system should then be inspected.*

Manual Steering Lubricant Checking

Although regularly scheduled lubricant changes are not necessary, the lubricant level should be checked at six-month intervals. Remove the filler plug from the top rear of the steering gear housing and check to make sure that there is sufficient lubricant to cover the worm gear. If necessary, add SAE 90 multipurpose gear oil and then refit the filler plug.

Power Steering Reservoir Checking

The fluid level in the power steering reservoir should be checked at every engine oil change (every three months or 4,000 miles). Locate the power steering pump in the engine compartment on the driver's side, below the cylinder head and adjacent to the block. Before removing the reservoir cover, wipe the outside of the cover and case so that no dirt can drop into the reservoir.

Check the fluid level when the engine is hot. Remove the reservoir cover. If it has a dipstick, the fluid level should be at the level indicated by the marks on the dipstick. If no dipstick is fitted, the correct fluid level is approximately 1/2–1 in. below the top of the filler neck. If necessary for either reservoir, add power steering fluid. *Do not use automatic transmission fluid.* Replace the reservoir cover.

Rear Axle Lubricant Checking

The rear axle lubricant level should be checked at every engine oil change (every three months or 4,000 miles). To check the level, jack the car and remove the axle filler plug. The correct lubricant level for each axle is indicated in the "Rear Axle Identification Chart." The manufacturer recommends that only multipurpose gear

Rear Axle Identification Chart

Axle Size (ring gear diameter)	Filler Location	Cover Fastening	Capacity (pints)	Lubricant Level
7¼	Cover	9 bolts	2.0	Bottom of filler hole to 5/8 in. below
8¼	Carrier right side	10 bolts	4.4	From 1/8 in. below filler hole to 1/4 in. below
8¾	Carrier right side	Welded	4.4	Maintain at bottom of filler hole
9¼ *	Cover *	10 bolts	4.0	Bottom of filler hole to 1/2 in. below
9¾	Cover	10 bolts	5.5	Bottom of filler hole to 1/2 in. below

* Used 1968 and 1969 models only

lubricant which meets the API GL-5 requirements to be used in both conventional and Sure-Grip differentials. Gear lubricant viscosity depends on the anticipated ambient temperature.

Anticipated Temperature Range	Viscosity Grade
Above 10° F	SAE 90
As low as —30° F	SAE 80
Below —30° F	SAE 75

If it is determined that the rear axle requires lubricant, add the appropriate amount and refit the filler plug. Lower the vehicle.

Cooling System Service

The coolant level in the radiator should be checked at monthly intervals. Because all cooling systems are pressurized, it is recommended that the engine be totally cold before proceeding. Find the radiator pressure cap at the top of the radiator. Turn the cap with a clean rag until it reaches its safety stop. If any pressure is noted escaping, allow ALL the pressure to escape before turning the cap any further. When the pressure has escaped, remove the cap. Visually check the radiator; if water is required, add as necessary to bring the coolant level to within 1¼ in. of the top of the radiator filler neck. Refit the pressure cap. Because all cooling systems have an overflow tube, some coolant may be noted on the ground for the first few days after the radiator has been filled. This is normal, and no cause for alarm.

In the Fall of the year, the cooling system antifreeze must be renewed. It is also recommended that the cooling system be flushed at this time. To accomplish this,

bring the vehicle to operating temperature, locate the petcock on the bottom of the radiator, and allow the coolant to drain. It is also recommended, though not mandatory, that the block also be drained. To do this, locate the drain plugs near the bottom of the cylinder block on the side. Unscrew and remove the plugs. If a commercial cooling system cleaner is to be used, follow the directions given. If not, run water through the radiator until the water coming out is clean. Close the radiator petcock and install the proper quantity of ethylene glycol antifreeze to make sure that the vehicle will not freeze in the lowest anticipated temperature. Top up the radiator with water and start the vehicle. Turn the vehicle's heater and blower motor to the maximum output position. If the car is equipped with air conditioning, place it in the "heat" position. Allow the vehicle to reach operating temperature. Watch the water level in the radiator closely and add as necessary. After the vehicle is thoroughly warmed, refit the radiator cap and road-test the car.

TIRE CARE

In order to obtain the most uniform tread wear, your vehicle's tires should be rotated no later than every other oil change. Examine the tires at this time for unusual wear patterns. Erratic wear can be the result of improper inflation, improper front end alignment, poor balance or worn suspension parts. Do not mistake the tread wear indicators or bars molded into the bottom of the tread grooves as indicative of mechanical problems; when these ½ in. wide staggered bars appear, tire replacement is in order.

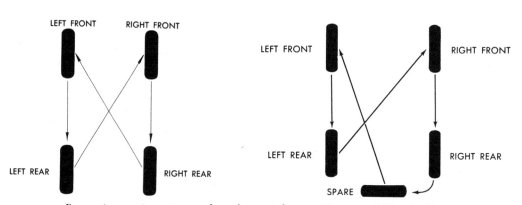

Proper tire rotation pattern and tread wear indicators (Courtesy of Chrysler Corp.)

A decal showing the recommended tire pressure and size for your vehicle is located on the rear body pillar on the left front door. Proper pressure, balance, and size are important to both tread life and safety. It should be noted that the original balance of the tire and wheel are gradually lost as the tires wear; balance is also lost after a tire has been repaired. If the vehicle is to be driven at speeds over 75 mph, increase the tire inflation pressure four psi over the normally recommended figure. However, in no case should inflation be increased over 32 psi for load range B tires. If the sticker on the car's body recommends a pressure differential between front and rear, it must be maintained.

When replacing your vehicle's tires, radial ply types may be selected; however, they must be used in sets of five and must never be mixed on a vehicle with tires of other than radial construction. Always select the recommended size radial.

If it becomes necessary to store your vehicle's tires, place them on their sidewalls on a flat surface. Permanent flat spotting can result if the tires are stored standing on their treads. If the tires are to be stored while mounted, inflation pressures should be reduced to 12–16 psi. Keep the tires away from water, oil, gasoline, electric motors (ozone), and heat.

BATTERY CARE

Your battery should be checked at monthly intervals for proper water level and terminal cleanliness.

To add water to the battery, remove the caps from each battery cell. Visually check the water level of each cell, and add *distilled water* to bring the level to approximately 3/8 in. above the top of the battery plates. Refit the battery caps.

NOTE: *If the temperature is below freezing, the vehicle must be driven several miles to thoroughly mix the water and battery electrolyte; otherwise, battery failure may result.*

To ensure good electrical connections, the battery cables and terminals must be free of corrosion. To clean them, prepare a solution of baking soda and water. Taking note of their positions, remove the battery cables with either a wrench or a battery cable puller. Apply the baking soda solution to the cables and terminals.

NOTE: *Be careful not to drip the baking soda solution into the battery cells. It will neutralize the batteries' acid and cause failure.*

Remove any corrosion with a stiff wire brush and a clean, dry rag. To prevent further corrosion, obtain a bottle of petroleum jelly or a commercial battery grease and apply it heavily to the cables and terminals. Connect the battery (be sure to replace the cables to their original terminals), and to ensure good electrical contact, road-test the vehicle.

NOTE: *Further battery information may be found in the "Tune-Up and Trouble-shooting Diagnosis" section.*

Pushing, Towing, and Jump Starting

If the vehicle is equipped with an automatic transmission, the car cannot be started by pushing. If the car is equipped with a manual transmission, place it in high gear, turn on the ignition, and depress the clutch. When car speed reaches 10 mph, release the clutch slowly.

If the vehicle must be towed, place the transmission in neutral. The towing distance/speed should not exceed 15 miles and 30 mph. If the transmission is not working, or the vehicle must be towed in excess of 15 miles, the driveshaft must be disconnected, or the rear wheels should be raised from the highway. If the towed vehicle requires steering control, place the steering lock (if so equipped) in the off position. If the windshield wipers, or other accessories, must be used while towing, turn the ignition key to the on position. If no ignition key is available for a vehicle equipped with a steering lock, a dolly must be placed under the rear wheels. In addition, the front wheels must be raised from the ground.

When jump-starting a vehicle, it is important to remember to connect the positive battery terminals together. The negative terminals should be connected in the same manner. Otherwise, serious electrical system damage can result.

Lubricant Changes

Rear Axle

Regular changes of the rear axle lubricant, for both standard and Sure-Grip differentials, are not recommended by the factory with the following exceptions: If the lubricant has become contaminated with water (water can enter the differential through the axle vent should the rear axle be submerged), or if the anticipated ambient temperature is much lower than average, as shown in the rear axle recommended lubricant chart.

To drain the axle, raise the car on a hoist and remove the filler plug. For 7¼, 8¼, and 8¾ in. axles, use a pump to siphon the oil lubricant from the axle. For the 9¼ and 9¾ in. axle, position a container under the differential, remove the drain plug from the bottom of the differential and drain the lubricant into the container. Refit the drain plug.

Fill the axle with the proper grade lubricant to the level indicated in the identification chart. Refit the filler plug and lower the car.

Manual Transmission

Although the manufacturer does not specifically recommend periodic lubricant changes in normal service, it is suggested that the lubricant be changed at regular intervals of 36,000 miles. Regularly scheduled lubricant changes are especially recommended if the car is used in competition or to tow a trailer.

To drain the lubricant, raise the car on a hoist or jack the front of the car and support it with suitable stands. Remove the filler plug from the right side of the transmission case. For A-745, A-230, and A-833 transmissions, position a container below the drain plug, located on the right side of the transmission case, and remove the plug, allowing the lubricant to drain into the container. A suction gun must be used on the A-903 transmission to siphon the old lubricant through the filler plug hole.

After draining, replace the drain plug and fill the transmission with the proper lubricant to the correct level. Refit the filler plug and lower the car.

Automatic Transmission

The automatic transmission fluid need not be changed for most models in normal service. For vehicles used in abnormal service, and for an extra measure of protection, fluid should be changed at 36,000 mile intervals. If the vehicle is used in competition or for trailer towing, it is recommended that the fluid be changed at 12,000 mile intervals.

In addition, Chrysler recommends that the bands be adjusted at the time of transmission draining, refilling, and filter service. To perform the above operations, please refer to the "Automatic Transmission" section.

To drain the transmission fluid, raise the car on a hoist or jack up the front of the car and support it with stands. Place a container, which has a large opening, under the transmission oil pan. Loosen the pan bolts at one corner, tap the pan to break the seal, and allow the fluid to drain. Remove the oil pan and filter. Remove the access plate from in front of the torque converter. With the aid of a socket wrench on the vibration damper bolt, rotate the engine clockwise to bring the converter drain to the bottom. Position the container under the converter, withdraw the drain plug, and allow the fluid to drain.

Refit the converter drain plug and torque it to 100 in. lbs. Install the access plate. Place a new filter on the bottom of the valve body and tighten the retaining screws to 35 in. lbs. Clean the oil pan, fit a new gasket, and install the assembly. Torque the pan bolts to 150 in. lbs. Remove the container and lower the car.

Fill the transmission with 6 qts of Dexron automatic transmission fluid. Start the engine and allow it to idle for at least two minutes. With the parking brake engaged, move the selector lever momentarily to each position, ending in the neutral position. Add enough fluid to bring the level to the "add one pint" mark on the dipstick. Road-test the vehicle to thoroughly warm up the transmission and recheck the fluid level with the engine idling and the parking brake engaged, after the transmission is at its normal operative temperature. The fluid level should then be between the "full" and "add one pint" marks.

CAUTION: *To prevent dirt from entering the transmission, be sure that the dipstick cap is fully seated onto the filler tube.*

Chassis Greasing

All Chrysler vehicles are equipped with nine ball joints or end fittings in the front suspension and steering system. They should be inspected for wear and damage twice yearly, and lubricated every 18,000 miles, for vehicles used in severe service, or 36,000 miles for vehicles used in normal service. For information on checking ball joint wear, please refer to the "Front Suspension" section. For lubrication procedures, see below.

1. With a clean rag, wipe all road dirt from the ball joint seal or end fitting.

2. Take the threaded plug from the ball joint and install a grease fitting (if applicable).

3. Fill the joint or fitting with lubricant. The joint is filled when grease freely flows

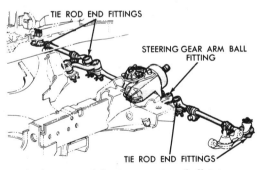

Typical steering lubrication points (ball joints not shown) (Courtesy of Chrysler Corp.)

from the bleed area at the base of the seal or fitting, or the seal begins to balloon. If high-pressure lubrication equipment is being used, be sure not to burst the seal.

Jacking and Hoisting

Jack the car at the front lower control arms and at the rear, under the axle housing. To lift at the frame, use adaptors so that contact will be made at the points shown. The lifting pads must extend beyond the sides of the supporting structure.

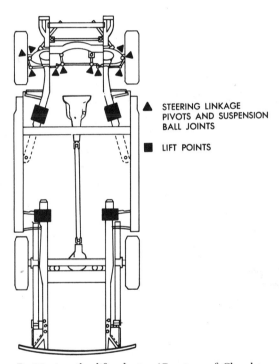

▲ STEERING LINKAGE PIVOTS AND SUSPENSION BALL JOINTS

■ LIFT POINTS

Positioning the lift adaptor (Courtesy of Chrysler Corp.)

Lubrication and Maintenance Schedule
1968–71

Service Interval	Item	Replace	Check Fluid Level	Inspect and/or Clean	Lubricate	Service
Every month	Battery		X			
	Cooling system		X			
3 months or 4,000 miles, whichever occurs first	Engine crankcase oil	X				
	Transmission		X			
	Rear axle		X			
	Universal joints			X		
Every engine oil change	Manifold heat control valve					X
	Power steering fluid		X			
	Carburetor air filter—paper					X
Every second oil change	Engine oil filter	X				
	Tire rotation					X
Every 6 months	Carburetor air filter—paper			X		
	Crankcase ventilation system			X		X
	Carburetor choke shaft			X		X
	Crankcase inlet air cleaner			X	X	
	Transmission		X			
	Rear axle		X			
	Steering gear (manual)		X			
	linkage			X		
	Suspension ball joints			X		
	Universal joints			X		
	Brake master cylinder		X			
	Brake hoses			X		
	Headlight aiming					X
	Hood latch and safety catch			X	X	
Every 12 months	Cooling system					X
	Crankcase ventilator valve	X				
	Carburetor air filter—paper	X				
	Throttle linkage				X	
Every 12 months or 12,000 miles, whichever occurs first	Engine performance evaluation					X
	Brakes			X		
	Front wheel bearing lubricant			X		
Every 24 months or 24,000 miles, whichever occurs first	Carburetor air filter	X				
	Fuel filter	X				
	Brake pedal linkage bushing			X	X	
Every 36 months or 36,000 miles, whichever occurs first	Front suspension ball joints				X	
	Steering tie rod ends				X	
	Clutch torque shaft bearings				X	
	Transmission fluid	X				
	Automatic transmission filter	X				
	Automatic transmission bands					X
	Rear axle lubricant	X				
When necessary	Distributor				X	
	Body mechanisms				X	

Lubrication and Maintenance Schedule (cont.)
1968–71

Service Interval	Item	Replace	Check Fluid Level	Inspect and/or Clean	Lubri- cate	Service
When necessary	Clutch drive lugs, release bearing sleeve, fork fingers and pivot				X	
	Column-mounted gearshift linkage				X	
	Floor-mounted gearshift controls				X	
	Parking brake mechanism				X	
	Speedometer cable				X	

Lubrication and Maintenance Schedule
1972–73

Service Interval	Item	Replace	Check Fluid Level	Inspect and/or Clean	Lubri- cate	Service
Every month	Battery		X			
	Cooling system		X			
3 months or 4,000 miles, whichever occurs first	Engine crankcase oil	X				
Every engine oil change	Power steering fluid		X			
	Carburetor air filter *			X		
Every second oil change	Engine oil filter	X				
	Tire rotation					X
Every 6 months	Carburetor choke shaft			X		X
	Manifold heat control valve					X
	Transmission		X			
	Rear axle		X			
	Gear (manual)		X			
	Steering linkage			X		
	Suspension ball joints			X		
	Universal joints			X		
	Brake master cylinder		X			
	Brake hoses			X		
	Headlight aiming					X
	Hood latch and safety catch			X	X	
Every 12 months	Carburetor air filter			X		
	Carburetor air filter *	X				
	Cooling system					X
	Crankcase ventilation system			X		X
	Crankcase inlet air cleaner			X		X
	Throttle linkage				X	
Every 12 months or 12,000 miles whichever occurs first	Brakes **			X		X
	Exhaust gas floor jet ***			X		
	Front wheel bearing lubricant			X	X	
	Fuel vapor storage canister					X

Lubrication and Maintenance Schedule (cont.)
1972–73

Service Interval	Item	Replace	Check Fluid Level	Inspect and/or Clean	Lubri-cate	Service
Every 18,000 miles	Spark plugs	X				
First 24,000 miles	Exhaust gas floor jet			X		
Every 24 months or 24,000 miles, whichever occurs first	Carburetor air filter—paper	X				
	Crankcase ventilator valve	X				
	Distributor				X	X
	Fuel filter	X				
	Brake pedal linkage bushings				X	X
Every 36 months or 36,000 miles, whichever occurs first	Front suspension ball joints				X	
	Steering tie rod ends				X	
	Clutch torque shaft bearings				X	
When necessary	Body mechanisms				X	
	Clutch release bearing sleeve, fork fingers and pivot				X	
	Column-mounted gearshift linkage				X	
	Floor mounted gearshift controls				X	
	Parking brake mechanism				X	
	Speedometer cable				X	

   * Vehicles equipped with Fresh Air Induction System
   ** Replace lining if necessary
   *** After first 24,000 miles

Trailer Towing And/Or Severe Service
1968–73

Service Interval	Item	Replace	Check Fluid Level	Inspect and/or Clean	Lubri-cate	Service
Every 3 months or 4,000 miles, whichever occurs first	Brake hose and tubing			X		
	Transmission		X			
	Rear axle		X			
	Universal joints			X		
Every 36,000 miles	Manual transmission fluid	X				
	Rear axle lubricant	X				
	Universal joints					X
Every 24,000 miles	Automatic transmission fluid, filter and band adjustment	X				X

2 · Tune-Up and Troubleshooting

Tune-Up Procedures

SPARK PLUGS AND WIRING

Clean any foreign material from around the spark plugs prior to removing them. Use a spark plug socket with a rubber insert to remove the plugs. This will prevent cracking the porcelain insulator. Each spark plug should be individually inspected and, if necessary, replaced. Refer to the spark plug diagnosis section for an analysis of plug tip conditions. Clean reusable spark plugs and file the center electrode flat.

Set the electrode gap by bending the outside electrode to the proper clearance. Never bend the center electrode.

Spark plugs should not be reset more than once because the center electrode wears back toward the insulator.

Carefully install each spark plug and tighten each to 30 ft lbs. When installing new spark plugs on a slant-six engine, do not use the metal gaskets supplied with the plug. If a rubber gasket is used on the spark plug, replace it with a new gasket when installing new plugs.

Label each spark plug cable and its corresponding terminal on the distributor cap according to the number of the cylinder to which it is connected. Remove the cables and clean them with a kerosine-moistened cloth. Wipe the cables dry and inspect them for brittle, cracked, gummy, or otherwise deteriorated insulation. Defective or old wiring should be replaced because it may cause engine misfires and/or cross-firing. Inspect and clean wire terminals, spark plug terminals, and distributor cap sockets to ensure perfect electrical contact.

BREAKER POINTS AND CONDENSER

Removal and Installation, Adjustment

Single-Point Distributor

Use the procedure described below to remove, install, and gap a single-contact point set.

1. Pull back the spring clips and lift off the distributor cap. Pull off the rotor.

Mechanical Valve Lifter Clearance

Year	Engine	Intake (Hot) In.	Exhaust (Hot) In.
1966–1973	All 6 cylinders	0.010	0.020
1966–1967	273 V8	0.013	0.021
1966	318 V8	0.013	0.021
1966–1969	426 Hemi	0.028(Cold)	0.032(Cold)

Tune-Up Specifications

When analyzing compression test results, look for uniformity among cylinders rather than specific pressures.

Year	ENGINE No. Cyl Displacement (cu in.)	hp	SPARK PLUGS Type §	Gap (in.)	DISTRIBUTOR Point Dwell (deg)	Point Gap (in.)	IGNITION TIMING (deg) ▲● Man Trans	Auto Trans	Valves Intake Opens (deg) ■	Fuel Pump Pressure (psi)	IDLE SPEED (rpm) ▲● Man Trans	Auto Trans
'68	6-225	145	N-14Y	0.035	43	0.029	5B(TDC)	5B(TDC)	10	3½–5	550(650)	550(650)
	8-273	190	N-14Y	0.035	31	0.017	5A	2½A	10	5–7	700	650
	8-318	230	N-14Y	0.035	31	0.017	5B(5A)	10B(2½)A	10	5–7	500(650)	500(600)
	8-383	290	J-14Y	0.035	31	0.017	TDC	7½B	18	3½–5	650	600
	8-383	330	J-11Y	0.035	31	0.017	TDC	5B	18	3½–5	650	650
	8-383	335	J-11Y	0.035	31	0.017	TDC	5B	21	3½–5	650	650
	8-426	425	N-10Y	0.035	30①	0.017	TDC	TDC	36	7–8½	750	650
	8-440	375	J-11Y	0.035	31①	0.017	TDC	5B	21	6–7½	650	650
'69	6-225	145	N-14Y	0.035	45	0.020	TDC	TDC	10	3½–5	700	650
	8-318	230	N-14Y	0.035	33	0.017	TDC	TDC	10	5–7	700	650
	8-383	290	J-14Y	0.035	33	0.017	TDC	7½B	18	3½–5	700	600
	8-383	330	J-11Y	0.035	33	0.017	TDC	5B	18	3½–5	700	650
	8-383	335	J-11Y	0.035	30①	0.017	TDC	5B	21	3½–5	700	650
	8-426	425	N-10Y	0.035	30①	0.017	TDC	TDC	36	7–8½	800	800

Year	Engine											
'70	8-440	375	J-11Y	0.035	33②	0.017	TDC	5B	21	6-7½	700	650
	6-225	145	N-14Y	0.035	44	0.020	TDC	TDC	10	3½-5	700	650
	8-318	230	N-14Y	0.035	32	0.017	TDC	TDC	10	5-7	750	700
	8-383	290	J-14Y	0.035	30	0.018	TDC	2½B	18	3½-5	750	650
	8-383	330	J-11Y	0.035	30	0.018	TDC	2½B	18	3½-5	750	750
	8-383	335	J-11Y	0.035	30	0.018	TDC	2½B	21	3½-5	750	750
	8-426	425	N-10Y	0.035	30①	0.017	TDC	5B	36	7-8½	900	900
	8-440	375	J-11Y	0.035	30	0.018	TDC	2½B	18	3½-5	900	800
	8-440	390	J-11Y	0.035	30①	0.017	5B	5B	21	6-7½	900	900
'71	6-225	145	N-14Y	0.035	44	0.020	TDC(2½B)	TDC(2½B)	16	3½-5	750	750
	8-318	230	N-14Y	0.035	32	0.017	TDC	TDC	10	5-7	750	700
	8-340	275	N-9Y	0.035	33②	0.017	5B	5B	22	5-7	900	900
	8-383	275	J-14Y	0.035	30	0.018	TDC	2½B	18	3½-5	750	700
	8-383	300	J-11Y	0.035	30	0.018	TDC	2½B	21	3½-5	900	800
	8-426	425	N-10Y	0.035	30①	0.017	TDC	2½B	36	7-8½	950	950
	8-440	370	J-11Y	0.035	30	0.018	TDC	2½B	18	3½-5	900	800
	8-440	385	J-11Y	0.035	30①	0.017	12½B	12½B	21	6-7½	900	900
'72	6-225	110	N-14Y	0.035	44	0.020	TDC	TDC	16	3½-5	750(700)	750(700)

Tune-Up Specifications (cont.)

When analyzing compression test results, look for uniformity among cylinders rather than specific pressures.

Year	ENGINE No. Cyl Displacement (cu in.)	hp	SPARK PLUGS Type §	Gap (in.)	DISTRIBUTOR Point Dwell (deg)	Point Gap (in.)	IGNITION TIMING (deg) ▲● Man Trans	Auto Trans	Valves Intake Opens (deg) ■	Fuel Pump Pressure (psi)	IDLE SPEED (rpm) ▲● Man Trans	Auto Trans
'72	8-318	150	N-13Y	0.035	32	0.017	TDC	TDC	10	5-7	750	750(700)
	8-340	240	N-9Y	0.035	Electronic		2½B	2½B	22	5-7	900(850)	750
	8-400	190	J-13Y	0.035	30	0.018	—	5B③	18	3½-5	—	700
	8-400	255④	J-11Y	0.035	Electronic		TDC(2½B)	10B(5B)	21	3½-5	900(800)	750
	8-440	290	J-11Y	0.035	Electronic		2½B	10B(5B)	21	3½-5	900(800)	900
'73	6-225	105	N-14Y	0.035	Electronic		TDC	TDC	16	4-5½	750	750
	8-318	150	N-13Y	0.035	Electronic		2½B	TDC	10	6-7½	750	700
	8-340	240	N-9Y	0.035	Electronic		5B	2½B	22	6-7½	850	850
	8-400	175	J-13Y	0.035	Electronic		—	10B	18	4-5½	—	700
	8-400	260	J-11Y	0.035	Electronic		2½B	10B	21	4-5½	900	850
	8-440	275	J-11Y	0.035	Electronic		—	10B	21	4-5½	—	800

▲ See text for procedure
● Figure in parentheses indicates California engine
■ All figures Before Top Dead Center
§ All spark plug listings are Champion original equipment numbers
① Adjust each set of points to this figure. With both sets connected, the total reading should be 40 degrees.

② For vehicles with manual transmission, adjust each set of points to 30 degrees. With both sets connected, the total reading should be 40 degrees.
③ For non-California vehicles built after February 2, 1972, adjust ignition timing to 7½ degrees Before Top Dead Center.
④ For non-California vehicles equipped with Fresh Air Packs, figure is 265 hp.
A After Top Dead Center
B Before Top Dead Center
TDC Top Dead Center
—— Not applicable

2. Loosen the terminal screw nut and remove the primary and condenser leads.

3. Remove the stationary contact lock-screw and remove the contact point set.

4. Remove the condenser retaining screw and lift out the condenser.

5. Install the new condenser and tighten its retaining screw.

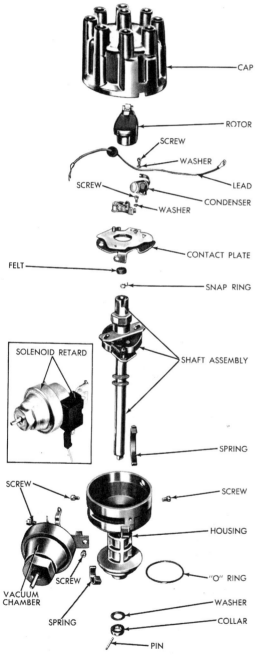

Chrysler V8 distributor (Courtesy of Chrysler Corp.)

6. Install the new point set but do not fully tighten its lockscrews.

7. Connect the condenser and primary leads.

8. If necessary, align the contacts by bending the stationary contact bracket only. *Never bend the movable contact arm to correct alignment.*

9. Attach a remote starter switch to the electrical system according to the switch manufacturer's instructions. Use this switch to crank the engine, rotating the distributor cam until the rubbing block of the movable contact arm rests on a peak of the cam lobe. If no remote starter switch is available, the same result may be obtained by gently tapping the ignition key to allow the starter to rotate the engine only a small amount. Adjust the points as above.

10. Insert the proper thickness feeler gauge between the contact points. If necessary, increase or decrease the gap by inserting a screwdriver in the "V" notch of the stationary contact base and using the screwdriver to move the stationary contact.

11. Tighten the lockscrew and recheck the gap setting. Reset if necessary.

12. Install the new rotor and refit the distributor cap. Check the point dwell.

DUAL-POINT DISTRIBUTOR

Removal and installation of dual contact points is the same as for single point set. However, adjustment of dual points is slightly different because one set of contacts must be blocked open with a clean insulator while the opposite points set is adjusted to specifications, using the single-point set adjustment procedure. When adjusted correctly, tighten the lockscrew. Block open this contact set and adjust the other set in the same manner as for the first. Check the point dwell. If the contacts have been installed and adjusted correctly, the dwell angle should be as specified for both contact sets.

DWELL ANGLE AND POINT GAP

Dwell angle is the number of degrees the distributor shaft rotates while the points are closed. The dwell angle is a function of the point gap. Increasing the point gap decreases the dwell angle, and decreasing the point gap increases the dwell angle. The dwell angle may be set with a feeler gauge as described in the

Breaker Point R & R procedure, however the use of a dwell meter is much more accurate.

The proper dwell angle is important because it determines the intensity of the spark at the spark plug if everything else in the ignition system is functioning properly.

NOTE: *The dwell angle must be set before the ignition timing is adjusted.*

If the contact points have been installed and gapped correctly the dwell angle should be within specifications.

1. Connect the dwell meter leads to the distributor terminal of the coil and ground.

2. Start the engine and run it at idle speed.

3. Note the dwell meter reading. If it is not within specifications, the point gap is incorrect. Readjust the contact points and recheck the dwell. Be sure that the correct point set has been installed.

Dwell Variation Checking

Excessive wear of the distributor mechanical parts may cause variations in dwell that affect ignition timing. The following is the procedure for a dwell variation test. A *good* quality dwell meter must be used for this test.

1. Disconnect the vacuum line at the distributor, connect the dwell meter, and run the engine at its idle speed.

2. *Slowly* increase engine speed to 1,500 rpm, and then slowly reduce to idle speed while noting the dwell meter reading.

If the dwell reading varies more than two degrees, wear in the distributor shaft, bushings, or breaker plate is probably excessive. The distributor will have to be removed for a complete inspection and test.

NOTE: *Dwell variation at speeds above 1,500 rpm does not necessarily indicate distributor wear.*

IGNITION TIMING

Ignition timing must be checked only when the engine is hot and running at its correct idle speed. Dwell angle or point gap *must* be set *before* ignition timing is checked.

1. Clean the timing indicator and the circumference of the vibration damper. Paint the correct timing mark on the indicator and the timing mark on the damper with white or luminescent (day-glo) paint.

2. Disconnect the vacuum line at the distributor.

3. Connect a stroboscopic timing light to no. 1 spark plug lead.

4. Start the engine and adjust the idle speed to specification with the *transmission in neutral.*

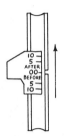

Timing marks—6 cyl. models (Courtesy of Chrysler Corp.)

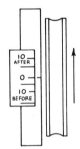

Timing marks—V8 models (Courtesy of Chrysler Corp.)

5. Loosen the distributor hold-down screw so the housing can be rotated.

6. Check the ignition timing by aiming the strobe light at the timing indicator and the vibration damper. If the timing is correct, the painted mark on the damper will appear opposite the painted timing indicator mark. If necessary, advance or retard the timing by rotating the distributor housing, until the correct timing is obtained.

7. Tighten the distributor hold-down screw and recheck the timing. Connect the vacuum line. Stop the engine and disconnect the timing light.

Electronic Ignition System

An electronic ignition system is either optional or standard equipment depending on the model prior to 1973. It is standard for all 1973 models. This type of ignition allows the points to be eliminated; consequently, there is no dwell adjustment. The only regular maintenance required is inspection of the wiring, spark plug re-

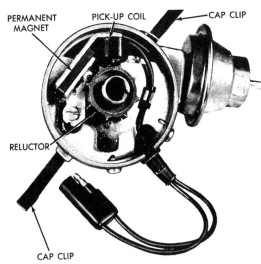

PERMANENT MAGNET

PICK-UP COIL

CAP CLIP

RELUCTOR

CAP CLIP

Internal view of the electronic ignition distributor (Courtesy of Chrysler Corp.)

placement timing adjustment, and inspection of the distributor cap.

To determine whether a car is equipped with electronic ignition, check for a double primary lead from the distributor, a dual ballast resistor located on the firewall, and a control unit located either on the left wheel housing or the firewall.

If the electronic ignition is not functioning properly, it is suggested that your local Plymouth dealer be consulted.

VALVE LASH

Adjustment

225 AND 273 CU IN. ENGINES

The six-cylinder engines and the pre-1970 273 cu in. V8 engine, used in various models, have mechanical valve tappets (lifters) and adjustable rocker arms. Therefore, the valve lash or valve clearance can be checked and adjusted to the specified values listed in the "Tune-Up Specifications" chart in the conventional manner for mechanical tappets. The valve lash adjustment should be performed only when the engine is hot. Before proceeding, be sure that you can properly identify which are intake and which are exhaust valves. The simplest way to determine this is to look at the intake or exhaust manifold and determine which manifold branch leads into that particular valve. If it is an exhaust branch, it is an exhaust valve; if it is an intake branch, it is an intake valve.

1. Warm the engine until it reaches its normal operating temperature (water temperature of about 185° F).

2. Set the engine idle speed to 550 rpm and run the engine at this speed for five minutes.

3. Stop the engine and remove the valve covers.

4. Adjust the valves for one cylinder at a time. Start with number one cylinder and work to number six.

5. Before attempting to adjust the valves for any cylinder, the piston must be at TDC on the compression stroke. To get a cylinder on TDC, rotate the crankshaft by hand until it is observed that both valves are closed. Then remove the spark plug for that cylinder and insert a screwdriver into the hole. Continue to rotate the crankshaft until the top of the piston can be felt and the piston has traveled to the highest point of the bore.

6. Using the proper thickness feeler gauge, measure the clearance between the valve stem tip and the end of the rocker arm adjusting screw at each valve. If necessary, turn the adjusting screw to obtain the correct valve clearance. Note that the exhaust valve and intake valve have different clearance specifications.

7. It is good practice to recheck each valve for proper adjustment. Replace the valve cover and use a new valve cover gasket.

426 HEMI

NOTE: *1968–69 models used mechanical lifters, while 1970–71 models used adjustable hydraulic lifters. Adjust the valves with the engine cold.*

1. Mark the crankshaft damper with chalk at TDC and 180° opposite TDC.

2. Rotate the crankshaft until no. 1 cylinder is at TDC on the compression stroke.

3. Remove the valve covers.

4. Each rocker arm has an adjusting screw secured by a locknut. Adjust each valve on no. 1 cylinder by loosening the locknut and inserting the proper thickness feeler gauge for 1968–69 models between the valve stem tip and the end of the rocker arm adjusting screw at each valve. If necessary, turn the adjusting screw to obtain the correct valve clearance. On 1970–71 models, zero lash is the proper setting, hence, no feeler gauge is required.

5. Before proceeding, be sure that you can properly identify which are intake and

which are exhaust valves. The simplest way to determine this is to look at the intake or exhaust manifold and determine which manifold branch leads into that particular valve. If it is an exhaust branch, it is an exhaust valve; if it is an intake branch, it is an intake valve.

6. Adjust the intake valves on no. 2 and no. 7 cylinders and exhaust on no. 4 and no. 8 cylinders. On 1968–69 engines, adjust the intake valve to have a clearance of 0.028 in. and the exhaust valves 0.032 in. with the engine COLD. On 1970–71 engines, adjust the valves to have zero lash, then tighten the adjustment screw an additional 1½ turns. Tighten the locknuts to 25 ft lbs.

7. Rotate the crankshaft 180° in the normal direction of rotation until points open to fire no. 4 cylinder.

8. Adjust the intake tappets on no. 1 and no. 8 cylinders and the exhaust tappets on no. 3 and no. 6 cylinders as in step 6.

9. Rotate the crankshaft 180° in the normal direction of rotation until points open to fire no. 6 cylinder.

10. Adjust the intake tappets on no. 3 and no. 4 cylinders and exhaust tappets on no. 5 and no. 7 cylinders as in step 6.

11. Rotate the crankshaft 180° in the normal direction of rotation until the points open to fire no. 7 cylinder.

12. Adjust the intake tappets on no. 5 and no. 6 clinders and the exhaust tappets on no. 1 and no. 2 cylinders as in step 6.

13. Set the ignition timing to specifications and install the rocker covers.

All Other Engines

Non-adjustable hydraulic valve lifters are used on all other engines. These lifters are properly adjusted when the rocker arm shaft attaching bolts are torqued to specifications.

If the engine will not start after the rocker arm assembly has been replaced, spin the engine with the starter to allow the lifters to adjust to their proper height.

CARBURETOR ADJUSTMENTS

NOTE: *These are the mixture and idle speed carburetor adjustment procedures. For more detailed information, please refer to the "Emission Controls and Fuel System" section.*

1968–73 with CAP or CAS Except 426 Hemi, and Multiple Carburetor Engines

Adjust with air cleaner installed.
NOTE: *This is the basic carburetor adjustment procedure. Any specific exceptions are listed below.*

1. Run the engine at fast idle to stabilize engine temperature.

2. Make sure the choke plate is fully released.

3. Attach a tachometer of known accuracy to the engine.

4. Connect an exhaust analyzer to the engine and insert the probe as far into the tailpipe as possible. On vehicles with dual exhausts, insert the probe into the left tailpipe as this is the side without the heat riser valve.

5. Check the dwell and ignition timing and adjust it as required to conform to specifications.

6. If your car is equipped with air conditioning, turn the air conditioner off. On models with six-cylinder engines, turn the headlights on high beam.

7. Place the transmission in the neutral position. Make sure the hot idle compensator valve is fully seated in the closed position.

8. Turn the engine idle speed adjustment screw in or out to adust idle speed to specification. If equipped with an electric solenoid throttle positioner, turn the solenoid adjusting screw in or out to obtain the specified idle rpm. Adjust the curb idle speed screw until it just touches the stop on the carburetor body. Back the curb idle speed adjusting screw out one full turn.

9. Turn each idle mixture adjustment screw $1/16$ turn richer (counterclockwise). Wait 10 seconds and observe the reading on the exhaust gas analyzer. Continue this procedure until the meter indicates a definite increase in the richness of the mixture.

NOTE: *This step is very important. A carburetor that is set too lean will cause the exhaust gas analyzer to give a false reading, indicating a rich mixture. Because of this, the carburetor must first be known to have a rich mixture to verify the reading on the exhaust gas analyzer.*

10. After verifying the reading obtained on the meter, adjust the mixture screws to get an air/fuel ratio of 14.2:1. Turn the mixture screws clockwise (leaner) to raise

the meter reading or counterclockwise (richer) to lower the meter reading.

1968–69 383 and 440 V8, Single Carburetor

The carburetors used on these engines (Ball & Ball 2V, Carter 4V, or Holley 4V) have lead or cup plugs installed over the idle mixture screws and an additional off idle mixture control screw added to the body of the carburetor. When adjusting the carburetor idle speed and mixture, use the off idle adjustment screw to alter the idle speed air/fuel mixture so it conforms to the 14.2:1 ratio specified. If unable to obtain an acceptable engine idle by adjusting this screw, the rough idle or low-speed surge can be the result of improper balance of the idle mixture adjustment in the right and left carburetor bores. Adjust the mixture screws within the limits of adjustment to smooth out the engine.

426 Hemi Dual 4 bbl.

Because each carburetor is equipped with a complete idle system, accurate carburetor synchronization is very important. After adjusting the idle speed and mixture, it should be rechecked and rebalanced as required in the outside ambient temperature after a road test.

Adjust with air cleaner removed.

1. Run the engine at fast idle to stabilize the engine's temperature.

2. Make sure that the choke plate is fully released.

3. Attach a tachometer of known accuracy to the engine.

4. If the engine has a hot idle compensator valve, make sure it is fully seated in the closed position.

5. Place the transmission in neutral.

6. Turn the idle speed adjustment screws in or out to adjust the engine idle speed to specifications. If equipped with an electric solenoid throttle positioner, turn the solenoid adjusting screw in or out to obtain the specified engine idle speed. Turn the curb idle speed adjusting screw clockwise until it just touches the stop on the carburetor throttle body. Back the curb idle speed adjusting screw out one full turn.

7. Adjust each idle mixture screw to obtain the highest possible rpm. Repeat this operation until all four mixture adjustment

screws have been properly adjusted and balanced.

8. If the idle mixture adjustment procedure has changed the engine idle speed, adjust the idle speed.

Balancing Multiple-Carburetor Installations

426 HEMI

There is no actual adjustment of the external carburetor linkage to synchronize the twin carburetors. Proper balancing of the carburetor idle speeds as described in the idle speed for the 426 Hemi will ensure correct mixture adjustment procedure and carburetor synchronization.

440 SIX PACK

Because only the center carburetor has provisions for adjusting the engine idle speed and fuel mixture, these adjustments are performed using the procedure for single-carburetor installations. The throttle

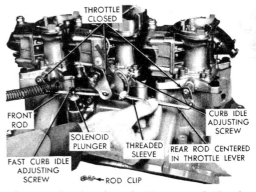

Adjusting the throttle rods (Courtesy of Chrysler Corp.)

rods which connect each outboard carburetor to the center carburetor can be adjusted for correct throttle synchronization by using the procedure below.

1. Remove the air cleaner.

2. Remove the outboard throttle rod securing clips and disengage the front and rear rods from the throttle levers.

3. Be sure that the ignition switch is turned off. (This de-energizes the fast curb idle solenoid so that clearance can be obtained between the plunger and the fast curb idle adjusting screw.)

4. Close the throttle valves of all three carburetors and hold them in the closed position.

5. Shorten or lengthen the front and

rear connector rods by turning each rod into or out of the threaded sleeve until the rod end can be inserted into the hole in the throttle lever smoothly.

6. Fit each throttle connector rod into its corresponding throttle lever and secure each rod with a clip.

Fast Curb Idle Speed Solenoid Adjustment

1970–72 MODELS (IF SO EQUIPPED)

1. Bring the engine to operating temperature and attach a tachometer.

2. With the engine running, adjust the fast curb idle screw to the proper rpm for the vehicle.

3. Adjust the slow curb idle screw until the screw end just contacts the stop. Back off the screw one full turn; this should return the vehicle to the slow curb idle setting.

4. Test the above procedure by disconnecting the solenoid wire at the connector. (Be sure not to let the lead short to the engine.) Reconnect the wire. The fast curb idle speed solenoid should not advance the throttle.

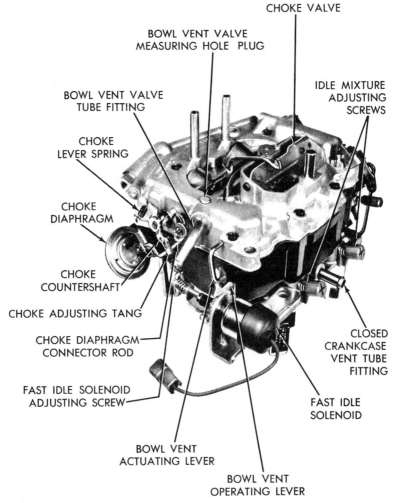

Carter Thermo–Quad, showing the fast idle solenoid (Courtesy of Chrysler Corp.)

Engine Tune-Up

Engine tune-up is a procedure performed to restore engine performance, deteriorated due to normal wear and loss of adjustment. The three major areas considered in a routine tune-up are compression, ignition, and carburetion, although valve adjustment may be included.

A tune-up is performed in three steps: *analysis*, in which it is determined whether normal wear is responsible for performance loss, and which parts require replacement or service; *parts replacement or service*; and *adjustment*, in which engine adjustments are returned to original specifications. Since the advent of emission control equipment, precision adjustment has become increasingly critical, in order to maintain pollutant emission levels.

Analysis

The procedures below are used to indicate where adjustments, parts service or replacement are necessary within the realm of a normal tune-up. If, following these tests, all systems appear to be functioning properly, proceed to the Troubleshooting Section for further diagnosis.

—Remove all spark plugs, noting the cylinder in which they were installed. Remove the air cleaner, and position the throttle and choke in the full open position. Disconnect the coil high tension lead from the coil and the distributor cap. Insert a compression gauge into the spark plug port of each cylinder, in succession, and crank the engine with

Maxi. Press. Lbs. Sq. In.	Min. Press. Lbs. Sq. In.	Max. Press. Lbs. Sq. In.	Min. Press. Lbs. Sq. In.
134	101	188	141
136	102	190	142
138	104	192	144
140	105	194	145
142	107	196	147
146	110	198	148
148	111	200	150
150	113	202	151
152	114	204	153
154	115	206	154
156	117	208	156
158	118	210	157
160	120	212	158
162	121	214	160
164	123	216	162
166	124	218	163
168	126	220	165
170	127	222	166
172	129	224	168
174	131	226	169
176	132	228	171
178	133	230	172
180	135	232	174
182	136	234	175
184	138	236	177
186	140	238	178

Compression pressure limits
© Buick Div. G.M. Corp.

the starter to obtain the highest possible reading. Record the readings, and compare the highest to the lowest on the compression pressure limit chart. If the difference exceeds the limits on the chart, or if all readings are excessively low, proceed to a wet compression check (see Troubleshooting Section).

—Evaluate the spark plugs according to the spark plug chart in the Troubleshooting Section, and proceed as indicated in the chart.

—Remove the distributor cap, and inspect it inside and out for cracks and/or carbon tracks, and inside for excessive wear or burning of the rotor contacts. If any of these faults are evident, the cap must be replaced.

—Check the breaker points for burning, pitting or wear, and the contact heel resting on the distributor cam for excessive wear. If defects are noted, replace the entire breaker point set.

—Remove and inspect the rotor. If the contacts are burned or worn, or if the rotor is excessively loose on the distributor shaft (where applicable), the rotor must be replaced.

—Inspect the spark plug leads and the coil high tension lead for cracks or brittleness. If any of the wires appear defective, the entire set should be replaced.

—Check the air filter to ensure that it is functioning properly.

Parts Replacement and Service

The determination of whether to replace or service parts is at the mechanic's discretion; however, it is suggested that any parts in questionable condition be replaced rather than reused.

—Clean and regap, or replace, the spark plugs as needed. Lightly coat the threads with engine oil and install the plugs. CAUTION: *Do not over-torque taper-seat spark plugs, or plugs being installed in aluminum cylinder heads.*

31

—If the distributor cap is to be reused, clean the inside with a dry rag, and remove corrosion from the rotor contact points with fine emery cloth. Remove the spark plug wires one by one, and clean the wire ends and the inside of the towers. If the boots are loose, they should be replaced.

If the cap is to be replaced, transfer the wires one by one, cleaning the wire ends and replacing the boots if necessary.

—If the original points are to remain in service, clean them lightly with emery cloth, lubricate the contact heel with grease specifically designed for this purpose. Rotate the crankshaft until the heel rests on a high point of the distributor cam, and adjust the point gap to specifications.

When replacing the points, remove the original points and condenser, and wipe out the inside of the distributor housing with a clean, dry rag. Lightly lubricate the contact heel and pivot point, and install the points and condenser. Rotate the crankshaft until the heel rests on a high point of the distributor cam, and adjust the point gap to specifications. NOTE: *Always replace the condenser when changing the points.*

—If the rotor is to be reused, clean the contacts with solvent. Do not alter the spring tension of the rotor center contact. Install the rotor and the distributor cap.

—Replace the coil high tension lead and/or the spark plug leads as necessary.

—Clean the carburetor using a spray solvent (e.g., Gumout Spray). Remove the varnish from the throttle bores, and clean the linkage. Disconnect and plug the fuel line, and run the engine until it runs out of fuel. Partially fill the float chamber with solvent, and reconnect the fuel line. In extreme cases, the jets can be pressure flushed by inserting a rubber plug into the float vent, running the spray nozzle through it, and spraying the solvent until it squirts out of the venturi fuel dump.

—Clean and tighten all wiring connections in the primary electrical circuit.

Additional Services

The following services *should* be performed in conjunction with a routine tune-up to ensure efficient performance.

—Inspect the battery and fill to the proper level with distilled water. Remove the cable clamps, clean clamps and posts thoroughly, coat the posts lightly with petroleum jelly, reinstall and tighten.

—Inspect all belts, replace and/or adjust as necessary.

—Test the PCV valve (if so equipped), and clean or replace as indicated. Clean all crankcase ventilation hoses, or replace if cracked or hardened.

—Adjust the valves (if necessary) to manufacturer's specifications.

Adjustments

—Connect a dwell-tachometer between the distributor primary lead and ground. Remove the distributor cap and rotor (unless equipped with Delco externally adjustable distributor). With the ignition off, crank the engine with a remote starter switch and measure the point dwell angle. Adjust the dwell angle to specifications. NOTE: *Increasing the gap decreases the dwell angle and* *vice-versa.* Install the rotor and distributor cap.

—Connect a timing light according to the manufacturer's specifications. Identify the proper timing marks with chalk or paint. NOTE: *Luminescent (day-glo) paint is excellent for this purpose.* Start the engine, and run it until it reaches operating temperature. Disconnect and plug any distributor vacuum lines, and adjust idle to the speed required to adjust timing, according to specifications. Loosen the distributor clamp and adjust timing to specifications by rotating the distributor in the engine. NOTE: *To advance timing, rotate distributor opposite normal direction of rotor rotation, and vice-versa.*

—Synchronize the throttles and mixture of multiple carburetors (if so equipped) according to procedures given in the individual car sections.

—Adjust the idle speed, mixture, and idle quality, as specified in the car sections. Final idle adjustments should be made with the air cleaner installed. CAUTION: *Due to strict emission control requirements on 1969 and later models, special test equipment (CO meter, SUN Tester) may be necessary to properly adjust idle mixture to specifications.*

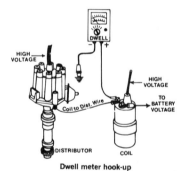

Dwell meter hook-up

Trouble-shooting

The following section is designed to aid in the rapid diagnosis of engine problems. The systematic format is used to diagnose problems ranging from engine starting difficulties to the need for engine overhaul. It is assumed that the user is equipped with basic hand tools and test equipment (tach-dwell meter, timing light, voltmeter, and ohmmeter).

Troubleshooting is divided into two sections. The first, *General Diagnosis*, is used to locate the problem area. In the second, *Specific Diagnosis*, the problem is systematically evaluated.

General Diagnosis

PROBLEM: Symptom	Begin diagnosis at Section Two, Number ——
Engine won't start:	
Starter doesn't turn	1.1, 2.1
Starter turns, engine doesn't	2.1
Starter turns engine very slowly	1.1, 2.4
Starter turns engine normally	3.1, 4.1
Starter turns engine very quickly	6.1
Engine fires intermittently	4.1
Engine fires consistently	5.1, 6.1
Engine runs poorly:	
Hard starting	3.1, 4.1, 5.1, 8.1
Rough idle	4.1, 5.1, 8.1
Stalling	3.1, 4.1, 5.1, 8.1
Engine dies at high speeds	4.1, 5.1
Hesitation (on acceleration from standing stop)	5.1, 8.1
Poor pickup	4.1, 5.1, 8.1
Lack of power	3.1, 4.1, 5.1, 8.1
Backfire through the carburetor	4.1, 8.1, 9.1
Backfire through the exhaust	4.1, 8.1, 9.1
Blue exhaust gases	6.1, 7.1
Black exhaust gases	5.1
Running on (after the ignition is shut off)	3.1, 8.1
Susceptible to moisture	4.1
Engine misfires under load	4.1, 7.1, 8.4, 9.1
Engine misfires at speed	4.1, 8.4
Engine misfires at idle	3.1, 4.1, 5.1, 7.1, 8.4

PROBLEM: Symptom	Probable Cause
Engine noises: ①	
Metallic grind while starting	Starter drive not engaging completely
Constant grind or rumble	*Starter drive not releasing, worn main bearings
Constant knock	Worn connecting rod bearings
Knock under load	Fuel octane too low, worn connecting rod bearings
Double knock	Loose piston pin
Metallic tap	*Collapsed or sticky valve lifter, excessive valve clearance, excessive end play in a rotating shaft
Scrape	*Fan belt contacting a stationary surface
Tick while starting	S.U. electric fuel pump (normal), starter brushes
Constant tick	*Generator brushes, shreaded fan belt
Squeal	*Improperly tensioned fan belt
Hiss or roar	*Steam escaping through a leak in the cooling system or the radiator overflow vent
Whistle	*Vacuum leak
Wheeze	Loose or cracked spark plug

①—It is extremely difficult to evaluate vehicle noises. While the above are general definitions of engine noises, those starred (*) should be considered as possibly originating elsewhere in the car. To aid diagnosis, the following list considers other potential sources of these sounds.

Metallic grind:
Throwout bearing; transmission gears, bearings, or synchronizers; differential bearings, gears; something metallic in contact with brake drum or disc.

Metallic tap:
U-joints; fan-to-radiator (or shroud) contact.

Scrape:
Brake shoe or pad dragging; tire to body contact; suspension contacting undercarriage or exhaust; something non-metallic contacting brake shoe or drum.

Tick:
Transmission gears; differential gears; lack of radio suppression; resonant vibration of body panels; windshield wiper motor or transmission; heater motor and blower.

Squeal:
Brake shoe or pad not fully releasing; tires (excessive wear, uneven wear, improper inflation); front or rear wheel alignment (most commonly due to improper toe-in).

Hiss or whistle:
Wind leaks (body or window); heater motor and blower fan.

Roar:
Wheel bearings; wind leaks (body and window).

Specific Diagnosis

This section is arranged so that following each test, instructions are given to proceed to another, until a problem is diagnosed.

INDEX

Group		Topic
1	*	Battery
2	*	Cranking system
3	*	Primary electrical system
4	*	Secondary electrical system
5	*	Fuel system
6	*	Engine compression
7	**	Engine vacuum
8	**	Secondary electrical system
9	**	Valve train
10	**	Exhaust system
11	**	Cooling system
12	**	Engine lubrication

*—The engine need not be running.
**—The engine must be running.

SAMPLE SECTION

Test and Procedure	Results and Indications	Proceed to
4.1—Check for spark: Hold each spark plug wire approximately ¼″ from ground with gloves or a heavy, dry rag. Crank the engine and observe the spark.	→ If no spark is evident:	4.2
	→ If spark is good in some cases:	4.3
	→ If spark is good in all cases:	4.6

DIAGNOSIS

1.1—Inspect the battery visually for case condition (corrosion, cracks) and water level.	If case is cracked, replace battery:	1.4
	If the case is intact, remove corrosion with a solution of baking soda and water (CAUTION: do not get the solution into the battery), and fill with water:	1.2
1.2—Check the battery cable connections: Insert a screwdriver between the battery post and the cable clamp. Turn the headlights on high beam, and observe them as the screwdriver is gently twisted to ensure good metal to metal contact.	If the lights brighten, remove and clean the clamp and post; coat the post with petroleum jelly, install and tighten the clamp:	1.4
	If no improvement is noted:	1.3

Testing battery cable connections using a screwdriver

1.3—Test the state of charge of the battery using an individual cell tester or hydrometer.	If indicated, charge the battery. NOTE: If no obvious reason exists for the low state of charge (i.e., battery age, prolonged storage), the charging system should be tested:	1.4

Spec. Grav. Reading	Charged Condition
1.260-1.280	Fully Charged
1.230-1.250	Three Quarter Charged
1.200-1.220	One Half Charged
1.170-1.190	One Quarter Charged
1.140-1.160	Just About Flat
1.110-1.130	All The Way Down

State of battery charge

Electrolyte temperature (° F)	Specific gravity correction
+ 120	+.016
	+.012
+ 100	+.008
	+.004
+ 80	no correction
	−.004
+ 60	−.008
	−.012
+ 40	−.016
	−.020
+ 20	−.024
	−.028
0	−.032
	−.036
− 20	−.040

ADD to reading

SUBTRACT from reading

The effect of temperature on the specific gravity of battery electrolyte

Test and Procedure	*Results and Indications*	*Proceed to*
1.4—Visually inspect battery cables for cracking, bad connection to ground, or bad connection to starter.	If necessary, tighten connections or replace the cables:	2.1

Tests in Group 2 are performed with coil high tension lead disconnected to prevent accidental starting.

2.1—Test the starter motor and solenoid: Connect a jumper from the battery post of the solenoid (or relay) to the starter post of the solenoid (or relay).	If starter turns the engine normally:	2.2
	If the starter buzzes, or turns the engine very slowly:	2.4
	If no response, replace the solenoid (or relay). If the starter turns, but the engine doesn't, ensure that the flywheel ring gear is intact. If the gear is undamaged, replace the starter drive.	3.1 3.1
2.2—Determine whether ignition override switches are functioning properly (clutch start switch, neutral safety switch), by connecting a jumper across the switch(es), and turning the ignition switch to "start".	If starter operates, adjust or replace switch:	3.1
	If the starter doesn't operate:	2.3
2.3—Check the ignition switch "start" position: Connect a 12V test lamp between the starter post of the solenoid (or relay) and ground. Turn the ignition switch to the "start" position, and jiggle the key.	If the lamp doesn't light when the switch is turned, check the ignition switch for loose connections, cracked insulation, or broken wires. Repair or replace as necessary:	3.1
	If the lamp flickers when the key is jiggled, replace the ignition switch.	3.3

Checking the ignition switch "start" position

2.4—Remove and bench test the starter, according to specifications in the car section.	If the starter does not meet specifications, repair or replace as needed:	3.1
	If the starter is operating properly:	2.5
2.5—Determine whether the engine can turn freely: Remove the spark plugs, and check for water in the cylinders. Check for water on the dipstick, or oil in the radiator. Attempt to turn the engine using an 18″ flex drive and socket on the crankshaft pulley nut or bolt.	If the engine will turn freely only with the spark plugs out, and hydrostatic lock (water in the cylinders) is ruled out, check valve timing:	9.2
	If engine will not turn freely, and it is known that the clutch and transmission are free, the engine must be disassembled for further evaluation:	Next Chapter

Tests and Procedures	*Results and Indications*	*Proceed to*
3.1—Check the ignition switch "on" position: Connect a jumper wire between the distributor side of the coil and ground, and a 12V test lamp between the switch side of the coil and ground. Remove the high tension lead from the coil. Turn the ignition switch on and jiggle the key.	If the lamp lights:	3.2
	If the lamp flickers when the key is jiggled, replace the ignition switch:	3.3
	If the lamp doesn't light, check for loose or open connections. If none are found, remove the ignition switch and check for continuity. If the switch is faulty, replace it:	3.3

Checking the ignition switch "on" position

Tests and Procedures	*Results and Indications*	*Proceed to*
3.2—Check the ballast resistor or resistance wire for an open circuit, using an ohmmeter.	Replace the resistor or the resistance wire if the resistance is zero.	3.3
3.3—Visually inspect the breaker points for burning, pitting, or excessive wear. Gray coloring of the point contact surfaces is normal. Rotate the crankshaft until the contact heel rests on a high point of the distributor cam, and adjust the point gap to specifications.	If the breaker points are intact, clean the contact surfaces with fine emery cloth, and adjust the point gap to specifications. If pitted or worn, replace the points and condenser, and adjust the gap to specifications: NOTE: *Always lubricate the distributor cam according to manufacturer's recommendations when servicing the breaker points.*	3.4
3.4—Connect a dwell meter between the distributor primary lead and ground. Crank the engine and observe the point dwell angle.	If necessary, adjust the point dwell angle: NOTE: *Increasing the point gap decreases the dwell angle, and vice-versa.*	3.6
	If dwell meter shows little or no reading:	3.5

Dwell meter hook-up

Dwell angle

Tests and Procedures	*Results and Indications*	*Proceed to*
3.5—Check the condenser for short: Connect an ohmmeter across the condenser body and the pigtail lead.	If any reading other than infinite resistance is noted, replace the condenser:	3.6

Checking the condenser for short

Test and Procedure	*Results and Indications*	*Proceed to*
3.6—Test the coil primary resistance: Connect an ohmmeter across the coil primary terminals, and read the resistance on the low scale. Note whether an external ballast resistor or resistance wire is utilized.	Coils utilizing ballast resistors or resistance wires should have approximately 1.0Ω resistance; coils with internal resistors should have approximately 4.0Ω resistance. If values far from the above are noted, replace the coil:	4.1
4.1—Check for spark: Hold each spark plug wire approximately ¼″ from ground with gloves or a heavy, dry rag. Crank the engine, and observe the spark.	If no spark is evident: If spark is good in some cylinders: If spark is good in all cylinders:	4.2 4.3 4.6
4.2—Check for spark at the coil high tension lead: Remove the coil high tension lead from the distributor and position it approximately ¼″ from ground. Crank the engine and observe spark. CAUTION: *This test should not be performed on cars equipped with transistorized ignition.*	If the spark is good and consistent: If the spark is good but intermittent, test the primary electrical system starting at 3.3: If the spark is weak or non-existent, replace the coil high tension lead, clean and tighten all connections and retest. If no improvement is noted:	4.3 3.3 4.4

4.3—Visually inspect the distributor cap and rotor for burned or corroded contacts, cracks, carbon tracks, or moisture. Also check the fit of the rotor on the distributor shaft (where applicable).	If moisture is present, dry thoroughly, and retest per 4.1:
	 If burned or excessively corroded contacts, cracks, or carbon tracks are noted, replace the defective part(s) and retest per 4.1:
	 If the rotor and cap appear intact, or are only slightly corroded, clean the contacts thoroughly (including the cap towers and spark plug wire ends) and retest per 4.1:
	     If the spark is good in all cases:
	     If the spark is poor in all cases:
		4.1
		
		 4.1
		
		 4.6
		 4.5

4.4—Check the coil secondary resistance: Connect an ohmmeter across the distributor side of the coil and the coil tower. Read the resistance on the high scale of the ohmmeter.	The resistance of a satisfactory coil should be between 4KΩ and 10KΩ. If the resistance is considerably higher (i.e., 40KΩ) replace the coil, and retest per 4.1: NOTE: *This does not apply to high performance coils.*	4.1

Testing the coil primary resistance

Testing the coil secondary resistance

Test and Procedure	*Results and Indications*	*Proceed to*
4.5—Visually inspect the spark plug wires for cracking or brittleness. Ensure that no two wires are positioned so as to cause induction firing (adjacent and parallel). Remove each wire, one by one, and check resistance with an ohmmeter.	Replace any cracked or brittle wires. If any of the wires are defective, replace the entire set. Replace any wires with excessive resistance (over 8000Ω per foot for suppression wire), and separate any wires that might cause induction firing.	4.6
4.6—Remove the spark plugs, noting the cylinders from which they were removed, and evaluate according to the chart below.	See below.	See below.

	Condition	*Cause*	*Remedy*	*Proceed to*
	Electrodes eroded, light brown deposits.	Normal wear. Normal wear is indicated by approximately .001″ wear per 1000 miles.	Clean and regap the spark plug if wear is not excessive: Replace the spark plug if excessively worn:	4.7
	Carbon fouling (black, dry, fluffy deposits).	If present on one or two plugs:		
		Faulty high tension lead(s).	Test the high tension leads:	4.5
		Burnt or sticking valve(s).	Check the valve train: (Clean and regap the plugs in either case.)	9.1
		If present on most or all plugs: Overly rich fuel mixture, due to restricted air filter, improper carburetor adjustment, improper choke or heat riser adjustment or operation.	Check the fuel system:	5.1
	Oil fouling (wet black deposits)	Worn engine components. NOTE: *Oil fouling may occur in new or recently rebuilt engines until broken in.*	Check engine vacuum and compression: Replace with new spark plug	6.1
	Lead fouling (gray, black, tan, or yellow deposits, which appear glazed or cinder-like).	Combustion by-products.	Clean and regap the plugs: (Use plugs of a different heat range if the problem recurs.)	4.7

	Condition	Cause	Remedy	Proceed to
	Gap bridging (deposits lodged between the electrodes).	Incomplete combustion, or transfer of deposits from the combustion chamber.	Replace the spark plugs:	4.7
	Overheating (burnt electrodes, and extremely white insulator with small black spots).	Ignition timing advanced too far.	Adjust timing to specifications:	8.2
		Overly lean fuel mixture.	Check the fuel system:	5.1
		Spark plugs not seated properly.	Clean spark plug seat and install a new gasket washer: (Replace the spark plugs in all cases.)	4.7
	Fused spot deposits on the insulator.	Combustion chamber blow-by.	Clean and regap the spark plugs:	4.7
	Pre-ignition (melted or severely burned electrodes, blistered or cracked insulators, or metallic deposits on the insulator).	Incorrect spark plug heat range.	Replace with plugs of the proper heat range:	4.7
		Ignition timing advanced too far.	Adjust timing to specifications:	8.2
		Spark plugs not being cooled efficiently.	Clean the spark plug seat, and check the cooling system:	11.1
		Fuel mixture too lean.	Check the fuel system:	5.1
		Poor compression.	Check compression:	6.1
		Fuel grade too low.	Use higher octane fuel:	4.7

Test and Procedure	Results and Indications	Proceed to
4.7—Determine the static ignition timing: Using the flywheel or crankshaft pulley timing marks as a guide, locate top dead center on the *compression* stroke of the No. 1 cylinder. Remove the distributor cap.	Adjust the distributor so that the rotor points toward the No. 1 tower in the distributor cap, and the points are just opening:	4.8
4.8—Check coil polarity: Connect a voltmeter negative lead to the coil high tension lead, and the positive lead to ground (NOTE: *reverse the hook-up for positive ground cars*). Crank the engine momentarily. **Checking coil polarity**	If the voltmeter reads up-scale, the polarity is correct:	5.1
	If the voltmeter reads down-scale, reverse the coil polarity (switch the primary leads):	5.1

Test and Procedure	Results and Indications	Proceed to
5.1—Determine that the air filter is functioning efficiently: Hold paper elements up to a strong light, and attempt to see light through the filter.	Clean permanent air filters in gasoline (or manufacturer's recommendation), and allow to dry. Replace paper elements through which light cannot be seen:	5.2
5.2—Determine whether a flooding condition exists: Flooding is identified by a strong gasoline odor, and excessive gasoline present in the throttle bore(s) of the carburetor.	If flooding is not evident:	5.3
	If flooding is evident, permit the gasoline to dry for a few moments and restart. If flooding doesn't recur:	5.6
	If flooding is persistant:	5.5
5.3—Check that fuel is reaching the carburetor: Detach the fuel line at the carburetor inlet. Hold the end of the line in a cup (not styrofoam), and crank the engine.	If fuel flows smoothly:	5.6
	If fuel doesn't flow (NOTE: *Make sure that there is fuel in the tank*), or flows erratically:	5.4
5.4—Test the fuel pump: Disconnect all fuel lines from the fuel pump. Hold a finger over the input fitting, crank the engine (with electric pump, turn the ignition or pump on); and feel for suction.	If suction is evident, blow out the fuel line to the tank with low pressure compressed air until bubbling is heard from the fuel filler neck. Also blow out the carburetor fuel line (both ends disconnected):	5.6
	If no suction is evident, replace or repair the fuel pump:	5.6
	NOTE: *Repeated oil fouling of the spark plugs, or a no-start condition, could be the result of a ruptured vacuum booster pump diaphragm, through which oil or gasoline is being drawn into the intake manifold (where applicable).*	
5.5—Check the needle and seat: Tap the carburetor in the area of the needle and seat.	If flooding stops, a gasoline additive (e.g., Gumout) will often cure the problem:	5.6
	If flooding continues, check the fuel pump for excessive pressure at the carburetor (according to specifications). If the pressure is normal, the needle and seat must be removed and checked, and/or the float level adjusted:	5.6
5.6—Test the accelerator pump by looking into the throttle bores while operating the throttle.	If the accelerator pump appears to be operating normally:	5.7
	If the accelerator pump is not operating, the pump must be reconditioned. Where possible, service the pump with the carburetor(s) installed on the engine. If necessary, remove the carburetor. Prior to removal:	5.7
5.7—Determine whether the carburetor main fuel system is functioning: Spray a commercial starting fluid into the carburetor while attempting to start the engine.	If the engine starts, runs for a few seconds, and dies:	5.8
	If the engine doesn't start:	6.1

Test and Procedures	*Results and Indications*	*Proceed to*
5.8—Uncommon fuel system malfunctions: See below:	If the problem is solved: If the problem remains, remove and recondition the carburetor.	6.1

Condition	*Indication*	*Test*	*Usual Weather Conditions*	*Remedy*
Vapor lock	Car will not restart shortly after running.	Cool the components of the fuel system until the engine starts.	Hot to very hot	Ensure that the exhaust manifold heat control valve is operating. Check with the vehicle manufacturer for the recommended solution to vapor lock on the model in question.
Carburetor icing	Car will not idle, stalls at low speeds.	Visually inspect the throttle plate area of the throttle bores for frost.	High humidity, 32-40° F.	Ensure that the exhaust manifold heat control valve is operating, and that the intake manifold heat riser is not blocked.
Water in the fuel	Engine sputters and stalls; may not start.	Pump a small amount of fuel into a glass jar. Allow to stand, and inspect for droplets or a layer of water.	High humidity, extreme temperature changes.	For droplets, use one or two cans of commercial gas dryer (Dry Gas) For a layer of water, the tank must be drained, and the fuel lines blown out with compressed air.

Test and Procedure	*Results and Indications*	*Proceed to*
6.1—Test engine compression: Remove all spark plugs. Insert a compression gauge into a spark plug port, crank the engine to obtain the maximum reading, and record.	If compression is within limits on all cylinders: If gauge reading is extremely low on all cylinders: If gauge reading is low on one or two cylinders: (If gauge readings are identical and low on two or more adjacent cylinders, the head gasket must be replaced.)	7.1 6.2 6.2

Testing compression
(© Chevrolet Div. G.M. Corp.)

Compression pressure limits
(© Buick Div. G.M. Corp.)

Maxi. Press. Lbs. Sq. In.	*Min. Press. Lbs. Sq. In.*	*Maxi. Press. Lbs. Sq. In.*	*Min. Press. Lbs. Sq. In.*	*Max. Press. Lbs. Sq. In.*	*Min. Press. Lbs. Sq. In.*	*Max. Press. Lbs. Sq. In.*	*Min. Press. Lbs. Sq. In.*
134	101	162	121	188	141	214	160
136	102	164	123	190	142	216	162
138	104	166	124	192	144	218	163
140	105	168	126	194	145	220	165
142	107	170	127	196	147	222	166
146	110	172	129	198	148	224	168
148	111	174	131	200	150	226	169
150	113	176	132	202	151	228	171
152	114	178	133	204	153	230	172
154	115	180	135	206	154	232	174
156	117	182	136	208	156	234	175
158	118	184	138	210	157	236	177
160	120	186	140	212	158	238	178

Test and Procedure	Results and Indications	Proceed to
6.2—Test engine compression (wet): Squirt approximately 30 cc. of engine oil into each cylinder, and retest per 6.1.	If the readings improve, worn or cracked rings or broken pistons are indicated:	Next Chapter
	If the readings do not improve, burned or excessively carboned valves or a jumped timing chain are indicated: NOTE: *A jumped timing chain is often indicated by difficult cranking.*	7.1
7.1—Perform a vacuum check of the engine: Attach a vacuum gauge to the intake manifold beyond the throttle plate. Start the engine, and observe the action of the needle over the range of engine speeds.	See below.	See below

	Reading	Indications	Proceed to
	Steady, from 17-22 in. Hg.	Normal.	8.1
	Low and steady.	Late ignition or valve timing, or low compression:	6.1
	Very low	Vacuum leak:	7.2
	Needle fluctuates as engine speed increases.	Ignition miss, blown cylinder head gasket, leaking valve or weak valve spring:	6.1, 8.3
	Gradual drop in reading at idle.	Excessive back pressure in the exhaust system:	10.1
	Intermittent fluctuation at idle.	Ignition miss, sticking valve:	8.3, 9.1
	Drifting needle.	Improper idle mixture adjustment, carburetors not synchronized (where applicable), or minor intake leak. Synchronize the carburetors, adjust the idle, and retest. If the condition persists:	7.2
	High and steady.	Early ignition timing:	8.2

Test and Procedure	Results and Indications	Proceed to
7.2—Attach a vacuum gauge per 7.1, and test for an intake manifold leak. Squirt a small amount of oil around the intake manifold gaskets, carburetor gaskets, plugs and fittings. Observe the action of the vacuum gauge.	If the reading improves, replace the indicated gasket, or seal the indicated fitting or plug:	8.1
	If the reading remains low:	7.3
7.3—Test all vacuum hoses and accessories for leaks as described in 7.2. Also check the carburetor body (dashpots, automatic choke mechanism, throttle shafts) for leaks in the same manner.	If the reading improves, service or replace the offending part(s):	8.1
	If the reading remains low:	6.1
8.1—Check the point dwell angle: Connect a dwell meter between the distributor primary wire and ground. Start the engine, and observe the dwell angle from idle to 3000 rpm.	If necessary, adjust the dwell angle. NOTE: *Increasing the point gap reduces the dwell angle and vice-versa.* If the dwell angle moves outside specifications as engine speed increases, the distributor should be removed and checked for cam accuracy, shaft endplay and concentricity, bushing wear, and adequate point arm tension (NOTE: *Most of these items may be checked with the distributor installed in the engine, using an oscilloscope*):	8.2
8.2—Connect a timing light (per manufacturer's recommendation) and check the dynamic ignition timing. Disconnect and plug the vacuum hose(s) to the distributor if specified, start the engine, and observe the timing marks at the specified engine speed.	If the timing is not correct, adjust to specifications by rotating the distributor in the engine: (Advance timing by rotating distributor opposite normal direction of rotor rotation, retard timing by rotating distributor in same direction as rotor rotation.)	8.3
8.3—Check the operation of the distributor advance mechanism(s): To test the mechanical advance, disconnect all but the mechanical advance, and observe the timing marks with a timing light as the engine speed is increased from idle. If the mark moves smoothly, without hesitation, it may be assumed that the mechanical advance is functioning properly. To test vacuum advance and/or retard systems, alternately crimp and release the vacuum line, and observe the timing mark for movement. If movement is noted, the system is operating.	If the systems are functioning:	8.4
	If the systems are not functioning, remove the distributor, and test on a distributor tester:	8.4
8.4—Locate an ignition miss: With the engine running, remove each spark plug wire, one by one, until one is found that doesn't cause the engine to roughen and slow down.	When the missing cylinder is identified:	4.1

Test and Procedure	Results and Indications	Proceed to
9.1—Evaluate the valve train: Remove the valve cover, and ensure that the valves are adjusted to specifications. A mechanic's stethoscope may be used to aid in the diagnosis of the valve train. By pushing the probe on or near push rods or rockers, valve noise often can be isolated. A timing light also may be used to diagnose valve problems. Connect the light according to manufacturer's recommendations, and start the engine. Vary the firing moment of the light by increasing the engine speed (and therefore the ignition advance), and moving the trigger from cylinder to cylinder. Observe the movement of each valve.	See below	See below

Observation	Probable Cause	Remedy	Proceed to
Metallic tap heard through the stethoscope.	Sticking hydraulic lifter or excessive valve clearance.	Adjust valve. If tap persists, remove and replace the lifter:	10.1
Metallic tap through the stethoscope, able to push the rocker arm (lifter side) down by hand.	Collapsed valve lifter.	Remove and replace the lifter:	10.1
Erratic, irregular motion of the valve stem.*	Sticking valve, burned valve.	Recondition the valve and/or valve guide:	Next Chapter
Eccentric motion of the pushrod at the rocker arm.*	Bent pushrod.	Replace the pushrod:	10.1
Valve retainer bounces as the valve closes.*	Weak valve spring or damper.	Remove and test the spring and damper. Replace if necessary:	10.1

*—When observed with a timing light.

Test and Procedure	Results and Indications	Proceed to
9.2—Check the valve timing: Locate top dead center of the No. 1 piston, and install a degree wheel or tape on the crankshaft pulley or damper with zero corresponding to an index mark on the engine. Rotate the crankshaft in its direction of rotation, and observe the opening of the No. 1 cylinder intake valve. The opening should correspond with the correct mark on the degree wheel according to specifications.	If the timing is not correct, the timing cover must be removed for further investigation:	

Test and Procedure	Results and Indications	Proceed to
10.1—Determine whether the exhaust manifold heat control valve is operating: Operate the valve by hand to determine whether it is free to move. If the valve is free, run the engine to operating temperature and observe the action of the valve, to ensure that it is opening.	If the valve sticks, spray it with a suitable solvent, open and close the valve to free it, and retest. If the valve functions properly:	10.2
	If the valve does not free, or does not operate, replace the valve:	10.2
10.2—Ensure that there are no exhaust restrictions: Visually inspect the exhaust system for kinks, dents, or crushing. Also note that gasses are flowing freely from the tailpipe at all engine speeds, indicating no restriction in the muffler or resonator.	Replace any damaged portion of the system:	11.1
11.1—Visually inspect the fan belt for glazing, cracks, and fraying, and replace if necessary. Tighten the belt so that the longest span has approximately $\frac{1}{2}''$ play at its midpoint under thumb pressure.	Replace or tighten the fan belt as necessary:	11.2

Checking the fan belt tension
(© Nissan Motor Co. Ltd.)

Test and Procedure	Results and Indications	Proceed to
11.2—Check the fluid level of the cooling system.	If full or slightly low, fill as necessary:	11.5
	If extremely low:	11.3
11.3—Visually inspect the external portions of the cooling system (radiator, radiator hoses, thermostat elbow, water pump seals, heater hoses, etc.) for leaks. If none are found, pressurize the cooling system to 14-15 psi.	If cooling system holds the pressure:	11.5
	If cooling system loses pressure rapidly, re-inspect external parts of the system for leaks under pressure. If none are found, check dipstick for coolant in crankcase. If no coolant is present, but pressure loss continues:	11.4
	If coolant is evident in crankcase, remove cylinder head(s), and check gasket(s). If gaskets are intact, block and cylinder head(s) should be checked for cracks or holes. If the gasket(s) is blown, replace, and purge the crankcase of coolant:	12.6
	NOTE: Occasionally, due to atmospheric and driving conditions, condensation of water can occur in the crankcase. This causes the oil to appear milky white. To remedy, run the engine until hot, and change the oil and oil filter.	

Test and Procedure	*Results and Indication*	*Proceed to*
11.4—Check for combustion leaks into the cooling system: Pressurize the cooling system as above. Start the engine, and observe the pressure gauge. If the needle fluctuates, remove each spark plug wire, one by one, noting which cylinder(s) reduce or eliminate the fluctuation. **Radiator pressure tester** (© American Motors Corp.)	Cylinders which reduce or eliminate the fluctuation, when the spark plug wire is removed, are leaking into the cooling system. Replace the head gasket on the affected cylinder bank(s).	
11.5—Check the radiator pressure cap: Attach a radiator pressure tester to the radiator cap (wet the seal prior to installation). Quickly pump up the pressure, noting the point at which the cap releases. **Testing the radiator pressure cap** (© American Motors Corp.)	If the cap releases within ± 1 psi of the specified rating, it is operating properly: If the cap releases at more than ± 1 psi of the specified rating, it should be replaced:	11.6 11.6
11.6—Test the thermostat: Start the engine cold, remove the radiator cap, and insert a thermometer into the radiator. Allow the engine to idle. After a short while, there will be a sudden, rapid increase in coolant temperature. The temperature at which this sharp rise stops is the thermostat opening temperature.	If the thermostat opens at or about the specified temperature: If the temperature doesn't increase: (If the temperature increases slowly and gradually, replace the thermostat.)	11.7 11.7
11.7—Check the water pump: Remove the thermostat elbow and the thermostat, disconnect the coil high tension lead (to prevent starting), and crank the engine momentarily.	If coolant flows, replace the thermostat and retest per 11.6: If coolant doesn't flow, reverse flush the cooling system to alleviate any blockage that might exist. If system is not blocked, and coolant will not flow, recondition the water pump.	11.6 —
12.1—Check the oil pressure gauge or warning light: If the gauge shows low pressure, or the light is on, for no obvious reason, remove the oil pressure sender. Install an accurate oil pressure gauge and run the engine momentarily.	If oil pressure builds normally, run engine for a few moments to determine that it is functioning normally, and replace the sender. If the pressure remains low: If the pressure surges: If the oil pressure is zero:	— 12.2 12.3 12.3

Test and Procedure	Results and Indications	Proceed to
12.2—Visually inspect the oil: If the oil is watery or very thin, milky, or foamy, replace the oil and oil filter.	If the oil is normal:	12.3
	If after replacing oil the pressure remains low:	12.3
	If after replacing oil the pressure becomes normal:	—
12.3—Inspect the oil pressure relief valve and spring, to ensure that it is not sticking or stuck. Remove and thoroughly clean the valve, spring, and the valve body.	If the oil pressure improves:	—
	If no improvement is noted:	12.4

Oil pressure relief valve
(© British Leyland Motors)

Test and Procedure	Results and Indications	Proceed to
12.4—Check to ensure that the oil pump is not cavitating (sucking air instead of oil): See that the crankcase is neither over nor underfull, and that the pickup in the sump is in the proper position and free from sludge.	Fill or drain the crankcase to the proper capacity, and clean the pickup screen in solvent if necessary. If no improvement is noted:	12.5
12.5—Inspect the oil pump drive and the oil pump:	If the pump drive or the oil pump appear to be defective, service as necessary and retest per 12.1:	12.1
	If the pump drive and pump appear to be operating normally, the engine should be disassembled to determine where blockage exists:	Next Chapter
12.6—Purge the engine of ethylene glycol coolant: Completely drain the crankcase and the oil filter. Obtain a commercial butyl cellosolve base solvent, designated for this purpose, and follow the instructions precisely. Following this, install a new oil filter and refill the crankcase with the proper weight oil. The next oil and filter change should follow shortly thereafter (1000 miles).		

3 · Engine and Engine Rebuilding

Engine Electrical

DISTRIBUTOR

Removal

1. Disconnect the vacuum advance line at the distributor.

2. Disconnect the primary wire at the coil.

3. Unfasten the distributor cap retaining clips and lift off the cap.

4. Mark the distributor body and the engine block to indicate the position of the body in the block. Scribe a mark on the edge of the distributor housing to indicate the position of the rotor on the distributor. These marks can be used as guides when installing the distributor in a correctly timed engine.

5. Remove the distributor hold-down clamp screw and clamp.

6. Carefully lift the distributor out of the block. Note the slight rotation of the distributor shaft as the distributor is removed. When installing the distributor the rotor must be in this position as the distributor is inserted into the block.

Installation
(Engine Has Not Been Rotated)

1. Install a new seal in the groove of the distributor shaft and carefully lower the distributor into the distributor bore.

2. With the rotor positioned slightly to the side of the mark on the distributor body, engage the distributor drive gear with the camshaft drive gear. As the distributor slides into place the rotor will rotate slightly and align with the mark on the body.

3. Install the distributor hold-down clamp and bolt. Do not tighten.

4. Install the distributor cap and coil primary wire.

5. Set the point gap and time the engine.

6. Tighten the distributor hold down clamp and install the vacuum advance hose.

Installation
(Engine Has Been Rotated)

If the crankshaft has been rotated or otherwise disturbed (as during engine rebuilding) after the distributor was removed, proceed as follows to install the distributor.

1. Bring the no. 1 piston to TDC by removing the no. 1 spark plug and inserting a finger over the hole while rotating the crankshaft. The compression pressure can be felt as the no. 1 piston approaches TDC on the compression stroke. The TDC timing mark on the crankshaft vibration damper should now be opposite the indicator on the timing chain case.

2. *For six-cylinder engines:* Note the position of the distributor cap (which should be connected to the engine by the spark plug cables). Hold the distributor so that the rotor will be in position *just ahead* of the distributor cap terminal for the no. 1 spark plug when the distributor is installed. Now lower the distributor into its engine block opening, engaging the distributor gear with the camshaft drive gear. Be sure that the rubber O-ring seal is in the groove in the distributor shank. When the distributor is properly seated, the rotor should be under the no. 1 distributor cap terminal with the contact points just opening. Proceed with step 4.

3. *For eight-cylinder engines:* Clean the top of the engine block around the distributor opening to ensure a good seal between the distributor base and the block. Note the position of the distributor cap. Hold the distributor so that the rotor will be in position *directly under* the distributor cap terminal for the no. 1 spark plug when the distributor is installed. Lower the distributor into its engine block opening, engaging the tongue of the distributor shaft with the slot in the distributor and oil pump drive gear.

4. Install the distributor hold-down clamp and tighten its retaining screw finger tight.

5. Check the point gap and refit the distributor cap. Connect the primary wire to the coil.

6. Check and adjust the point dwell and the ignition timing using the procedures described in the tune-up section.

7. Connect the vacuum advance line to the distributor.

ALTERNATOR

The alternator is basically an alternating current (AC) generator with solid state rectifiers which convert AC current to DC current (direct current) for charging the battery. The solid state rectifiers are located between the battery alternator coils

Firing Order

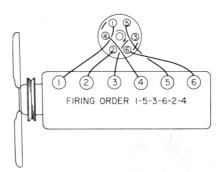

All 6 cyl. engines (Courtesy of Chrysler Corp.)

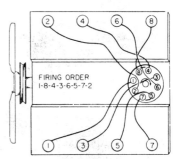

273, 318, 340 V8 (Courtesy of Chrysler Corp.)

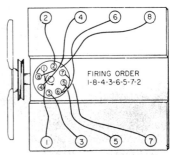

383, 426, 413, 400, 440 cu. in. V8 with Chrysler dist. (Move No. 1 one space CW for Autolite and Prestolite dist.) (Courtesy of Chrysler Corp.)

and, since they are one-way current flow devices, the rectifiers eliminate any need for a cutout relay in the charging circuit.

Be sure to read and follow the "Alternator Service Precautions" before servicing the vehicle charging system.

Alternator Service Precautions

Because alternator (AC) systems differ from DC systems, special care must be taken when servicing the charging system.

1. Battery polarity should be checked before any connections, such as jumper ca-

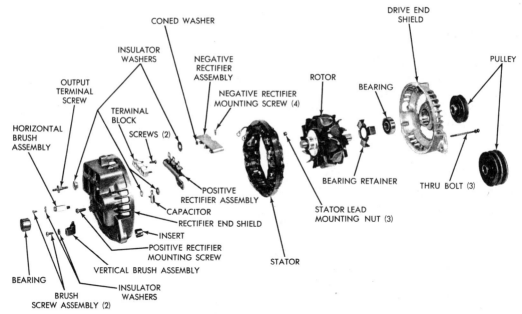

CONED WASHER

INSULATOR WASHERS

NEGATIVE RECTIFIER ASSEMBLY

OUTPUT TERMINAL SCREW

NEGATIVE RECTIFIER MOUNTING SCREW (4)

TERMINAL BLOCK

ROTOR

DRIVE END SHIELD

BEARING

PULLEY

HORIZONTAL BRUSH ASSEMBLY

SCREWS (2)

POSITIVE RECTIFIER ASSEMBLY

CAPACITOR

RECTIFIER END SHIELD

INSERT

POSITIVE RECTIFIER MOUNTING SCREW

VERTICAL BRUSH ASSEMBLY

BEARING

BRUSH SCREW ASSEMBLY (2)

INSULATOR WASHERS

STATOR LEAD MOUNTING NUT (3)

BEARING RETAINER

STATOR

THRU BOLT (3)

383, 400, 426, and 440 V8 (Courtesy of Chrysler Corp.)

bles or battery charger leads, are made. Reversed battery connections will damage the diode rectifiers. It is recommended that the battery cables be disconnected before connecting a battery charger.

2. The battery must *never* be disconnected while the alternator is running.

3. Always disconnect the battery ground lead before replacing the alternator.

4. Do not attempt to polarize an alternator, or the regulator of an alternator equipped car.

5. Do not short across or ground any alternator terminals.

6. Always disconnect the battery ground lead before removing the alternator output cable, whether the engine is running or not.

7. If electric arc welding has to be done on the car, first disconnect the battery and alternator cables. Never start the car with the welding unit attached.

Removal and Installation

1. Disconnect both battery cables at the battery terminals.

2. Disconnect the alternator output BAT and field (FLD) leads, and disconnect the ground wire.

3. Remove the alternator mounting bracket bolts and remove the alternator.

4. Installation is the reverse of the above. Adjust the alternator drive belt ten-

sion. Check the alternator and regulator circuits and perform any necessary adjustments.

VOLTAGE REGULATOR

The function of the voltage regulator is to limit the output voltage by controlling the flow of current in the alternator rotor field coil which, in effect, controls the strength of the rotor magnetic field. On all models, the output voltage is limited by two different types of voltage regulators.

The 1968–69 models use a mechanical voltage regulator, i.e., the regulator has contact points which are adjustable.

All 1970–73 models are equipped with a solid-state (silicon transistor) voltage regulator which is not adjustable.

Removal and Installation

Both types of voltage regulators can be removed and installed by using the same procedure.

1. Disconnect the cables from the battery posts.

2. Label and disconnect each electrical lead from the voltage regulator.

3. Remove the regulator by withdrawing its securing screws.

4. Installation is the reverse of the above. Be sure that the electrical leads are connected to the correct terminals and that all connections are clean and tight. If

Alternator and Regulator Specifications

| Year | ALTERNATOR | | | REGULATOR | | | | | | |
| | Part No. or Manufacturer | Field Current @ 12 V | Output (amps) | Part No. or Manufacturer | Field Relay | | | Regulator | | |
					Air Gap (in.)	Point Gap (in.)	Volts to Close	Air Gap (in.)	Point Gap (in.)	Volts @ 75°
'68–'69	6 Cyl. Models	2.38–2.75	26 ± 3	2098300①	0.050①	0.014	13.8	0.015	0.050	13.8–14.4
	V8 Std.—All	2.38–2.75	34.5 ± 3	2098300①	0.050①	0.014	13.8	0.015	0.050	13.8–14.4
	Heavy Duty, A/C	2.38–2.75	44 ± 3②	2098300①	0.050①	0.014	13.8	0.015	0.050	13.8–14.4
'70–'71	6 Cyl. Models	2.38–2.75	26 ± 3	3438150	Not Adjustable					13.8–14.4
	V8 Std.—All	2.38–2.75	34.5 ± 3	3438150	Not Adjustable					13.8–14.4
	Heavy Duty, A/C	2.38–2.75	44.5 ± 3	3438150	Not Adjustable					13.8–14.4
	Special Equip.	2.38–2.75	51 ± 3	3438150	Not Adjustable					13.8–14.4
'72–'73	6 Cyl. Models	2.5–3.1	26	3438150	Not Adjustable					13.8–14.4
	V8 Std.	2.5–3.1	39	3438150	Not Adjustable					13.8–14.4
	Heavy Duty, A/C	2.5–3.1	50	3438150	Not Adjustable					13.8–14.4
	Special Equip.	2.5–3.1	60	3438150	Not Adjustable					13.8–14.4

① Chrysler built—used interchangeably with #2444900, which is Essex wire built. Air gap setting is 0.032–0.042 in, all other dimensions are identical with #2098300

② 51 amp special equipment model available

possible, test the voltage regulator to be sure that the output is correct.

Voltage Regulator Adjustments—1968–69

Adjust the *upper contact* voltage setting as follows:

1. Remove the regulator cover.

2. Use an insulated tool to adjust the upper contact voltage as necessary by bending the regulator lower spring hanger *down* to *increase* the voltage setting or *up* to *decrease* the voltage setting.

3. If the voltage reading is now correct, refit the regulator cover.

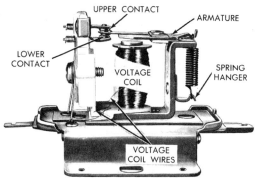

1968–69 regulator with cover removed (Courtesy of Chrysler Corp.)

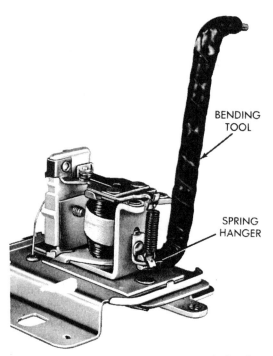

Adjusting the spring tension (Courtesy of Chrysler Corp.)

Adjust the *lower contact* voltage setting as follows:

1. Remove the regulator cover.

2. Measure the lower contact point gap with a feeler gauge. The lower contact gap should be 0.014 in. plus or minus 0.002 in. If necessary, adjust the contact gap by bending the lower stationary contact bracket while making sure that the contacts remain in alignment.

3. If the voltage reading is now correct, refit the regulator cover. If the lower contact gap is correct but the voltage reading is still outside the 0.2–0.7 volt increase, continue this procedure to adjust the lower contacts air gap.

4. Connect a small dry cell and test lamp in series with the IGN and FLD terminals of the voltage regulator.

5. Insert a 0.048 in. wire gauge between the regulator armature and the core of the voltage coil next to the stop pin on the armature.

6. Press down on the armature (not on the contact reed) until the armature contacts the wire gauge. The upper contacts should just open and the test lamp should be dim.

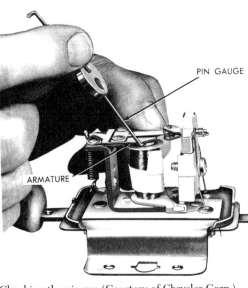

Checking the air gap (Courtesy of Chrysler Corp.)

7. Insert a 0.052 in. wire gauge between the armature and the voltage coil core, next to the stop pin on the armature.

8. Press down on the armature until it contacts the wire gauge. The upper contacts should remain closed and the test lamp should remain bright.

9. To obtain the correct difference of 0.2–0.7 volt increase of the lower contact's voltage over the upper contact voltage, adjust the lower contact's air gap by loosening the stationary contact bracket screw and moving the bracket up or down to obtain the proper air gap setting as follows:

If the difference is above 0.7 volt (V), reduce the air gap to a minimum of 0.045 in. with the contacts open and the test lamp dim. At 0.048 in., the contacts should close and the test lamp should be bright.

If the difference is below 0.2 V, increase the air gap to a maximum of 0.055 in., the contacts should be open and the test lamp should be dim.

Be certain that the air gap is measured with the stationary contact bracket attaching screw fully tightened.

10. When all adjustments are complete, refit the regulator cover.

Transistorized Voltage Regulator

This voltage regulator maintains correct charging voltage by varying the duty cycle of a series of pulses to the alternator field. The pulse frequency is controlled by the ignition frequency of the engine. The regulator has no moving parts and requires no adjustment after it is set internally at the factory. If the unit is found to be defective, it must be removed and replaced with a new regulator.

Voltage Regulator Test

1. Clean the battery terminals and check the specific gravity of the battery electrolyte. If the specific gravity is below 1.200, charge the battery before performing the voltage regulator test as it must be above 1.200 to allow a prompt, regulated voltage check.

2. Connect the positive lead of the test voltmeter to the ignition no. 1 terminal of the ballast resistor. (The end with one or two blue wires connected to it.)

3. Connect the voltmeter negative lead to a good body ground.

4. Start and operate the engine at 1,250 rpm with all lights and accessories switched off. Observe the voltmeter reading. The regulator is working properly if the voltage readings are in accordance with the following chart.

Ambient Temp Near Regulator	Voltage Range
Below 20° F	14.3–15.3
80° F	13.8–14.4
140° F	13.3–14.0
Above 140° F	Less than 13.8

5. If the voltage reading is below the specified limits, check for a bad voltage regulator ground. Using the low voltage scale of the test meter, check for a voltage drop between the regulator cover and body.

If the reading is still low, switch off the ignition and disconnect the voltage regulator connector. Switch on the ignition but do not start the car. Check for battery voltage at the wiring harness terminal connected to the blue and green leads. *Disconnect the wiring harness from the voltage regulator when checking the leads.* Switch off the ignition. If there is no voltage at either lead, the problem is in the vehicle wiring or alternator field circuit. If voltage is present, change the voltage regulator and repeat step 4.

6. If the voltage reading is above the specified limits, check the ground between the voltage regulator and the vehicle body, and between the vehicle body and the engine. Check the ignition switch circuit between the switch battery terminal and the voltage regulator. If the voltage reading is still high (more than ½ V above the specified limits), change the voltage regulator and repeat step 4.

7. Remove the test voltmeter.

STARTER

Chrysler Corporation cars use only two types of starter: a direct-drive type or a 3.5:1 reduction gear type. The reduction gear type may be identified by the battery terminal on the starter being installed at a 45° angle in relation to the case; the direct-drive type starter battery terminal is parallel to the starter case.

Both types have solenoids which are mounted directly on the starter assembly. The starter must be removed from the car to service the solenoid and motor brushes.

Removal and Installation

1. Disconnect the ground cable at the battery.

2. Remove the cable from the starter.

3. Disconnect the solenoid leads at their solenoid terminals.

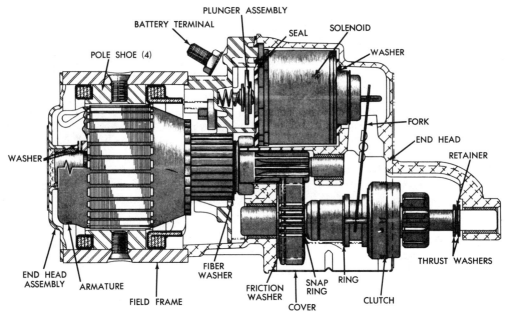

Cutaway view of the reduction gear starter (Courtesy of Chrysler Corp.)

4. Remove the starter securing bolts and withdraw the starter from the engine flywheel housing. On some models with automatic transmissions, the oil cooler tube bracket will interfere with starter removal. In this case, remove the starter securing bolts, slide the cooler tube bracket off the stud, then withdraw the starter.

5. Installation is the reverse of the above. Be sure that the starter and flywheel housing mating surfaces are free of dirt and oil.

Solenoid and Brush Service

REDUCTION GEAR STARTER

1. Remove the starter from the car and support the starter gear housing in a vise with soft jaws. DO NOT CLAMP.

2. Remove the two thru-bolts and the starter end assembly.

3. Carefully pull the armature up and out of the gear housing and the starter frame and field assembly.

4. Carefully pull the frame and field assembly up just enough to expose the terminal screw (which connects the series field coils to one pair of motor brushes) and support it with two blocks.

5. Support the terminal by placing a finger behind the terminal and remove the terminal screw.

6. Unwrap the shunt field coil lead

from the other starter brush terminal. Unwrap the solenoid lead wire from the brush terminals.

7. Remove the steel and fiber thrust washer.

8. Remove the nut, steel washer, and insulating washer from the solenoid terminal.

9. Straighten the solenoid wire and remove the brush holder plate with the brushes and solenoid as an assembly.

10. Inspect the starter brushes. Brushes that are worn more than one-half the length of new brushes or are oil-soaked, should be replaced.

11. Assemble the starter using the reverse of the above procedure. When resoldering the shunt field and solenoid leads, make a strong, low-resistance connection using a high-temperature solder and resin flux. *Do not break the shunt field wire units when removing and installing the brushes.*

DIRECT-DRIVE STARTER

1. Remove the starter from the car and support it in a vise with soft jaws. DO NOT CLAMP.

2. Remove the thru-bolts and tap the commutator and head from the field frame.

3. Remove the thrust washers from the armature shaft.

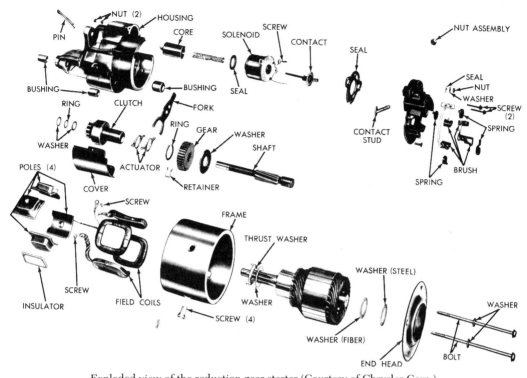

Exploded view of the reduction gear starter (Courtesy of Chrysler Corp.)

4. Lift the brush holder springs and remove the brushes from the brush holders. Remove the brush plate.

5. Disconnect the field coil leads at the solenoid connector.

6. Inspect the starter brushes. Brushes that are worn more than one-half the length of new brushes or are oil-soaked should be replaced. To replace the brushes, continue this procedure as follows.

7. Remove the ground brush terminal screw and carefully remove the ground brush set to prevent breaking the shunt field lead. Remove the shunt field lead from the old brush set to provide as much length as possible.

8. Remove the field terminal plastic covering and remove the old brushes. Use side cutters to break the weld by rolling the stranded wire off the terminal.

9. Drill a 0.174–0.184 in. hole in the series coil terminal $\frac{3}{16}$ in. from the top of the terminal to the centerline of the hole. (Use a no. 16 drill.)

CAUTION: *Do not damage the field coil during the drilling operation.*

10. Attach the insulated brush set to the series field terminal with a flat washer and no. 8 self-tapping screw. Attach the shunt field lead to the new ground brush set by making a loop around the terminal and soldering the lead to the terminal with resin core solder.

11. Attach the ground brush terminal to the field frame with the securing screw. Fold the extra shunt field lead back along the brush lead and secure it with electrical tape.

12. Assemble the starter using the reverse of steps 1–5.

BATTERY

Removal and Installation

1. Protect the paint finish with fender covers.

2. Disconnect the battery cables at the battery terminal posts.

3. Remove the battery hold-down clamp and remove the battery from the vehicle. Reverse the procedure to install. Make sure the battery connections are clean and that bright is showing on the battery posts and cable ends.

Battery and Starter Specifications

		BATTERY			STARTERS						
					Lock Test			No-Load Test			Brush Spring Tension (oz)
Year	Engine Displacement (cu in.)	Ampere Hour Capacity	Volts	Terminal Grounded	Amps	Volts	Torque (ft lbs)	Amps	Volts	RPM	
'68– '69	6-225, 8-318, 273	48	12	Neg.	400–450	4	——	90	11	1,925–2,600	32–36
	8-361	59	12	Neg.	400–450	4	——	90	11	1,925–2,600	32–36
	8-383, 426, 440	70	12	Neg.	400–450	4	——	90	11	1,925–2,600	32–36
	Opt. all others										
	8-426	70	12	Neg.	310–445	4	——	78	11	3,800	32–36
'70– '73	6-225, 8-318, 340	46	12	Neg.	400–450	4	——	90	11	1,925–2,600	32–36
	8-360, 383, 400	59①	12	Neg.	400–450	4	——	90	11	1,925–2,600	32–36
	8-426, 440	70	12	Neg.	400–450	4	——	90	11	1,925–2,600	32–36
	Opt. all others										

① 55 amps for '72 8-360, 8-400

Engine Mechanical

DESIGN

The standard equipment engine in most Plymouth models is the 225 cu in. slant-six. Although this engine has a very long stroke by modern standards, it presents a low profile because the block is canted 30° to the right.

The 273, 318, and 340 cu in. engines make up Chrysler's A block series of V8s. The 273 and 318 cu in. engines answer the need for small, reliable, economy power-plants, while the 340 is chosen where more power is desired.

Chrysler Corporation's B block line is really two series of engines, the low-block and high-block series. These subseries differ in block deck height, main journal diameter, connecting rod length, and push-rod length. Otherwise, they are similar and many parts interchange. The 383 and 400 cu in. engines are low-block types, while the 440 cu in. V8 is of raised-block construction. All these engines are conventional V8s with wedge-shaped combustion chambers and deep blocks that extend well below the crankshaft centerline.

The 426 Hemi is Plymouth's largest, heaviest, most complicated, and most powerful engine. It is basically a B series, raised-block engine, but with so many differences that it must be treated as a completely separate engine. It has hemispherical combustion chambers with 2.25 in. intake and 1.95 in. exhaust valves actuated by rocker arms mounted on separate intake and exhaust rocker shafts. The spark plugs are centrally located in the combustion chambers and aluminum tubes protect the plugs and wires from oil where they pass through the rocker covers. Because of the huge intake ports, there is no room for head bolts on the intake side. Instead, studs are mounted in the head which extend down into the valley between the cylinder heads. To reduce piston side thrust, Hemis use longer connecting rods than other raised-block B engines; to strengthen the lower end, the main caps are cross-bolted. The Hemi engine was discontinued in 1971.

General Engine Specifications

Year	Engine Cu In. Displacement	Carburetor Type	Advertised Horsepower @ rpm ∎	Advertised Torque @ rpm (ft lbs) ∎	Bore and Stroke (in.)	Advertised Compression Ratio	Oil Pressure @ 2000 rpm (psi)
'68	6-225	1 bbl	145 @ 4000	215 @ 2400	3.400 x 4.125	8.40 : 1	55
	8-273	2 bbl	190 @ 4400	260 @ 2000	3.625 x 3.310	9.00 : 1	55
	8-318	2 bbl	230 @ 4400	340 @ 2400	3.910 x 3.310	9.20 : 1	55
	8-383	2 bbl	290 @ 4400	390 @ 2800	4.250 x 3.375	9.20 : 1	55
	8-383	4 bbl	330 @ 5000	425 @ 3200	4.250 x 3.375	10.00 : 1	55
	8-383	4 bbl	335 @ 5200	425 @ 3400	4.250 x 3.375	10.00 : 1	55
	8-426 Hemi	2 x 4 bbl	425 @ 5000	490 @ 4000	4.250 x 3.750	10.25 : 1	55
	8-440	4 bbl	350 @ 4400	480 @ 2800	4.320 x 3.750	10.01 : 1	55
	8-440 HP	4 bbl	375 @ 4600	480 @ 3200	4.320 x 3.750	10.01 : 1	55
'69	6-225	1 bbl	195 @ 4000	215 @ 2400	3.400 x 4.125	8.40 : 1	55
	8-318	2 bbl	230 @ 4400	340 @ 2400	3.910 x 3.310	9.20 : 1	55
	8-383	2 bbl	290 @ 4400	390 @ 2800	4.250 x 3.375	9.20 : 1	55
	8-383	4 bbl	330 @ 5000	425 @ 3200	4.250 x 3.375	10.00 : 1	55
	8-383	4 bbl	335 @ 5200	425 @ 3400	4.250 x 3.375	10.00 : 1	55
	8-426 Hemi	2 x 4 bbl	425 @ 5000	490 @ 4000	4.250 x 3.750	10.25 : 1	55
	8-440	4 bbl	350 @ 4400	480 @ 2800	4.320 x 3.750	10.01 : 1	55
	8-440 HP	4 bbl	375 @ 4600	480 @ 3200	4.320 x 3.750	10.01 : 1	55
'70	6-225	1 bbl	145 @ 4000	215 @ 2400	3.400 x 4.125	8.40 : 1	55
	8-318	2 bbl	230 @ 4400	320 @ 2000	3.910 x 3.310	8.80 : 1	55
	8-383	2 bbl	290 @ 4400	390 @ 2800	4.250 x 3.375	8.70 : 1	55
	8-383	4 bbl	330 @ 5000	425 @ 3200	4.250 x 3.375	9.50 : 1	55
	8-383 HP	4 bbl	335 @ 5200	425 @ 3400	4.250 x 3.375	9.50 : 1	55
	8-426 Hemi	2 x 4 bbl	425 @ 5000	490 @ 4000	4.250 x 3.750	10.20 : 1	55
	8-440	4 bbl	350 @ 4400	480 @ 2800	4.320 x 3.750	9.70 : 1	55
	8-440 HP	4 bbl	375 @ 4600	480 @ 3200	4.320 x 3.750	9.70 : 1	55

General Engine Specifications (cont.)

Year	Engine Cu In. Displacement	Carburetor Type	Advertised Horsepower @ rpm ■	Advertised Torque @ rpm ■ (ft lbs)	Bore and Stroke (in.)	Advertised Compression Ratio	Oil Pressure @ 2000 rpm (psi)
'70	8-440	3 x 2 bbl	390 @ 4700	490 @ 3200	4.320 x 3.750	10.50 : 1	55
'71	6-225	1 bbl	145 @ 4000	215 @ 2400	3.400 x 4.125	8.40 : 1	55
	8-318	2 bbl	230 @ 4400	320 @ 2000	3.910 x 3.310	8.60 : 1	55
	8-340	4 bbl	275 @ 5000	340 @ 3200	4.040 x 3.310	10.30 : 1	55
	8-383	2 bbl	275 @ 4400	375 @ 2800	4.250 x 3.375	8.50 : 1	55
	8-383 HP	4 bbl	300 @ 4800	410 @ 3400	4.250 x 3.375	8.50 : 1	55
	8-426 Hemi	2 x 4 bbl	425 @ 5000	490 @ 4000	4.250 x 3.750	10.20 : 1	55
	8-440	4 bbl	335 @ 4400	460 @ 3200	4.320 x 3.750	8.50 : 1	55
	8-440 HP	4 bbl	375 @ 4600	480 @ 3200	4.320 x 3.750	9.50 : 1	55
	8-440	3 x 2 bbl	385 @ 4700	490 @ 3200	4.320 x 3.750	10.30 : 1	55
'72	6-225	1 bbl	110 @ 4000①	185 @ 2000②	3.400 x 4.125	8.40 : 1	55
	8-318	2 bbl	150 @ 4000	260 @ 1600	3.910 x 3.310	8.60 : 1	55
	8-340	4 bbl	240 @ 4800	290 @ 3600	4.040 x 3.310	8.50 : 1	55
	8-400	2 bbl	190 @ 4400③	310 @ 2400④	4.340 x 3.380	8.20 : 1	55
	8-400	4 bbl	255 @ 4800⑤	340 @ 3200⑥	4.340 x 3.380	8.20 : 1	55
	8-400⑪	4 bbl	265 @ 4800	345 @ 3200	4.340 x 3.380	8.20 : 1	55
	8-440	4 bbl	225 @ 4400⑦	345 @ 3200⑧	4.320 x 3.750	8.20 : 1	55
	8-440	4 bbl	280 @ 4800⑨	375 @ 3200⑩	4.320 x 3.750	8.20 : 1	55
	8-440⑪	4 bbl	290 @ 4800	380 @ 3200	4.320 x 3.750	8.20 : 1	55
'73	6-225	1 bbl	105 @ 4000	185 @ 1600	3.400 x 4.125	8.40 : 1	55
	8-318	2 bbl	150 @ 3600	265 @ 2000	3.910 x 3.310	8.60 : 1	55
	8-340	2 bbl	240 @ 4800	295 @ 3600	4.040 x 3.310	8.50 : 1	55
	8-340	4 bbl	240 @ 4800	295 @ 3600	4.040 x 3.310	8.50 : 1	55
	8-400	2 bbl	185 @ 3600	310 @ 2400	4.340 x 3.380	8.20 : 1	55

General Engine Specifications (cont.)

Year	Engine Cu In. Displacement	Carburetor Type	Advertised Horsepower @ rpm ■	Advertised Torque @ rpm (ft lbs) ■	Bore and Stroke (in.)	Advertised Compression Ratio	Oil Pressure @ 2000 rpm (psi)
'73	8-400	4 bbl	260 @ 4800	335 @ 3600	4.340 x 3.380	8.20 : 1	55
	8-440	4 bbl	220 @ 3600	350 @ 2400	4.320 x 3.750	8.20 : 1	55
	8-440	4 bbl	275 @ 4800	380 @ 3200	4.320 x 3.750	8.20 : 1	55

■ 1972–73 horsepower and torque are SAE net figures. They are measured at the rear of the transmission with all accessories installed and operating. Since the figures vary when a given engine is installed in different models, some are representative rather than exact.

① For California vehicles, advertised horsepower is 97 @ 4000 rpm

② For California vehicles, advertised torque is 180 @ 2000 rpm

③ For California vehicles, advertised horsepower is 181 @ 4400 rpm

④ For California vehicles, advertised torque is 305 @ 2400 rpm

⑤ For California vehicles, advertised horsepower is 246 @ 4800 rpm

⑥ For California vehicles, advertised torque is 335 @ 3200 rpm

⑦ For California vehicles, advertised horsepower is 216 @ 4400 rpm

⑧ For California vehicles, advertised torque is 340 @ 3200 rpm

⑨ For California vehicles, advertised horsepower is 271 @ 4800 rpm

⑩ For California vehicles, advertised torque is 370 @ 3200 rpm

⑪ Not available in California

HP High Performance

Valve Specifications

Year	Engine No. Cyl Displacement (cu in.)	Seat Angle (deg)	Face Angle (deg)	Spring Test Pressure (lbs @ in.)	Spring Installed Height (in.)	STEM TO GUIDE Clearance (in.) Intake	STEM TO GUIDE Clearance (in.) Exhaust	STEM Diameter (in.) Intake	STEM Diameter (in.) Exhaust
'68	6-225	45	45①	144 @ 1.31	1¹¹⁄₁₆	0.0010–0.0030	0.0020–0.0040	0.3725	0.3715
	8-273	45	45①	177 @ 1.31	1¹¹⁄₁₆	0.0010–0.0030	0.0020–0.0040	0.3725	0.3715
	8-318	45	45①	177 @ 1.31	1¹¹⁄₁₆	0.0010–0.0030	0.0020–0.0040	0.3725	0.3715
	8-383③	45	45	200 @ 1.44	1⅞	0.0010–0.0030	0.0020–0.0040	0.3725	0.3715
	8-383④	45	45	230 @ 1.41	1⅞	0.0010–0.0030	0.0020–0.0040	0.3725	0.3715
	8-426	45	45	280 @ 1.38	1⅞	0.0020–0.0040	0.0030–0.0050	0.3090	0.3080
	8-440	45	45	200 @ 1.44	1⅞	0.0010–0.0030	0.0020–0.0040	0.3725	0.3715
	8-440⑥	45	45	230 @ 1.41	1⅞	0.0010–0.0030	0.0020–0.0040	0.3725	0.3715
'69	6-225	45	45①	144 @ 1.31	1¹¹⁄₁₆	0.0010–0.0030	0.0020–0.0040	0.3725	0.3715
	8-318	45	45①	177 @ 1.31	1¹¹⁄₁₆	0.0010–0.0030	0.0020–0.0040	0.3725	0.3715
	8-383③	45	45	200 @ 1.44	1⅞	0.0010–0.0030	0.0020–0.0040	0.3725	0.3715

Valve Specifications (cont.)

Year	Engine No. Cyl Displacement (cu in.)	Seat Angle (deg)	Face Angle (deg)	Spring Test Pressure (lbs @ in.)	Spring Installed Height (in.)	STEM TO GUIDE Clearance (in.)		STEM Diameter (in.)	
						Intake	Exhaust	Intake	Exhaust
'69	8-383④	45	45	246 @ 1.36	1⅞	0.0010–0.0030	0.0020–0.0040	0.3725	0.3715
	8-426	45	45	280 @ 1.38	1⅞	0.0020–0.0040	0.0030–0.0050	0.3090	0.3080
	8-440	45	45	200 @ 1.44	1⅞	0.0010–0.0030	0.0020–0.0040	0.3725	0.3715
	8-440⑥	45	45	246 @ 1.36	1⅞	0.0010–0.0030	0.0020–0.0040	0.3725	0.3715
'70	6-225	45	45①	144 @ 1.31	1¹¹⁄₁₆	0.0010–0.0030	0.0020–0.0040	0.3725	0.3715
	8-318	45	45①	177 @ 1.31	1¹¹⁄₁₆	0.0010–0.0030	0.0020–0.0040	0.3725	0.3715
	8-383③	45	45	200 @ 1.44	1⅞	0.0010–0.0030	0.0020–0.0040	0.3727	0.3717
	8-383④	45	45	246 @ 1.72	1⅞	0.0015–0.0032	0.0025–0.0042	0.3722	0.3712
	8-426	45	45	200 @ 1.44	1⅞	0.0020–0.0040	0.0030–0.0050	0.3090	0.3080
	8-440	45	45	246 @ 1.72	1⅞	0.0010–0.0030	0.0020–0.0040	0.3727	0.3717
	8-440⑥	45	45	310 @ 1.38	1⅞	0.0015–0.0032	0.0025–0.0042	0.3722	0.3712
'71	6-225	45	45①	144 @ 1.31	1¹¹⁄₁₆	0.0010–0.0030	0.0020–0.0040	0.3725	0.3715
	8-318	45	45①	177 @ 1.31	1¹¹⁄₁₆	0.0010–0.0030	0.0020–0.0040	0.3725	0.3715
	8-340	45	45①	238 @ 1.31	1¹¹⁄₁₆	0.0015–0.0035	0.0025–0.0045	0.3720	0.3710
	8-383③	45	45	200 @ 1.44	1⅞	0.0010–0.0030	0.0020–0.0040	0.3727	0.3717
	8-383④	45	45	246 @ 1.72	1⅞	0.0015–0.0032	0.0025–0.0042	0.3722	0.3712
	8-426	45	45	310 @ 1.28	1⅞	0.0020–0.0040	0.0030–0.0050	0.3090	0.3080
	8-440	45	45	200 @ 1.44	1⅞	0.0010–0.0030	0.0020–0.0040	0.3722	0.3717
	8-440⑥	45	45	246 @ 1.72	1⅞	0.0015–0.0032	0.0025–0.0042	0.3722	0.3712
'72	6-225	45	45①	144 @ 1.31	1¹¹⁄₁₆	0.0010–0.0030	0.0020–0.0040	0.3725	0.3715
	8-318	45	45①	177 @ 1.31	1¹¹⁄₁₆	0.0010–0.0030	0.0020–0.0040	0.3725	0.3715
	8-340	45	45①	208 @ 1.31	1¹¹⁄₁₆	0.0015–0.0035	0.0025–0.0045	0.3720	0.3710
	8-400③	45	45	200 @ 1.44	1⅞	0.0010–0.0030	0.0020–0.0040	0.3727	0.3717
	8-400④	45	45	246 @ 1.72	1⅞	0.0015–0.0032	0.0025–0.0042	0.3722	0.3712

Valve Specifications (cont.)

Year	Engine No. Cyl Displacement (cu in.)	Seat Angle (deg)	Face Angle (deg)	Spring Test Pressure (lbs @ in.)	Spring Installed Height (in.)	STEM TO GUIDE Clearance (in.)		STEM Diameter (in.)	
						Intake	Exhaust	Intake	Exhaust
'72	8-440	45	45	200 @ 1.44	1⅞	0.0010–0.0030	0.0020–0.0040	0.3727	0.3717
	8-440⑥	45	45	246 @ 1.72	1⅞	0.0015–0.0032	0.0025–0.0042	0.3722	0.3712
'73	6-225	45	45②	160 @ 1.24	1$\frac{21}{32}$	0.0010–0.0030	0.0020–0.0040	0.3725	0.3715
	8-318	45	45②	189 @ 1.28	1$\frac{21}{32}$	0.0010–0.0030	0.0020–0.0040	0.3725	0.3715
	8-340	45	45②	238 @ 1.22	1$\frac{21}{32}$	0.0015–0.0035	0.0025–0.0045	0.3720	0.3710
	8-400③	45	45	200 @ 1.42	1$\frac{55}{64}$	0.0010–0.0027	⑦	0.3727	⑨
	8-400④	45	45	234 @ 1.40	1$\frac{55}{64}$	0.0015–0.0032	⑧	0.3722	⑩
	8-440	45	45	200 @ 1.42	1$\frac{55}{64}$	0.0010–0.0027	⑦	0.3727	⑨
	8-440⑥	45	45	234 @ 1.40	1$\frac{55}{64}$	0.0015–0.0032	⑧	0.3722	⑩

① Exhaust 43°
② Exhaust 47°
③ 2 bbl carburetor
④ 4 bbl carburetor
⑤ Hemi
⑥ Hi-Performance

⑦ Hot end—0.0020–0.0037, cold end—0.0010–0.0027
⑧ Hot end—0.0025–0.0042, cold end—0.0015–0.0032
⑨ Hot end—0.3716, cold end—0.3726
⑩ Hot end—0.3711, cold end—0.3721

Ring Gap

Year	Engine	Top Compression	Bottom Compression	Year	Engine	Oil Control
'68–'72	6-225, 8-273 318, 340, 8-383, 400, 426, 440	0.010–0.020 0.013–0.023	0.010–0.020 0.013–0.023	'68–'73	All engines	0.015–0.055
'73	6-225, 8-318	0.010–0.020	0.010–0.020			
'73	8-340, 400, 440	0.013–0.023	0.013–0.023			

Ring Side Clearance

Year	Engine	Top Compression	Bottom Compression	Year	Engine	Oil Control
'68–'73	All engines	0.0015–0.0030	0.0015–0.0030	'68–'73	6-225, 8-273, 318, 426, 340	0.0002–0.0050
					8-383, 440, 400	0.0000–0.0050

Crankshaft and Connecting Rod Specifications

All measurements are given in in.

Year	Engine Displacement (cu in.)	CRANKSHAFT				CONNECTING ROD		
		Main Brg. Journal Dia	Main Brg. Oil Clearance	Shaft End-Play	Thrust on No.	Journal Diameter	Oil Clearance	Clearance Side
'68–'73	6-225	2.7495–2.7505	0.0005–0.0015	0.002–0.007	3	2.1865–2.1875	0.0005–0.0015	0.006–0.012
'68	8-273, 318	2.4495–2.5005	0.0005–0.0015	0.002–0.007	3	2.1240–2.1250	0.0005–0.0025	0.006–0.014
'68–'73	8-318, 340	2.4495–2.5005	0.0005–0.0015	0.002–0.007	3	2.1240–2.1250	0.0005–0.0025	0.009–0.017
'68–'73	8-361, 383, 400	2.6245–2.6255	0.0005–0.0015	0.002–0.007	3	2.3740–2.3750	0.0005–0.0015	0.009–0.017
'68–'73	426, 440	2.7495–2.7505	0.0005–0.0015	0.002–0.007	3	2.3740–2.3750	0.0010–0.0020	0.009–0.017
'68	426 Hemi	2.7495–2.7505	0.0015–0.0025	0.002–0.007	3	2.3740–2.3750	0.0015–0.0025	0.009–0.013
'69–'70	426 Hemi	2.7495–2.7505	0.0015–0.0025	0.002–0.007	3	2.3740–2.3750	0.0015–0.0025	0.009–0.017
'71	426 Hemi	2.7490–2.7500	0.0015–0.0030	0.002–0.007	3	2.3738–2.3745	0.0015–0.0025	0.013–0.017

Torque Specifications
All readings in ft lbs

Year	Engine Displacement (cu in.)	Cylinder Head Bolts	Rod Bearing Bolts	Main Bearing Bolts	Crankshaft Pulley Bolt	Flywheel to Crankshaft Bolts	MANIFOLD	
							Intake	Exhaust
'68–'73	6—All	70	45	85	Press fit	55	10①	10
'68–'73	8-273, 318, 340	95	45	85	135②	65	40	30
	8-361, 383, 400, 440	70	45	85	135②	55	40	30
'68–'72	8-426	75	75	100③	135	70	④	35

① Intake to exhaust bolts—20 ft. lbs.
② '71 318, 340, cu in. engines—100 ft. lbs.
③ Cross bolt mains—45 ft. lbs.
④ 4 center bolts on either side—6 ft. lbs., others 40 ft. lbs.

ENGINE REMOVAL AND INSTALLATION

1. Scribe the outline of the hood hinge brackets on the bottom of the hood and remove the hood.
2. Drain the cooling system and remove the radiator.
3. Remove the battery.
4. Taking note of their positions, remove the fuel lines from the pump and plug the lines.
5. Being sure to take note of their positions, remove all wires and hoses that attach to the engine (except air conditioning hoses). Remove all emission control equipment that may be damaged by the engine removal procedure.
6. If the vehicle is equipped with air conditioning and/or power steering, remove the unit from the engine and position it out of the way *without disconnecting the lines.*
7. On six-cylinder models, attach a lifting sling to the engine cylinder head. On V8 models (except the Hemi), remove the carburetor and attach the engine lifting fixture to the carburetor flange studs on the intake manifold. On models with the Hemi engine, never attempt to remove the engine with the lifting sling attached to the intake manifold. Instead, attach a lifting sling to the front of the left cylinder head, and the rear strap to the rear of the right cylinder head.
8. Raise the vehicle on a hoist and install an engine support fixture to support the rear of the engine.

9. On models with automatic transmissions, drain the transmission and torque converter. On models with standard transmissions, disconnect the clutch torque shaft from the engine.
10. Disconnect the exhaust pipe from the exhaust manifold.
11. Remove the driveshaft.
12. Disconnect the transmission linkage and any wiring or cables that attach to the transmission.
13. Remove the engine rear support crossmember and remove the transmission.
14. Remove the bolts that attach the motor mounts to the chassis.
15. Lower the vehicle and, with a suitable hoist attached, carefully remove the engine from the vehicle.
16. Reverse the above procedure to install. To properly install the transmission to the engine, refer to the appropriate transmission installation procedure in the "Transmission" section of this book.

CYLINDER HEAD

Removal and Installation

6 CYLINDER MODELS

1. Disconnect the battery.
2. The entire cooling system must be drained by opening the drain cock in the radiator and removing the drain plug on the side of the engine block.
3. Remove the vacuum line at the carburetor and distributor.
4. Disconnect the accelerator linkage.
5. Remove the spark plug wires at the plug.

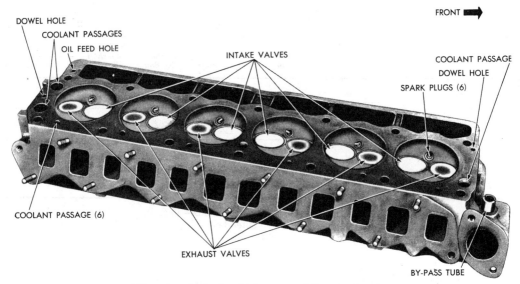

DOWEL HOLE
COOLANT PASSAGES
OIL FEED HOLE
INTAKE VALVES
FRONT
COOLANT PASSAGE
DOWEL HOLE
SPARK PLUGS (6)
COOLANT PASSAGE (6)
EXHAUST VALVES
BY-PASS TUBE

Slant six cylinder head (Courtesy of Chrysler Corp.)

6. Taking note of their positions, disconnect the heater hoses.

7. Disconnect the temperature sending wire.

8. Disconnect the exhaust pipe at the exhaust manifold flange.

9. Disconnect the diverter valve vacuum at the intake manifold and take the air tube assembly from the cylinder head (if so equipped).

10. Remove the PCV and evaporative control system (if so equipped).

11. Remove the intake/exhaust manifold and carburetor as an assembly. Remove the valve cover.

12. Remove the rocker arms and shaft assembly.

13. Remove the pushrods, being sure to take note of their location so they may be installed in their original location.

14. Remove 14 head bolts and the cylinder head.

15. Installation is the reverse of the above. While the head is off, check it for warpage with a straightedge. In addition, install the head gasket with a good quality sealer and be sure to torque the head bolts in the proper sequence to the specified torque. Torque the bolts in three stages.

273, 318, 340, 383, 400, AND 440 CU IN. ENGINES

1. Drain the cooling system and disconnect the battery ground cable.

2. Remove the alternator, air cleaner, and fuel line.

3. Disconnect the accelerator linkage.

4. Remove the vacuum advance line from between the carburetor and the distributor.

5. Remove the distributor cap and wires as an assembly.

6. Disconnect the coil wires, water temperature sending unit, heater hoses, and by-pass hose.

7. Remove the closed ventilation system, the evaporative control system (if so equipped), and the valve covers.

8. Remove the intake manifold, ignition coil, and carburetor as an assembly.

9. Remove the exhaust manifolds.

10. Remove the rocker and shaft assemblies.

11. Remove the pushrods and keep them in order to ensure installation in their original locations.

12. Remove the head bolts from each cylinder head and remove the cylinder heads.

To install the cylinder heads, proceed as follows:

1. Clean all the gasket surfaces of the engine block and the cylinder heads. Install the spark plugs.

2. Coat new cylinder head gaskets with sealer, install the gaskets, and refit the cylinder heads.

3. Install the cylinder head bolts. For 273, 318, and 340 cu in. engines, torque the cylinder head bolts to 50 ft lbs in the sequence indicated in the illustration. Repeat this sequence and torque all the cyl-

inder head bolts to 85 ft lbs for the 273 and 318 cu in. engines or to 95 ft lbs for the 340 cu in. engine. For 383, 400, and 440 cu in. engines, torque the cylinder head bolts to 40 ft lbs in the sequence indicated. Repeat this sequence and re-torque all the cylinder head bolts to 70 ft lbs.

4. Reverse the removal procedure (steps 1–12) to complete the installation.

426 HEMI ENGINE

1. Disconnect the battery ground cable and drain the cooling system.

2. Remove the air cleaner, and also the distributor cap and the cable assembly.

3. Remove the cables from the spark plugs and remove the spark plugs.

4. Disconnect the brake lines at the master cylinder and remove the cotter pin and the clevis pin from the linkage at the rear of the power brake unit.

5. Remove the four nuts securing the brake booster to its mounting bracket and remove the power brake and master cylinder assembly.

6. Remove the valve covers and gaskets.

7. Remove the rocker and shaft assemblies.

8. Remove the pushrods and keep them in order to ensure installation in their original locations.

9. Remove the alternator and disconnect the accelerator cable and transmission throttle rod from the upper bellcrank.

10. Disconnect the fuel line at the "T" fitting.

11. Disconnect the intake manifold heat tubes located at the rear of the manifold. Remove the air tube between the automatic choke and the exhaust manifold.

12. Remove the intake manifold securing bolts. (There are three locating dowels at each end of the manifold.)

13. Remove the intake manifold with the ignition coil, both carburetors, fuel lines, fuel filters, throttle linkage, and the upper bellcrank as an assembly.

14. Disconnect the exhaust headers from the cylinder heads and tie them out of the way.

15. Remove the lower eight cylinder head bolts.

16. Remove the four stud nuts from the cylinder head studs inside the tappet chamber.

17. Remove the cylinder heads and place them on suitable supports. *To protect the studs, do not set the cylinder head down on the studs at any time.*

To install the cylinder heads, proceed as follows:

1. Clean all the gasket surfaces of the engine block and the cylinder heads.

2. Coat new cylinder head gaskets with sealer and install the gaskets with their raised beads toward the engine block. If the cylinder head studs were removed or worked loose, the studs will have to be coated with sealer and torqued to 20 ft lbs. Replace the cylinder heads on the engine block.

3. Install the cylinder head stud nuts inside the tappet chamber and the eight short lower cylinder head bolts. *Do not tighten at this time.*

4. Install the rocker arm and shaft assemblies and, after refitting the five *long* cylinder head bolts, torque all the head bolts and stud nuts to 50 ft lbs in the sequence indicated in the illustration. Repeat this sequence to torque all the bolts and stud nuts to 75 ft lbs.

5. Reverse the removal procedure to complete the installation.

Cylinder Head Torque Sequences

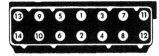

6 cyl. models (Courtesy of Chrysler Corp.)

273, 318, 340 V8's (Courtesy of Chrysler Corp.)

383, 400, 440 V8's (Courtesy of Chrysler Corp.)

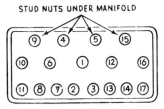

426 Hemi V8 (Courtesy of Chrysler Corp.)

ROCKER SHAFTS

Removal and Installation

6 CYLINDER MODELS

1. Remove the closed ventilation system.
2. Remove the evaporative control system (if so equipped).
3. Remove the valve cover with its gasket.
4. Take out the rocker arm and shaft assembly securing bolts and remove the rocker arm and shaft.
5. Reverse the above for installation. The flat on the end of the shaft must be on top and point toward the front of the engine to provide proper lubrication to the rocker arms. Torque the rocker arm bolts to 25 ft lbs and be sure to adjust the valves.

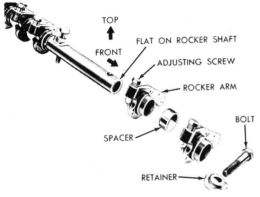

6 cyl. rocker shaft and arm. Note the adjusting screw and rocker shaft flat locations. (Courtesy of Chrysler Corp.)

273, 318, 340, 383, 400, AND 440 CU IN. ENGINES

The stamped steel rocker arms are arranged on one rocker arm shaft per cylinder head. Because the angle of the pushrods tends to force the rocker arm pairs toward each other, oilite spacers are fitted to absorb the side thrust at each rocker arm. To remove the rocker arm and shaft, adhere to the following procedure.

1. Disconnect the spark plug wires.
2. Disconnect the closed ventilation and evaporative control system (if so equipped).
3. Remove the valve covers with their gaskets.
4. Remove the rocker shaft bolts and retainers, and lift off the rocker arm assembly.

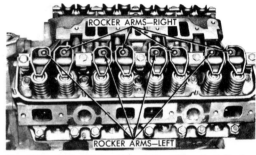

On 318, 340, 383, 400, 440, V8's, install the rocker arms as shown (Courtesy of Chrysler Corp.)

5. Reverse the above procedure to install. The notch on the end of both rocker shafts should point to the engine centerline and toward the front of the engine on the left cylinder head, or toward the rear on the right cylinder head. Torque the rocker shaft bolts on the 273 engine to 30 ft lbs, on the 318 and 340 engines to 210 in. lbs, and, on the 383, 400, and 440 cu in. engines, to 25 ft lbs.

426 HEMI ENGINE

1. Disconnect the battery and remove the air cleaner, distributor cap, and spark plug cables. Remove the spark plugs.
2. Disconnect the brake lines at the master cylinder and remove the cotter pin and clevis pin from the linkage at the rear of the power brake unit.
3. Remove the nuts securing the brake booster to its mounting bracket and remove the power brake and master cylinder assembly.
4. Remove the valve cover with its gasket.
5. Remove the bolts that retain the rocker arm support brackets to the cylinder head and engine block. Remove the rocker arm assembly.
6. Reverse the above for installation. When installing, be sure to note the positions of the oil holes in the no. 2 and no. 4 brackets; they must not be obstructed.

INTAKE MANIFOLD

Removal and Installation

6 CYLINDER COMBINATION MANIFOLD

1. Remove the air cleaner and the fuel line from the carburetor.
2. Disconnect the accelerator linkage.
3. Disconnect the exhaust pipe at the exhaust manifold flange.

4. Withdraw the manifold assembly-to-cylinder head bolts and remove the intake and exhaust manifolds with the carburetor as a single unit. The manifolds may be separated by removing the three bolts which hold them together.

5. Installation is the reverse of the above. When installing the manifold assembly, use new gaskets and a good commercial sealer. Loosen the three bolts that secure the intake manifold to the exhaust manifold to maintain proper alignment in relation to each other and the block. Torque these three bolts to 15 ft lbs. in this sequence: inner bolts first, then the outer two bolts. Torque the manifold assembly to cylinder head bolts to 10 ft lbs.

ALL V8s EXCEPT 426 HEMI

1. Drain the cooling system and disconnect the battery.

2. Remove the air cleaner and fuel line from the carburetor.

3. Disconnect the accelerator linkage.

4. Remove the vacuum control between the carburetor and distributor.

5. Remove the distributor cap and wires.

6. Disconnect the coil wires, temperature sending unit wires, and heater and by-pass hoses.

7. Remove the intake manifold securing bolts and remove the manifold and carburetor as an assembly.

8. To install the manifold, reverse the removal procedure. Be sure to torque the manifold in three steps and remember to use a good commercial sealer on new manifold gaskets.

426 HEMI

1. Drain the cooling system and disconnect the battery.

2. Remove the air cleaner and fuel lines from the carburetors.

3. Disconnect the accelerator linkage.

4. Remove the vacuum control line between the carburetor and distributor. Remove the distributor cap and wires.

5. Disconnect the coil wires, heater hoses, and by-pass hose.

6. Remove the two stud nuts and washers which retain the intake manifold inlet heat tube to the right-hand exhaust header.

7. Remove the screws attaching the upper end of the inlet tube to the rear face of the intake manifold.

8. Remove the inlet tube and discard the gaskets.

9. Remove the nut, washer, and bolt from the tube clamp at the exhaust pipe. Remove the clamp from the outlet tube.

10. Remove the screws attaching the heat shield and outlet tube to the rear face of the intake manifold and remove the tube and shield.

11. Remove the intake manifold securing bolts and remove the manifold with the carburetors and coil as an assembly.

12. To install the manifold, reverse the removal procedure. Be sure to torque the manifold in the proper sequence and to use a good-quality commercial sealer on the new manifold gaskets. Since the manifold is made from aluminum, be careful not to strip the bolt threads when tightening.

Intake Manifold Torque Sequences

NOTE: *Torque the manifold in two steps.*

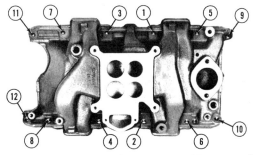

All V8 models except the 426 Hemi (Courtesy of Chrysler Corp.)

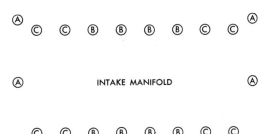

426 Hemi (Courtesy of Chrylser Corp.)

EXHAUST MANIFOLD

Removal and Installation

6 CYLINDER MODELS

Because the intake and exhaust manifolds are combined in one unit on this engine, please refer to the intake manifold removal procedure.

V8 MODELS

1. Disconnect the exhaust manifold at the flange where it mates to the exhaust pipe.

2. If the vehicle is equipped with air injection and/or a carburetor-heated air stove, remove them.

3. Remove the exhaust manifold by removing the securing bolts and washers. To reach these bolts, it may be necessary to jack the engine slightly off its front mounts. When the exhaust manifold is removed, sometimes the securing studs will screw out with the nuts. If this occurs, the studs must be replaced with the aid of sealing compound on the coarse thread ends. If this is not done, water leaks may develop at the studs. To install the exhaust manifold, reverse the removal procedure.

TIMING COVER, CHAIN, AND CAMSHAFT

On both six-cylinder and V8 models, it is normal to find particles of rubber collected between the seal retainer and the crankshaft oil slinger after the seal has been in service. It is recommended, whenever any internal engine service is performed, that a 1 qt container of Chrysler High-Performance Additive (Sulfurized Ester) be added to the engine oil to aid in initial break-in.

Timing Cover and Timing Chain Removal

6 CYLINDER MODELS

1. Disconnect the battery and drain the cooling system.

2. Remove the radiator and fan.

3. Remove the vibration damper with a puller.

4. Loosen the oil pan bolts to allow clearance and remove the timing case cover and gasket.

5. Slide the crankshaft oil slinger off the front of the crankshaft.

6. Remove the camshaft sprocket bolt.

7. Remove the timing chain with the camshaft sprocket.

8. To begin the installation procedure, rotate the crankshaft to line up the timing mark on the crankshaft sprocket with the centerline of the camshaft (without the chain).

9. Remove the camshaft sprocket and reinstall with the chain. Torque the sprocket to 35 ft lbs.

10. Replace the oil slinger.

11. From this point, reverse the removal procedure.

V8 MODELS

When installing a timing chain on a V8 engine, have an assistant support the camshaft with a screwdriver to prevent the camshaft from contacting the welch plug in the rear of the engine block. Remove the distributor and the oil pump/distributor drive gear.

Position the screwdriver against the rear of the cam gear and be careful not to damage the cam lobes.

1. Disconnect the battery and drain the cooling system.

2. Remove the vibration damper and pulley. On 273, 318, and 340 cu in. engines, remove the fuel lines and fuel pump, then loosen the oil pan bolts and remove the front bolt on each side.

3. Remove the timing gear cover and the crankshaft oil slinger.

4. On 273, 318, and 340 cu in. engines, remove the camshaft sprocket lockbolt, securing cup washer, and fuel pump eccentric. Remove the timing chain. On 383, 400, and 440 cu in. engines, remove the camshaft sprocket lockbolt and remove the timing chain with the camshaft and crankshaft sprockets.

5. To begin the installation procedure, place the camshaft and crankshaft sprockets on a flat surface with the timing indicators on an imaginary centerline through both sprocket bores. Place the timing chain around both sprockets. Be sure the timing marks are in alignment.

6. Turn the crankshaft and camshaft to align them with the keyway location in the crankshaft sprocket and the dowel hole in the camshaft sprocket.

7. Lift the sprockets and timing chain while keeping the sprockets tight against the chain in the correct position. Slide

both sprockets evenly onto their respective shafts.

8. Use a straightedge to measure the alignment of the sprocket timing marks. They must be perfectly aligned.

9. On 273, 318, and 340 cu in. engines, install the fuel pump eccentric, cup washer, and camshaft sprocket lockbolt, and torque to 35 ft lbs. On 383, 400, 426, and 440 V8s, install the washer and camshaft sprocket lockbolt and then torque the lockbolt to 35 ft lbs. Check to make sure that the rear face of the camshaft sprocket is flush with the camshaft end.

On the 426 Hemi, install the washers and camshaft lockbolt. Torque the lockbolt to 40 ft lbs.

Checking Timing Chain Slack

1. Position a scale next to the timing chain to detect any movement in the chain.

2. Place a torque wrench and socket on the camshaft sprocket attaching bolt.

Checking timing chain slack (Courtesy of Chrylser Corp.)

Apply either 30 ft lbs (if the cylinder heads are installed on the engine) or 15 ft lbs (cylinder heads removed) of force to the bolt and rotate the bolt in the direction of crankshaft rotation in order to remove all slack from the chain.

3. While applying torque to the camshaft sprocket bolt, the crankshaft should not be allowed to rotate. It may be necessary to block the crankshaft to prevent rotation.

4. Position the scale over the edge of a timing chain link and apply an equal amount of torque in the opposite direction. If the movement of the chain exceeds $3/16$ in., replace the chain.

Camshaft Removal and Installation

6 Cylinder Models

1. Remove the cylinder head, timing gear cover, camshaft sprocket, and timing chain.

Valve timing marks, all 6 cylinder (Courtesy of Chrysler Corp.)

2. Remove the valve tappets, keeping them in order to ensure installation in their original locations.

3. Remove the crankshaft sprocket.

4. Remove the distributor and oil pump.

5. Remove the fuel pump.

6. Fit a long bolt into the front of the camshaft to facilitate its removal.

7. Remove the camshaft, being careful not to damage the cam bearings with the cam lobes.

8. Lubricate the camshaft lobes and bearing journals with camshaft lubricant. In addition, it is recommended that 1 qt of Chrysler High-Performance Additive (Sulfurized Ester) be added to the initial crankcase oil fill.

9. Install the camshaft in the engine block. From this point, reverse the removal procedure.

V8 Models

1. Remove the cylinder heads. Remove the timing gear cover, the camshaft and crankshaft sprocket, and the timing chain.

2. Remove the valve tappets, keeping them in order to ensure installation in their original location.

3. Remove the distributor and lift out the oil pump and distributor driveshaft.

4. Remove the camshaft thrust plate (if so equipped).

5. Fit a long bolt into the front of the camshaft and remove the camshaft, being careful not to damage the cam bearings with the cam lobes.

6. Lubricate the camshaft lobes and

Valve timing marks, all V8 (Courtesy of Chrysler Corp.)

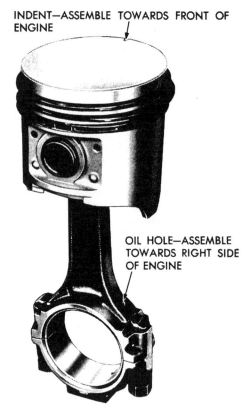

INDENT—ASSEMBLE TOWARDS FRONT OF ENGINE

OIL HOLE—ASSEMBLE TOWARDS RIGHT SIDE OF ENGINE

6 cylinder piston and connecting rod locating marks (Courtesy of Chrysler Corp.)

bearing journals with camshaft lubricant. In addition, it is recommended that 1 qt of Chrysler High-Performance Additive (Sulferized Ester) be added to the initial crankcase oil fill. Insert the camshaft into the engine block within 2 in. of its final position in the block.

7. Have an assistant support the camshaft with a screwdriver to prevent the camshaft from contacting the freeze plug in the rear of the engine block. Remove the distributor and the oil pump/ distributor drive gear. Position the screwdriver against the rear side of the cam gear and be careful not to damage the cam lobes.

8. Refit the camshaft thrust plate (if so equipped).

9. Install the oil pump and distributor driveshaft. Install the distributor. (Refer to the distributor "Installation" procedure.)

10. Inspect the crown of all the tappet faces with a straightedge. Replace any tappets that have dished or worn surfaces. Install the tappets.

11. Install the timing gear, gear cover, and the cylinder heads.

PISTONS AND CONNECTING RODS

Removal and Installation

ALL ENGINES

1. Remove the cylinder heads, intake and exhaust manifolds, and oil pan.

2. Use a ridge reamer to remove the ring ridge at the top of the cylinder bores. Keep the piston tops covered during the reaming operation.

3. Make note of the piston and connecting rod identification marks. These marks must face the same direction when the engine is reassembled. All piston and connecting rod assemblies must be returned to their original bores.

4. Rotate the crankshaft so that the piston and connecting rod to be removed are at bottom dead center.

5. Remove the connecting rod cap.

6. Push the piston and connecting rod assembly out of the top of the bore.

7. Reverse the above steps to install. Torque all bolts to proper specifications. Make sure all piston and connecting rods are in their original bores and facing proper direction.

NOTE: *See the engine rebuilding section for bearing renewal and ring renewal procedures.*

Piston and Connecting Rod Identification

To maintain correct balance, all pistons are the same weight, whether or not they are oversize. Oversize pistons are available for honed or rebored cylinders. Available sizes are: 0.005, 0.020, 0.040 in.

Piston sizes are stamped on the top of the piston.

Piston and Connecting Rod Positioning

For all models except 426 Hemi, the notch on the top of each piston must face the front of the engine. On 426 Hemi engines, the arrow on the piston top points toward the front of the engine.

To position the connecting rod correctly, the oil squirt hole should point to the right side on all six cylinder engines. On all V8 engines except the 426 Hemi, the larger chamber of the lower connecting rod bore must face toward the crankpin journal fillet. On the 426 Hemi, the connecting rod locating tang must face outboard.

Engine Lubrication

OIL PAN

Removal and Installation

6 CYLINDER

1. Jack up the front of the car and drain the oil. Disconnect the battery.
2. Remove the ball joints from the steering linkage center link and position the link forward out of the way.
3. Remove the front motor mount bolts.
4. Raise the engine 2 in. Remove the dust shield.
5. Remove the pan bolts.
6. Remove the pan. It may be necessary to rotate the crankshaft to get enough clearance to remove the pan.
7. Reverse the above steps to install. Use a new pan gasket and a good gasket sealer.

V8

1. Disconnect the battery. Remove the dipstick.
2. Raise the front of the car and drain the oil. Remove the engine-to-converter left housing brace.
3. Remove the idler arm and steering arm ball joints from the center steering link and position the link out of the way.
4. Disconnect the crossover pipe from the exhaust manifolds. In some cases it may be necessary to remove the pipe from the car.

5. Remove the converter dust cover.
6. Remove the oil pan bolts and remove the oil pan. It may be necessary to rotate the crankshaft to obtain clearance.
7. Reverse the above steps to install. Use a new gasket and a good gasket sealer. Torque the oil pan bolts to 200 in. lbs. The oil pump strainer must touch the bottom of the oil pan.

REAR MAIN BEARING OIL SEAL

Replacement oil seals are the split rubber type. Both halves of the seal must be replaced at the same time.

1. Remove the oil pan. On V8 engines remove the oil pump.
2. Remove the rear main bearing cap and seal retainer.
3. Remove the lower half rope seal from the bearing cap. Remove the upper half by driving on either exposed end with a short piece of $3/16$ in. brazing wire. As the end of the seal becomes exposed, grasp it with a pair of pliers and pull it gently from the block.
4. Loosen the crankshaft main bearing caps just enough to allow the crankshaft to drop $1/16$ in. Do not allow the crankshaft to drop enough to permit the main bearings to become displaced.
5. Wipe the crankshaft clean and lightly oil the crankshaft and new seal before installation.
6. Hold the seal tightly against the crankshaft (with the paint stripe to the rear) and install the upper seal half into its groove. If necessary, rotate the crankshaft as the seal is pushed in place.
7. Install the lower seal half into the rear main bearing cap, with the paint stripe to the rear.
8. Install the rear main bearing cap. CAUTION: *Make sure all main bearings are properly located before tightening the rest of the bearing caps.*
9. Tighten the rest of the bearing caps.
10. Install the oil pump, if removed, and oil pan.

OIL PUMP

Removal and Installation

6 CYLINDER

1. Drain the radiator, disconnect its upper and lower hoses, and remove the fan shroud.
2. Raise the vehicle and remove the

front engine mounting bolts. Jack the engine up 2 in.

3. Remove the oil filter, oil pump attaching bolts, and pump assembly.

4. Installation is the reverse of the removal procedures. Always use new O-ring and gaskets. Torque bolts to 200 in. lbs.

273, 318, 340 V8 Engines

1. Remove the oil pan.

2. Remove the oil pump from the rear main bearing cap.

3. Reverse the above steps to install. Torque the bolts to the proper specifications.

383, 400, 440 V8

1. The oil pump is on the outside of the block near the front of the engine.

2. Remove the oil pump attaching bolts.

3. Remove the oil pump.

4. Reverse the above steps to install. Use new O-rings and gaskets.

Engine Cooling

RADIATOR

Removal and Installation

1. Drain the cooling system. Detach the oil cooling lines for the automatic transmission if so equipped.

2. Disconnect the hose clamps and remove the upper and lower radiator hoses from the radiator.

3. Remove the fan shroud if so equipped. Slide the fan rearward over the fan and rest it on the engine.

4. Remove the radiator attaching bolts and lift the radiator out of the car.

5. Reverse the above steps to install. On automatic transmission equipped cars, check the fluid level. Fill the cooling system with the proper mixture of glycol antifreeze and water.

WATER PUMP

Removal and Installation

1. Drain the cooling system.

2. Remove the fan shroud securing screws and remove the shroud or position it out of the way.

3. It may be necessary to remove the radiator on some models to gain working space.

4. Remove the alternator belt by loosening the alternator securing bolts. Remove all other accessory drive belts.

5. Remove the fan, spacer or fluid drive, and the water pump pulley. Do not rest the fluid drive with its shaft pointing downward as this will cause the silicon drive fluid to drain down into the fan bearing and cause a bearing failure.

6. On some models, it may be necessary to remove the alternator or compressor mounting brackets to gain access to the water pump bolts.

CAUTION: *On cars equipped with air conditioning do not disconnect any refrigerant hoses. Serious injury could result from the high pressure liquid freon contained in these hoses.*

7. Remove the water pump securing bolts and remove the water pump.

8. Install a new water pump on the block using a new gasket and gasket sealer on both sides of the gasket. After tightening the bolts, make sure the pump still rotates.

9. Refit the alternator and/or compressor brackets if removed.

10. Install the fan, spacer or fluid drive, and pulley.

11. Install all drive belts and tighten to proper tension, 1/4 in. deflection at the mid-point of the longest distance between pulleys.

12. Install the radiator and fan shroud. Fill the cooling system.

THERMOSTAT

Removal and Installation

1. Partially drain the cooling system to a level slightly below the thermostat. The thermostat is located in the block at the end of the upper radiator hose.

EIGHT CYLINDER   SIX CYLINDER

Install the thermostat with the end at the bottom of the illustration in the block (Courtesy of Chrysler Corp.)

2. Remove the upper radiator hose from the thermostat housing.

3. Remove the thermostat housing bolts. Remove the housing.

4. Remove the thermostat from the block.

5. To install, reverse the above steps. Use a new gasket and gasket sealer. Always place the thermostat with the temperature sensing end facing into the block.

Testing

1. Make sure the thermostat is fully closed when cold. It may be held open by foreign material. If, after cleaning, the thermostat will not close, replace the thermostat.

2. To check for proper operation, immerse the thermostat in boiling water. Do not allow the thermostat to touch the sides or bottom of the pan.

3. The thermostat should open in the boiling water. If it does not, replace the thermostat. When reinstalling the thermostat make sure it is facing the proper direction as improper installation will cause malfunctions similar to a failed thermostat.

Engine Rebuilding

This section describes, in detail, the procedures involved in rebuilding a typical engine. The procedures specifically refer to an inline engine, however, they are basically identical to those used in rebuilding engines of nearly all design and configurations. Procedures for servicing atypical engines (i.e., horizontally opposed) are described in the appropriate section, although in most cases, cylinder head reconditioning procedures described in this chapter will apply.

The section is divided into two sections. The first, Cylinder Head Reconditioning, assumes that the cylinder head is removed from the engine, all manifolds are removed, and the cylinder head is on a workbench. The camshaft should be removed from overhead cam cylinder heads. The second section, Cylinder Block Reconditioning, covers the block, pistons, connecting rods and crankshaft. It is assumed that the engine is mounted on a work stand, and the cylinder head and all accessories are removed.

Procedures are identified as follows:

Unmarked—Basic procedures that must be performed in order to successfully complete the rebuilding process.

Starred (*)—Procedures that should be performed to ensure maximum performance and engine life.

Double starred (**)—Procedures that may be performed to increase engine performance and reliability. These procedures are usually reserved for extremely heavy-duty or competition usage.

In many cases, a choice of methods is also provided. Methods are identified in the same manner as procedures. The choice of method for a procedure is at the discretion of the user.

The tools required for the basic rebuilding procedure should, with minor exceptions, be those

TORQUE (ft. lbs.) *

U.S.

Bolt Diameter (inches)	Bolt Grade (SAE)				Wrench Size (inches)	
	1 and 2	5	6	8	Bolt	Nut
1/4	5	7	10	10.5	3/8	7/16
5/16	9	14	19	22	1/2	9/16
3/8	15	25	34	37	9/16	5/8
7/16	24	40	55	60	5/8	3/4
1/2	37	60	85	92	3/4	13/16
9/16	53	88	120	132	7/8	7/8
5/8	74	120	167	180	15/16	1
3/4	120	200	280	296	1-1/8	1-1/8
7/8	190	302	440	473	1-5/16	1-5/16
1	282	466	660	714	1-1/2	1-1/2

Metric

Bolt Diameter (mm)	Bolt Grade				Wrench Size (mm)
	5D	8G	10K	12K	Bolt and Nut
6	5	6	8	10	10
8	10	16	22	27	14
10	19	31	40	49	17
12	34	54	70	86	19
14	55	89	117	137	22
16	83	132	175	208	24
18	111	182	236	283	27
22	182	284	394	464	32
24	261	419	570	689	36

*—Torque values are for lightly oiled bolts. CAUTION: Bolts threaded into aluminum require much less torque.

General Torque Specifications

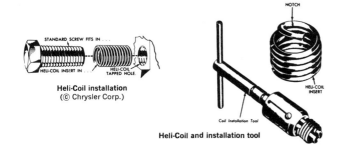

Heli-Coil installation
(© Chrysler Corp.)

Heli-Coil and installation tool

Heli-Coil Insert		Drill	Tap	Insert. Tool	Extract- ing Tool
Thread Size	Part No.	Insert Length (In.)	Size	Part No.	Part No.	Part No.
1/2 -20	1185-4	3/8	17/64 (.266)	4 CPB	528-4N	1227-6
5/16-18	1185-5	15/32	Q (.332)	5 CPB	528-5N	1227-6
3/8 -16	1185-6	9/16	X (.397)	6 CPB	528-6N	1227-6
7/16-14	1185-7	21/32	29/64 (.453)	7 CPB	528-7N	1227-16
1/2 -13	1185-8	3/4	33/64 (.516)	8 CPB	528-8N	1227-16

Heli-Coil Specifications

included in a mechanic's tool kit. An accurate torque wrench, and a dial indicator (reading in thousandths) mounted on a universal base should be available. Bolts and nuts with no torque specification should be tightened according to size (see chart). Special tools, where required, all are readily available from the major tool suppliers (i.e., Craftsman, Snap-On, K-D). The services of a competent automotive machine shop must also be readily available.

When assembling the engine, any parts that will be in frictional contact must be pre-lubricated, to provide protection on initial start-up. Vortex Pre-Lube, STP, or any product specifically formulated for this purpose may be used. NOTE: *Do not use engine oil.* Where semi-permanent (locked but removable) installation of bolts or nuts is desired, threads should be cleaned and coated with Loctite. Studs may be permanently installed using Loctite Stud and Bearing Mount.

Aluminum has become increasingly popular for use in engines, due to its low weight and excellent heat transfer characteristics. The following precautions must be observed when handling aluminum engine parts:
—Never hot-tank aluminum parts.
—Remove all aluminum parts (identification tags, etc.) from engine parts before hot-tanking (otherwise they will be removed during the process).
—Always coat threads lightly with engine oil or anti-seize compounds before installation, to prevent seizure.
—Never over-torque bolts or spark plugs in aluminum threads. Should stripping occur, threads can be restored according to the following procedure, using Heli-Coil thread inserts:

Tap drill the hole with the stripped threads to the specified size (see chart). Using the specified tap (NOTE: *Heli-Coil tap sizes refer to the size thread being replaced, rather than the actual tap size*), tap the hole for the Heli-Coil. Place the insert on the proper installation tool (see chart). Apply pressure on the insert while winding it clockwise into the hole, until the top of the insert is one turn below the surface. Remove the installation tool, and break the installation tang from the bottom of the in-

sert by moving it up and down. If the Heli-Coil must be removed, tap the removal tool firmly into the hole, so that it engages the top thread, and turn the tool counter-clockwise to extract the insert.

Snapped bolts or studs may be removed, using a stud extractor (unthreaded) or Vise-Grip pliers (threaded). Penetrating oil (e.g., Liquid Wrench) will often aid in breaking frozen threads. In cases where the stud or bolt is flush with, or below the surface, proceed as follows:

Drill a hole in the broken stud or bolt, approximately ½ its diameter. Select a screw extractor (e.g., Easy-Out) of the proper size, and tap it into the stud or bolt. Turn the extractor counter-clockwise to remove the stud or bolt.

Magnaflux and Zyglo are inspection techniques used to locate material flaws, such as stress cracks. Magnafluxing coats the part with fine magnetic particles, and subjects the part to a magnetic field. Cracks cause breaks

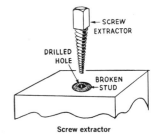

Screw extractor

in the magnetic field, which are outlined by the particles. Since Magnaflux is a magnetic process, it is applicable only to ferrous materials. The Zyglo process coats the material with a fluorescent dye penetrant, and then subjects it to blacklight inspection, under which cracks glow bright-

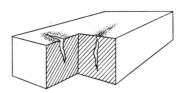

Magnaflux indication of cracks

ly. Parts made of any material may be tested using Zyglo. While Magnaflux and Zyglo are excellent for general inspection, and locating hidden defects, specific checks of suspected cracks may be made at lower cost and more readily using spot check dye. The dye is sprayed onto the suspected area, wiped off, and the area is then sprayed with a developer. Cracks then will show up bright-ly. Spot check dyes will only indicate surface cracks; therefore, structural cracks below the surface may escape detection. When questionable, the part should be tested using Magnaflux or Zyglo.

CYLINDER HEAD RECONDITIONING

Procedure	Method
Identify the valves:  **Valve identification** (© SAAB)	Invert the cylinder head, and number the valve faces front to rear, using a permanent felt-tip marker.
Remove the rocker arms:	Remove the rocker arms with shaft(s) or balls and nuts. Wire the sets of rockers, balls and nuts together, and identify according to the corresponding valve.
Remove the valves and springs:	Using an appropriate valve spring compressor (depending on the configuration of the cylinder head), compress the valve springs. Lift out the keepers with needlenose pliers, release the compressor, and remove the valve, spring, and spring retainer.
Check the valve stem-to-guide clearance:  **Checking the valve stem-to-guide clearance** (© American Motors Corp.)	Clean the valve stem with lacquer thinner or a similar solvent to remove all gum and varnish. Clean the valve guides using solvent and an expanding wire-type valve guide cleaner. Mount a dial indicator so that the stem is at 90° to the valve stem, as close to the valve guide as possible. Move the valve off its seat, and measure the valve guide-to-stem clearance by moving the stem back and forth to actuate the dial indicator. Measure the valve stems using a micrometer, and compare to specifications, to determine whether stem or guide wear is responsible for excessive clearance.
De-carbon the cylinder head and valves: 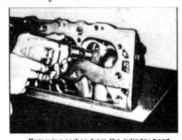 **Removing carbon from the cylinder head** (© Chevrolet Div. G.M. Corp.)	Chip carbon away from the valve heads, combustion chambers, and ports, using a chisel made of hardwood. Remove the remaining deposits with a stiff wire brush. NOTE: *Ensure that the deposits are actually removed, rather than burnished.*

Procedure	Method
Hot-tank the cylinder head:	Have the cylinder head hot-tanked to remove grease, corrosion, and scale from the water passages. NOTE: *In the case of overhead cam cylinder heads, consult the operator to determine whether the camshaft bearings will be damaged by the caustic solution.*
Degrease the remaining cylinder head parts:	Using solvent (i.e., Gunk), clean the rockers, rocker shaft(s) (where applicable), rocker balls and nuts, springs, spring retainers, and keepers. Do not remove the protective coating from the springs.
Check the cylinder head for warpage:  **Checking the cylinder head for warpage** (© Ford Motor Co.)	Place a straight-edge across the gasket surface of the cylinder head. Using feeler gauges, determine the clearance at the center of the straight-edge. Measure across both diagonals, along the longitudinal centerline, and across the cylinder head at several points. If warpage exceeds .003″ in a 6″ span, or .006″ over the total length, the cylinder head must be resurfaced. NOTE: *If warpage exceeds the manufacturers maximum tolerance for material removal, the cylinder head must be replaced.* When milling the cylinder heads of V-type engines, the intake manifold mounting position is altered, and must be corrected by milling the manifold flange a proportionate amount.
** Porting and gasket matching:  **Marking the cylinder head for gasket matching** (© Petersen Publishing Co.)  **Port configuration before and after gasket matching** (© Petersen Publishing Co.)	** Coat the manifold flanges of the cylinder head with Prussian blue dye. Glue intake and exhaust gaskets to the cylinder head in their installed position using rubber cement and scribe the outline of the ports on the manifold flanges. Remove the gaskets. Using a small cutter in a hand-held power tool (i.e., Dremel Moto-Tool), gradually taper the walls of the port out to the scribed outline of the gasket. Further enlargement of the ports should include the removal of sharp edges and radiusing of sharp corners. Do not alter the valve guides. NOTE: *The most efficient port configuration is determined only by extensive testing. Therefore, it is best to consult someone experienced with the head in question to determine the optimum alterations.*

Procedure	*Method*
** Polish the ports:	** Using a grinding stone with the above mentioned tool, polish the walls of the intake and exhaust ports, and combustion chamber. Use progressively finer stones until all surface imperfections are removed. NOTE: *Through testing, it has been determined that a smooth surface is more effective than a mirror polished surface in intake ports, and vice-versa in exhaust ports.*

Relieved and polished ports
((© Petersen Publishing Co.)

Polished combustion chamber
((© Petersen Publishing Co.)

| * Knurling the valve guides: | * Valve guides which are not excessively worn or distorted may, in some cases, be knurled rather than replaced. Knurling is a process in which metal is displaced and raised, thereby reducing clearance. Knurling also provides excellent oil control. The possibility of knurling rather than replacing valve guides should be discussed with a machinist. |

Cut-away view of a knurled valve guide
((© Petersen Publishing Co.)

| Replacing the valve guides: NOTE: *Valve guides should only be replaced if damaged or if an oversize valve stem is not available.* | Depending on the type of cylinder head, valve guides may be pressed, hammered, or shrunk in. In cases where the guides are shrunk into the head, replacement should be left to an equipped machine shop. In other cases, the guides are replaced as follows: Press or tap the valve guides out of the head using a stepped drift (see illustration). Determine the height above the boss that the guide must extend, and obtain a stack of washers, their I.D. similar to the guide's O.D., of that height. Place the stack of washers on the guide, and insert the guide into the boss. NOTE: *Valve guides are often tapered or beveled for installation.* Using the stepped installation tool (see illustration), press or tap the guides into position. Ream the guides according to the size of the valve stem. |

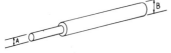

A-VALVE GUIDE I.D.
B-SLIGHTLY SMALLER THAN VALVE GUIDE O.D.

Valve guide removal tool

WASHERS

A-VALVE GUIDE I.D.
B-LARGER THAN THE VALVE GUIDE O.D.

Valve guide installation tool (with washers used during installation)

Procedure	*Method*
Replacing valve seat inserts:	Replacement of valve seat inserts which are worn beyond resurfacing or broken, if feasible, must be done by a machine shop.
Resurfacing (grinding) the valve face:   **Grinding a valve** (© Subaru) 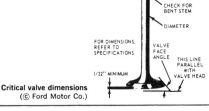 **Critical valve dimensions** (© Ford Motor Co.)	Using a valve grinder, resurface the valves according to specifications. CAUTION: *Valve face angle is not always identical to valve seat angle.* A minimum margin of 1/32″ should remain after grinding the valve. The valve stem tip should also be squared and resurfaced, by placing the stem in the V-block of the grinder, and turning it while pressing lightly against the grinding wheel.
Resurfacing the valve seats using reamers:  **Reaming the valve seat** (© S.p.A. Fiat) **Valve seat width and centering** (© Ford Motor Co.)	Select a reamer of the correct seat angle, slightly larger than the diameter of the valve seat, and assemble it with a pilot of the correct size. Install the pilot into the valve guide, and using steady pressure, turn the reamer clockwise. CAUTION: *Do not turn the reamer counter-clockwise.* Remove only as much material as necessary to clean the seat. Check the concentricity of the seat (see below). If the dye method is not used, coat the valve face with Prussian blue dye, install and rotate it on the valve seat. Using the dye marked area as a centering guide, center and narrow the valve seat to specifications with correction cutters. NOTE: *When no specifications are available, minimum seat width for exhaust valves should be 5/64″, intake valves 1/16″.* After making correction cuts, check the position of the valve seat on the valve face using Prussian blue dye.
* Resurfacing the valve seats using a grinder:  **Grinding a valve seat** (© Subaru)	Select a pilot of the correct size, and a coarse stone of the correct seat angle. Lubricate the pilot if necessary, and install the tool in the valve guide. Move the stone on and off the seat at approximately two cycles per second, until all flaws are removed from the seat. Install a fine stone, and finish the seat. Center and narrow the seat using correction stones, as described above.

Procedure	Method
Checking the valve seat concentricity : 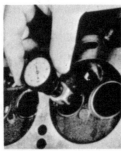 **Checking the valve seat concentricity using a dial gauge** (ⓒ American Motors Corp.)	Coat the valve face with Prussian blue dye, install the valve, and rotate it on the valve seat. If the entire seat becomes coated, and the valve is known to be concentric, the seat is concentric.
	* Install the dial gauge pilot into the guide, and rest the arm on the valve seat. Zero the gauge, and rotate the arm around the seat. Run-out should not exceed .002″.
* Lapping the valves : NOTE : *Valve lapping is done to ensure efficient sealing of resurfaced valves and seats. Valve lapping alone is not recommended for use as a resurfacing procedure.*  **Hand lapping the valves** 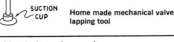 HAND DRILL ROD SUCTION CUP **Home made mechanical valve lapping tool**	* Invert the cylinder head, lightly lubricate the valve stems, and install the valves in the head as numbered. Coat valve seats with fine grinding compound, and attach the lapping tool suction cup to a valve head (NOTE : *Moisten the suction cup*). Rotate the tool between the palms, changing position and lifting the tool often to prevent grooving. Lap the valve until a smooth, polished seat is evident. Remove the valve and tool, and rinse away all traces of grinding compound.
	** Fasten a suction cup to a piece of drill rod, and mount the rod in a hand drill. Proceed as above, using the hand drill as a lapping tool. CAUTION : *Due to the higher speeds involved when using the hand drill, care must be exercised to avoid grooving the seat.* Lift the tool and change direction of rotation often.
Check the valve springs : 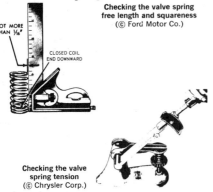 **Checking the valve spring free length and squareness** (ⓒ Ford Motor Co.) NOT MORE THAN 1/16″ CLOSED COIL END DOWNWARD **Checking the valve spring tension** (ⓒ Chrysler Corp.)	Place the spring on a flat surface next to a square. Measure the height of the spring, and rotate it against the edge of the square to measure distortion. If spring height varies (by comparison) by more than 1/16″ or if distortion exceeds 1/16″, replace the spring.
	** In addition to evaluating the spring as above, test the spring pressure at the installed and compressed (installed height minus valve lift) height using a valve spring tester. Springs used on small displacement engines (up to 3 liters) should be ± 1 lb. of all other springs in either position. A tolerance of ± 5 lbs. is permissible on larger engines.

Procedure	Method
* Install valve stem seals:  **Valve stem seal installation** (© Ford Motor Co.) SEAL	* Due to the pressure differential that exists at the ends of the intake valve guides (atmospheric pressure above, manifold vacuum below), oil is drawn through the valve guides into the intake port. This has been alleviated somewhat since the addition of positive crankcase ventilation, which lowers the pressure above the guides. Several types of valve stem seals are available to reduce blow-by. Certain seals simply slip over the stem and guide boss, while others require that the boss be machined. Recently, Teflon guide seals have become popular. Consult a parts supplier or machinist concerning availability and suggested usages. NOTE: *When installing seals, ensure that a small amount of oil is able to pass the seal to lubricate the valve guides; otherwise, excessive wear may result.*
Install the valves:	Lubricate the valve stems, and install the valves in the cylinder head as numbered. Lubricate and position the seals (if used, see above) and the valve springs. Install the spring retainers, compress the springs, and insert the keys using needlenose pliers or a tool designed for this purpose. NOTE: *Retain the keys with wheel bearing grease during installation.*
Checking valve spring installed height: 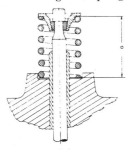  **Valve spring installed height dimension** (© Porsche) **Measuring valve spring installed height** (© Petersen Publishing Co.)	Measure the distance between the spring pad and the lower edge of the spring retainer, and compare to specifications. If the installed height is incorrect, add shim washers between the spring pad and the spring. CAUTION: *Use only washers designed for this purpose.*
** CC'ing the combustion chambers:	** Invert the cylinder head and place a bead of sealer around a combustion chamber. Install an apparatus designed for this purpose (burette mounted on a clear plate; see illustration) over the combustion chamber, and fill with the specified fluid to an even mark on the burette. Record the burette reading, and fill the combustion chamber with fluid. (NOTE: *A hole drilled in the plate will permit air to escape*). Subtract the burette reading, with the combustion chamber filled, from the previous reading, to determine combustion chamber volume in cc's. Duplicate this procedure in all combustion

Procedure	*Method*

CC'ing the combustion chamber
(© Petersen Publishing Co.)

chambers on the cylinder head, and compare the readings. The volume of all combustion chambers should be made equal to that of the largest. Combustion chamber volume may be increased in two ways. When only a small change is required (usually), a small cutter or coarse stone may be used to remove material from the combustion chamber. NOTE: *Check volume frequently.* Remove material over a wide area, so as not to change the configuration of the combustion chamber. When a larger change is required, the valve seat may be sunk (lowered into the head). NOTE: *When altering valve seat, remember to compensate for the change in spring installed height.*

Inspect the rocker arms, balls, studs, and nuts (where applicable):

 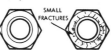

Stress cracks in rocker nuts
(© Ford Motor Co.)

Visually inspect the rocker arms, balls, studs, and nuts for cracks, galling, burning, scoring, or wear. If all parts are intact, liberally lubricate the rocker arms and balls, and install them on the cylinder head. If wear is noted on a rocker arm at the point of valve contact, grind it smooth and square, removing as little material as possible. Replace the rocker arm if excessively worn. If a rocker stud shows signs of wear, it must be replaced (see below). If a rocker nut shows stress cracks, replace it. If an exhaust ball is galled or burned, substitute the intake ball from the same cylinder (if it is intact), and install a new intake ball. NOTE: *Avoid using new rocker balls on exhaust valves.*

Replacing rocker studs:

Reaming the stud bore for oversize rocker studs
(© Buick Div. G.M. Corp.)

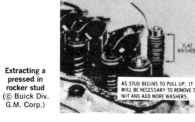

Extracting a pressed in rocker stud
(© Buick Div. G.M. Corp.)

In order to remove a threaded stud, lock two nuts on the stud, and unscrew the stud using the lower nut. Coat the lower threads of the new stud with Loctite, and install.

Two alternative methods are available for replacing pressed in studs. Remove the damaged stud using a stack of washers and a nut (see illustration). In the first, the boss is reamed .005-.006″ oversize, and an oversize stud pressed in. Control the stud extension over the boss using washers, in the same manner as valve guides. Before installing the stud, coat it with white lead and grease. To retain the stud more positively, drill a hole through the stud and boss, and install a roll pin. In the second method, the boss is tapped, and a threaded stud installed. Retain the stud using Loctite Stud and Bearing Mount.

Procedure	Method
Inspect the rocker shaft(s) and rocker arms (where applicable):  **Disassembled rocker shaft parts arranged for inspection** (© American Motors Corp.) 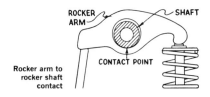 ROCKER ARM · SHAFT CONTACT POINT Rocker arm to rocker shaft contact	Remove rocker arms, springs and washers from rocker shaft. NOTE: *Lay out parts in the order they are removed.* Inspect rocker arms for pitting or wear on the valve contact point, or excessive bushing wear. Bushings need only be replaced if wear is excessive, because the rocker arm normally contacts the shaft at one point only. Grind the valve contact point of rocker arm smooth if necessary, removing as little material as possible. If excessive material must be removed to smooth and square the arm, it should be replaced. Clean out all oil holes and passages in rocker shaft. If shaft is grooved or worn, replace it. Lubricate and assemble the rocker shaft.
Inspect the camshaft bushings and the camshaft (overhead cam engines):	See next section.
Inspect the pushrods:	Remove the pushrods, and, if hollow, clean out the oil passages using fine wire. Roll each pushrod over a piece of clean glass. If a distinct clicking sound is heard as the pushrod rolls, the rod is bent, and must be replaced.
	* The length of all pushrods must be equal. Measure the length of the pushrods, compare to specifications, and replace as necessary.
Inspect the valve lifters: 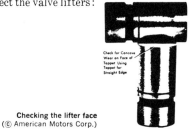 Check for Concave Wear on Face of Tappet Using Tappet for Straight Edge **Checking the lifter face** (© American Motors Corp.)	Remove lifters from their bores, and remove gum and varnish, using solvent. Clean walls of lifter bores. Check lifters for concave wear as illustrated. If face is worn concave, replace lifter, and carefully inspect the camshaft. Lightly lubricate lifter and insert it into its bore. If play is excessive, an oversize lifter must be installed (where possible). Consult a machinist concerning feasibility. If play is satisfactory, remove, lubricate, and reinstall the lifter.
* Testing hydraulic lifter leak down:  Lock Ring Plunger Cap Push Rod Socket Metering Disc Plunger Valve Seat Valve Valve Spring Valve Retainer Plunger Return Spring Tappet Body **Exploded view of a typical hydraulic lifter** (© American Motors Corp.)	Submerge lifter in a container of kerosene. Chuck a used pushrod or its equivalent into a drill press. Position container of kerosene so pushrod acts on the lifter plunger. Pump lifter with the drill press, until resistance increases. Pump several more times to bleed any air out of lifter. Apply very firm, constant pressure to the lifter, and observe rate at which fluid bleeds out of lifter. If the fluid bleeds very quickly (less than 15 seconds), lifter is defective. If the time exceeds 60 seconds, lifter is sticking. In either case, recondition or replace lifter. If lifter is operating properly (leak down time 15-60 seconds), lubricate and install it.

CYLINDER BLOCK RECONDITIONING

Procedure	*Method*
Checking the main bearing clearance:	Invert engine, and remove cap from the bearing to be checked. Using a clean, dry rag, thoroughly clean all oil from crankshaft journal and bearing insert. NOTE: *Plastigage is soluble in oil; therefore, oil on the journal or bearing could result in erroneous readings.* Place a piece of Plastigage along the full length of journal, reinstall cap, and torque to specifications. Remove bearing cap, and determine bearing clearance by comparing width of Plastigage to the scale on Plastigage envelope. Journal taper is determined by comparing width of the Plastigage strip near its ends. Rotate crankshaft 90° and retest, to determine journal eccentricity. NOTE: *Do not rotate crankshaft with Plastigage installed.* If bearing insert and journal appear intact, and are within tolerances, no further main bearing service is required. If bearing or journal appear defective, cause of failure should be determined before replacement.

Plastigage installed on main bearing journal
(© Chevrolet Div. G.M. Corp.)

Measuring Plastigage to determine
main bearing clearance
(© Chevrolet Div. G.M. Corp.)

Causes of bearing failure
(© Ford Motor Co.)

* Remove crankshaft from block (see below). Measure the main bearing journals at each end twice (90° apart) using a micrometer, to determine diameter, journal taper and eccentricity. If journals are within tolerances, reinstall bearing caps at their specified torque. Using a telescope gauge and micrometer, measure bearing I.D. parallel to piston axis and at 30° on each side of piston axis. Subtract journal O.D. from bearing I.D. to determine oil clearance. If crankshaft journals appear defective, or do not meet tolerances, there is no need to measure bearings; for the crankshaft will require grinding and/or undersize bearings will be required. If bearing appears defective, cause for failure should be determined prior to replacement.

Checking the connecting rod bearing clearance:	Connecting rod bearing clearance is checked in the same manner as main bearing clearance, using Plastigage. Before removing the crankshaft, connecting rod side clearance also should be measured and recorded.

Plastigage installed on connecting rod
bearing journal
(© Chevrolet Div. G.M. Corp.)

* Checking connecting rod bearing clearance, using a micrometer, is identical to checking main bearing clearance. If no other service

Procedure	*Method*
**Measuring Plastigage to determine connecting rod bearing clearance** (© Chevrolet Div. G.M. Corp.)	is required, the piston and rod assemblies need not be removed.
Removing the crankshaft: **Connecting rod matching marks** (© Ford Motor Co.)	Using a punch, mark the corresponding main bearing caps and saddles according to position (i.e., one punch on the front main cap and saddle, two on the second, three on the third, etc.). Using number stamps, identify the corresponding connecting rods and caps, according to cylinder (if no numbers are present). Remove the main and connecting rod caps, and place sleeves of plastic tubing over the connecting rod bolts, to protect the journals as the crankshaft is removed. Lift the crankshaft out of the block.
Remove the ridge from the top of the cylinder: 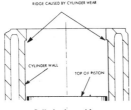**Cylinder bore ridge** (© Pontiac Div. G.M. Corp.)	In order to facilitate removal of the piston and connecting rod, the ridge at the top of the cylinder (unworn area; see illustration) must be removed. Place the piston at the bottom of the bore, and cover it with a rag. Cut the ridge away using a ridge reamer, exercising extreme care to avoid cutting too deeply. Remove the rag, and remove cuttings that remain on the piston. CAUTION: *If the ridge is not removed, and new rings are installed, damage to rings will result.*
Removing the piston and connecting rod: **Removing the piston** (© SAAB)	Invert the engine, and push the pistons and connecting rods out of the cylinders. If necessary, tap the connecting rod boss with a wooden hammer handle, to force the piston out. CAUTION: *Do not attempt to force the piston past the cylinder ridge* (see above).

Procedure	Method
Service the crankshaft:	Ensure that all oil holes and passages in the crankshaft are open and free of sludge. If necessary, have the crankshaft ground to the largest possible undersize.
	** Have the crankshaft Magnafluxed, to locate stress cracks. Consult a machinist concerning additional service procedures, such as surface hardening (e.g., nitriding, Tuftriding) to improve wear characteristics, cross drilling and chamfering the oil holes to improve lubrication, and balancing.
Removing freeze plugs:	Drill a small hole in the center of the freeze plugs. Thread a large sheet metal screw into the hole and remove the plug with a slide hammer.
Remove the oil gallery plugs:	Threaded plugs should be removed using an appropriate (usually square) wrench. To remove soft, pressed in plugs, drill a hole in the plug, and thread in a sheet metal screw. Pull the plug out by the screw using a slide hammer.
Hot-tank the block:	Have the block hot-tanked to remove grease, corrosion, and scale from the water jackets. NOTE: *Consult the operator to determine whether the camshaft bearings will be damaged during the hot-tank process.*
Check the block for cracks:	Visually inspect the block for cracks or chips. The most common locations are as follows: Adjacent to freeze plugs. Between the cylinders and water jackets. Adjacent to the main bearing saddles. At the extreme bottom of the cylinders. Check only suspected cracks using spot check dye (see introduction). If a crack is located, consult a machinist concerning possible repairs.
	** Magnaflux the block to locate hidden cracks. If cracks are located, consult a machinist about feasibility of repair.
Install the oil gallery plugs and freeze plugs:	Coat freeze plugs with sealer and tap into position using a piece of pipe, slightly smaller than the plug, as a driver. To ensure retention, stake the edges of the plugs. Coat threaded oil gallery plugs with sealer and install. Drive replacement soft plugs into block using a large drift as a driver.
	* Rather than reinstalling lead plugs, drill and tap the holes, and install threaded plugs.

Procedure	*Method*

Check the bore diameter and surface:

Visually inspect the cylinder bores for roughness, scoring, or scuffing. If evident, the cylinder bore must be bored or honed oversize to eliminate imperfections, and the smallest possible oversize piston used. The new pistons should be given to the machinist with the block, so that the cylinders can be bored or honed exactly to the piston size (plus clearance). If no flaws are evident, measure the bore diameter using a telescope gauge and micrometer, or dial gauge, parallel and perpendicular to the engine centerline, at the top (below the ridge) and bottom of the bore. Subtract the bottom measurements from the top to determine taper, and the parallel to the centerline measurements from the perpendicular measurements to determine eccentricity. If the measurements are not within specifications, the cylinder must be bored or honed, and an oversize piston installed. If the measurements are within specifications the cylinder may be used as is, with only finish honing (see below). NOTE: *Prior to submitting the block for boring, perform the following operation(s).*

1, 2, 3 Piston skirt seizure resulted in this pattern. Engine must be rebored

4. Piston skirt and oil ring seizure caused this damage. Engine must be rebored

5, 6 Score marks caused by a split piston skirt. Damage is not serious enough to warrant reboring

7. Ring seized longitudinally, causing a score mark 1 3/16" wide, on the land side of the piston groove. The honing pattern is destroyed and the cylinder must be rebored

8. Result of oil ring seizure. Engine must be rebored

9. Oil ring seizure here was not serious enough to warrant reboring. The honing marks are still visible

Cylinder wall damage
(© Daimler-Benz A.G.)

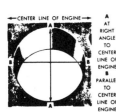

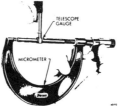

Cylinder bore measuring positions
(© Ford Motor Co.)

Measuring the cylinder bore with a telescope gauge
(© Buick Div. G.M. Corp.)

Determining the cylinder bore by measuring the telescope gauge with a micrometer
(© Buick Div. G.M. Corp.)

Measuring the cylinder bore with a dial gauge
(© Chevrolet Div. G.M. Corp.)

Procedure	*Method*
Check the block deck for warpage:	Using a straightedge and feeler gauges, check the block deck for warpage in the same manner that the cylinder head is checked (see Cylinder Head Reconditioning). If warpage exceeds specifications, have the deck resurfaced. NOTE: *In certain cases a specification for total material removal (Cylinder head and block deck) is provided. This specification must not be exceeded.*
* Check the deck height:	The deck height is the distance from the crankshaft centerline to the block deck. To measure, invert the engine, and install the crankshaft, retaining it with the center main cap. Measure the distance from the crankshaft journal to the block deck, parallel to the cylinder centerline. Measure the diameter of the end (front and rear) main journals, parallel to the centerline of the cylinders, divide the diameter in half, and subtract it from the previous measurement. The results of the front and rear measurements should be identical. If the difference exceeds .005″, the deck height should be corrected. NOTE: *Block deck height and warpage should be corrected concurrently.*
Check the cylinder block bearing alignment:  **Checking main bearing saddle alignment** (© Petersen Publishing Co.)	Remove the upper bearing inserts. Place a straightedge in the bearing saddles along the centerline of the crankshaft. If clearance exists between the straightedge and the center saddle, the block must be align-bored.
Clean and inspect the pistons and connecting rods: 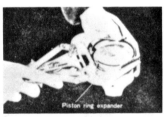 **Removing the piston rings** (© Subaru)	Using a ring expander, remove the rings from the piston. Remove the retaining rings (if so equipped) and remove piston pin. NOTE: *If the piston pin must be pressed out, determine the proper method and use the proper tools; otherwise the piston will distort.* Clean the ring grooves using an appropriate tool, exercising care to avoid cutting too deeply. Thoroughly clean all carbon and varnish from the piston with solvent. CAUTION: *Do not use a wire brush or caustic solvent on pistons.* Inspect the pistons for scuffing, scoring, cracks, pitting, or excessive ring groove wear. If wear is evident, the piston must be replaced. Check the connecting rod length by measuring the rod from the inside of the large end to the inside of the small end using calipers (see

Procedure	*Method*

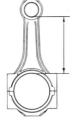

Ring Groove Cleaner

Cleaning the piston ring grooves
(© Ford Motor Co.)

A1404-C

Connecting rod length checking dimension

illustration). All connecting rods should be equal length. Replace any rod that differs from the others in the engine.

* Have the connecting rod alignment checked in an alignment fixture by a machinist. Replace any twisted or bent rods.

* Magnaflux the connecting rods to locate stress cracks. If cracks are found, replace the connecting rod.

Fit the pistons to the cylinders:

90° FROM PISTON PIN

Measuring the cylinder with a telescope gauge for piston fitting
(© Buick Div. G.M. Corp.)

60.91

Measuring the piston for fitting
(© Buick Div. G.M. Corp.)

90°   60.90

Using a telescope gauge and micrometer, or a dial gauge, measure the cylinder bore diameter perpendicular to the piston pin, 2½″ below the deck. Measure the piston perpendicular to its pin on the skirt. The difference between the two measurements is the piston clearance. If the clearance is within specifications or slightly below (after boring or honing), finish honing is all that is required. If the clearance is excessive, try to obtain a slightly larger piston to bring clearance within specifications. Where this is not possible, obtain the first oversize piston, and hone (or if necessary, bore) the cylinder to size.

Assemble the pistons and connecting rods:

Installing piston pin lock rings
(© Nissan Motor Co., Ltd.)

Inspect piston pin, connecting rod small end bushing, and piston bore for galling, scoring, or excessive wear. If evident, replace defective part(s). Measure the I.D. of the piston boss and connecting rod small end, and the O.D. of the piston pin. If within specifications, assemble piston pin and rod. CAUTION: *If piston pin must be pressed in, determine the proper method and use the proper tools; otherwise the piston will distort.* Install the lock rings; ensure that they seat properly. If the parts are not within specifications, determine the service method for the type of engine. In some cases, piston and pin are serviced as an assembly when either is defective. Others specify reaming the piston and connecting rods for an oversize pin. If the connecting rod bushing is worn, it may in many cases be replaced. Reaming the piston and replacing the rod bushing are machine shop operations.

Procedure	*Method*

Clean and inspect the camshaft:

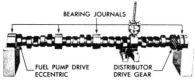

BEARING JOURNALS

FUEL PUMP DRIVE ECCENTRIC   DISTRIBUTOR DRIVE GEAR

**Checking the camshaft
for straightness**
(© Chevrolet Motor
Div. G.M. Corp.)

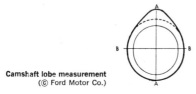

Camshaft lobe measurement
(© Ford Motor Co.)

Degrease the camshaft, using solvent, and clean out all oil holes. Visually inspect cam lobes and bearing journals for excessive wear. If a lobe is questionable, check all lobes as indicated below. If a journal or lobe is worn, the camshaft must be reground or replaced. NOTE: *If a journal is worn, there is a good chance that the bushings are worn.* If lobes and journals appear intact, place the front and rear journals in V-blocks, and rest a dial indicator on the center journal. Rotate the camshaft to check straightness. If deviation exceeds .001″, replace the camshaft.

* Check the camshaft lobes with a micrometer, by measuring the lobes from the nose to base and again at 90° (see illustration). The lift is determined by subtracting the second measurement from the first. If all exhaust lobes and all intake lobes are not identical, the camshaft must be reground or replaced.

Replace the camshaft bearings:

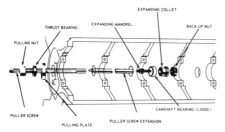

EXPANDING COLLET

THRUST BEARING   EXPANDING MANDREL   BACK-UP NUT

PULLING NUT

CAMSHAFT BEARING (LOOSE)

PULLER SCREW   PULLER SCREW EXTENSION

PULLING PLATE

Camshaft removal and installation tool (typical)
(© Ford Motor Co.)

If excessive wear is indicated, or if the engine is being completely rebuilt, camshaft bearings should be replaced as follows: Drive the camshaft rear plug from the block. Assemble the removal puller with its shoulder on the bearing to be removed. Gradually tighten the puller nut until bearing is removed. Remove remaining bearings, leaving the front and rear for last. To remove front and rear bearings, reverse position of the tool, so as to pull the bearings in toward the center of the block. Leave the tool in this position, pilot the new front and rear bearings on the installer, and pull them into position. Return the tool to its original position and pull remaining bearings into position. NOTE: *Ensure that oil holes align when installing bearings.* Replace camshaft rear plug, and stake it into position to aid retention.

Finish hone the cylinders:

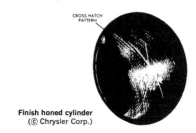

CROSS-HATCH PATTERN

Finish honed cylinder
(© Chrysler Corp.)

Chuck a flexible drive hone into a power drill, and insert it into the cylinder. Start the hone, and move it up and down in the cylinder at a rate which will produce approximately a 60° cross-hatch pattern (see illustration). NOTE: *Do not extend the hone below the cylinder bore.* After developing the pattern, remove the hone and recheck piston fit. Wash the cylinders with a detergent and water solution to remove abrasive dust, dry, and wipe several times with a rag soaked in engine oil.

Procedure	Method
Check piston ring end-gap:  **Checking ring end-gap** (© Chevrolet Motor Div. G.M. Corp.)	Compress the piston rings to be used in a cylinder, one at a time, into that cylinder, and press them approximately 1″ below the deck with an inverted piston. Using feeler gauges, measure the ring end-gap, and compare to specifications. Pull the ring out of the cylinder and file the ends with a fine file to obtain proper clearance. CAUTION: *If inadequate ring end-gap is utilized, ring breakage will result.*
Install the piston rings: 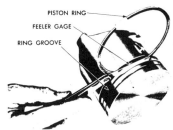 **Checking ring side clearance** (© Chrysler Corp.) 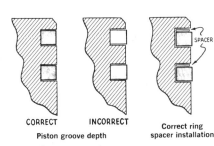 CORRECT INCORRECT **Correct ring spacer installation** Piston groove depth	Inspect the ring grooves in the piston for excessive wear or taper. If necessary, recut the groove(s) for use with an overwidth ring or a standard ring and spacer. If the groove is worn uniformly, overwidth rings, or standard rings and spacers may be installed without recutting. Roll the outside of the ring around the groove to check for burrs or deposits. If any are found, remove with a fine file. Hold the ring in the groove, and measure side clearance. If necessary, correct as indicated above. NOTE: *Always install any additional spacers above the piston ring.* The ring groove must be deep enough to allow the ring to seat below the lands (see illustration). In many cases, a "go-no-go" depth gauge will be provided with the piston rings. Shallow grooves may be corrected by recutting, while deep grooves require some type of filler or expander behind the piston. Consult the piston ring supplier concerning the suggested method. Install the rings on the piston, lowest ring first, using a ring expander. NOTE: *Position the ring markings as specified by the manufacturer (see car section).*
Install the camshaft:	Liberally lubricate the camshaft lobes and journals, and slide the camshaft into the block. CAUTION: *Exercise extreme care to avoid damaging the bearings when inserting the camshaft.* Install and tighten the camshaft thrust plate retaining bolts.
Check camshaft end-play:  **Checking camshaft end-play with a feeler gauge** (© Ford Motor Co.)	Using feeler gauges, determine whether the clearance between the camshaft boss (or gear) and backing plate is within specifications. Install shims behind the thrust plate, or reposition the camshaft gear and retest end-play.

Procedure	*Method*

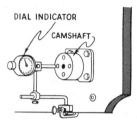

Checking camshaft end-play with a
dial indicator

 Mount a dial indicator stand so that the stem of the dial indicator rests on the nose of the camshaft, parallel to the camshaft axis. Push the camshaft as far in as possible and zero the gauge. Move the camshaft outward to determine the amount of camshaft end-play. If the end-play is not within tolerance, install shims behind the thrust plate, or reposition the camshaft gear and retest.

Install the rear main seal (where applicable):

Seating the rear
main seal
(© Buick Div. G.M. Corp.)

Position the block with the bearing saddles facing upward. Lay the rear main seal in its groove and press it lightly into its seat. Place a piece of pipe the same diameter as the crankshaft journal into the saddle, and firmly seat the seal. Hold the pipe in position, and trim the ends of the seal flush if required.

Install the crankshaft:

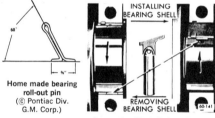

Home made bearing
roll-out pin
(© Pontiac Div.
G.M. Corp.)

Removal and installation of upper
bearing insert using a roll-out pin
(© Buick Div. G.M. Corp.)

Thoroughly clean the main bearing saddles and caps. Place the upper halves of the bearing inserts on the saddles and press into position. NOTE: *Ensure that the oil holes align.* Press the corresponding bearing inserts into the main bearing caps. Lubricate the upper main bearings, and lay the crankshaft in position. Place a strip of Plastigage on each of the crankshaft journals, install the main caps, and torque to specifications. Remove the main caps, and compare the Plastigage to the scale on the Plastigage envelope. If clearances are within tolerances, remove the Plastigage, turn the crankshaft 90°, wipe off all oil and retest. If all clearances are correct, remove all Plastigage, thoroughly

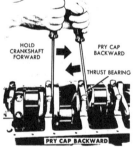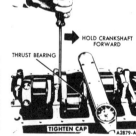

Aligning the thrust bearing
(© Ford Motor Co.)

Procedure	*Method*
	lubricate the main caps and bearing journals, and install the main caps. If clearances are not within tolerance, the upper bearing inserts may be removed, without removing the crankshaft, using a bearing roll out pin (see illustration). Roll in a bearing that will provide proper clearance, and retest. Torque all main caps, excluding the thrust bearing cap, to specifications. Tighten the thrust bearing cap finger tight. To properly align the thrust bearing, pry the crankshaft the extent of its axial travel several times, the last movement held toward the front of the engine, and torque the thrust bearing cap to specifications. Determine the crankshaft end-play (see below), and bring within tolerance with thrust washers.
Measure crankshaft end-play:  **Checking crankshaft end-play with a dial indicator** (© Ford Motor Co.) A 2908-A **Checking crankshaft end-play with a feeler gauge** (© Chevrolet Div. (G.M. Corp.)	Mount a dial indicator stand on the front of the block, with the dial indicator stem resting on the nose of the crankshaft, parallel to the crankshaft axis. Pry the crankshaft the extent of its travel rearward, and zero the indicator. Pry the crankshaft forward and record crankshaft end-play. NOTE: *Crankshaft end-play also may be measured at the thrust bearing, using feeler gauges* (see illustration).
Install the pistons:	Press the upper connecting rod bearing halves into the connecting rods, and the lower halves into the connecting rod caps. Position the piston ring gaps according to specifications (see car section), and lubricate the pistons. Install a ring compresser on a piston, and press two long (8") pieces of plastic tubing over the rod bolts. Using the plastic tubes as a guide, press the pistons into the bores and onto the crankshaft with a wooden hammer handle. After seating the rod on the crankshaft journal, remove the tubes and install the cap finger tight. Install the remaining pistons in the same man-

Procedure	*Method*

Tubing used as guide when installing
a piston
(© Oldsmobile Div. G.M. Corp.)

ner. Invert the engine and check the bearing clearance at two points (90° apart) on each journal with Plastigage. NOTE: *Do not turn the crankshaft with Plastigage installed.* If clearance is within tolerances, remove *all* Plastigage, thoroughly lubricate the journals, and torque the rod caps to specifications. If clearance is not within specifications, install different thickness bearing inserts and recheck. CAUTION: *Never shim or file the connecting rods or caps.* Always install plastic tube sleeves over the rod bolts when the caps are not installed, to protect the crankshaft journals.

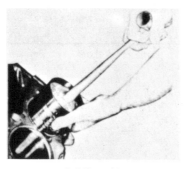

Installing a piston
(© Chevrolet Div. G.M. Corp.)

Check connecting rod side clearance:

Checking connecting rod side clearance
(© Chevrolet Div. G.M. Corp.)

Determine the clearance between the sides of the connecting rods and the crankshaft, using feeler gauges. If clearance is below the minimum tolerance, the rod may be machined to provide adequate clearance. If clearance is excessive, substitute an unworn rod, and recheck. If clearance is still outside specifications, the crankshaft must be welded and reground, or replaced.

Inspect the timing chain:

Visually inspect the timing chain for broken or loose links, and replace the chain if any are found. If the chain will flex sideways, it must be replaced. Install the timing chain as specified. NOTE: *If the original timing chain is to be reused, install it in its original position.*

Procedure	Method
Check timing gear backlash and runout:  **Checking camshaft gear backlash** (ⓒ Chevrolet Div. G.M. Corp.)  **Checking camshaft gear runout** (ⓒ Chevrolet Div. G.M. Corp.)	Mount a dial indicator with its stem resting on a tooth of the camshaft gear (as illustrated). Rotate the gear until all slack is removed, and zero the indicator. Rotate the gear in the opposite direction until slack is removed, and record gear backlash. Mount the indicator with its stem resting on the edge of the camshaft gear, parallel to the axis of the camshaft. Zero the indicator, and turn the camshaft gear one full turn, recording the runout. If either backlash or runout exceed specifications, replace the worn gear(s).

Completing the Rebuilding Process

Following the above procedures, complete the rebuilding process as follows:

Fill the oil pump with oil, to prevent cavitating (sucking air) on initial engine start up. Install the oil pump and the pickup tube on the engine. Coat the oil pan gasket as necessary, and install the gasket and the oil pan. Mount the flywheel and the crankshaft vibrational damper or pulley on the crankshaft. NOTE: *Always use new bolts when installing the flywheel.* Inspect the clutch shaft pilot bushing in the crankshaft. If the bushing is excessively worn, remove it with an expanding puller and a slide hammer, and tap a new bushing into place.

Position the engine, cylinder head side up. Lubricate the lifters, and install them into their bores. Install the cylinder head, and torque it as specified in the car section. Insert the pushrods (where applicable), and install the rocker shaft(s) (if so equipped) or position the rocker arms on the pushrods. If solid lifters are utilized, adjust the valves to the "cold" specifications.

Mount the intake and exhaust manifolds, the carburetor(s), the distributor and spark plugs. Adjust the point gap and the static ignition timing. Mount all accessories and install the engine in the car. Fill the radiator with coolant, and the crankcase with high quality engine oil.

Break-in Procedure

Start the engine, and allow it to run at low speed for a few minutes, while checking for leaks. Stop the engine, check the oil level, and fill as necessary. Restart the engine, and fill the cooling system to capacity. Check the point dwell angle and adjust the ignition timing and the valves. Run the engine at low to medium speed (800-2500 rpm) for approximately ½ hour, and retorque the cylinder head bolts. Road test the car, and check again for leaks.

Follow the manufacturer's recommended engine break-in procedure and maintenance schedule for new engines.

4 · Emission Controls and Fuel System

Emission Controls

NOTE: *The Evaporative Emission Control System (ECS), Exhaust Gas Recirculation System (EGR), the Air Injection Reactor (AIR), and the Temperature operated vacuum by-pass valve are used in conjunction with the systems listed below. A description of these systems is found after the 1973 section.*

1968–69

The Clean Air Package (CAP) was introduced at this time. The CAP uses specially calibrated carburetors and modified distributors. The positive crankcase ventilation valve (PCV) is used to control crankcase emissions.

The carburetors deliver a leaner idle mixture to improve low-speed emissions. The basic ignition timing is retarded and the entire advance curve is modified in some cases. A vacuum control valve is also incorporated into the vacuum advance system of some models. This valve gives full vacuum advance on deceleration by closing the carburetor vacuum port and opening a manifold vacuum port. During deceleration the vacuum advance unit on the distributor is operated by intake manifold vacuum instead of carburetor vacuum, as is the case in all other operations.

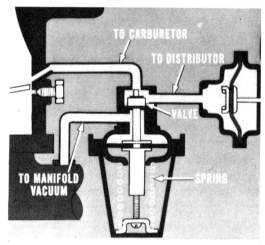

The CAP vacuum control valve (Courtesy of Chrysler Corp.)

1970–72

The Cleaner Air System (CAS) was introduced at this time and superseded the CAP. The CAS, however, did incorporate some of the features of the CAP with some new features. The primary components of the CAS are: a manifold heat valve, a more extensively modified carburetor, heated air intake, reduced compression ratios, and a solenoid in the distributor to control vacuum advance.

The heated air intake is used to maintain a 100° intake air temperature, minimize carburetor icing, and improve engine

96

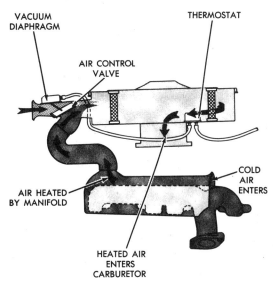

VACUUM
DIAPHRAGM

THERMOSTAT

AIR CONTROL
VALVE

COLD
AIR
ENTERS

AIR HEATED
BY MANIFOLD

HEATED AIR
ENTERS
CARBURETOR

Heated air intake system (Courtesy of Chrysler Corp.)

warm-up characteristics. A sensor unit, which is located on the clean air side of the air filter, senses the temperature of the air passing over it and regulates the vacuum supplied to a vacuum diaphragm in the inlet tube of the air cleaner. The colder the air, the greater the amount of the vacuum supplied to the vacuum diaphragm. The vacuum diaphragm opens or closes a damper door in the inlet tube of the air cleaner. If the door is open, it allows air from the engine compartment to go to the carburetor. If the door is closed, air flows over the heat stove located on the exhaust manifold, heating the air, into the carburetor. In this way heated air is supplied to the carburetor during cold days and when first starting the engine and warming it up.

All carburetors have leaner mixtures and better gasoline distribution and atomization characteristics. There is also a new, faster-acting choke. This choke opens faster after the engine starts to warm up. It incorporates an electric heater in the choke thermostat which heats the thermostat, causing it to open the choke earlier. This electric heater is called the manifold heat valve.

An idle stop solenoid is used to prevent run-on when the ignition is turned off. Run-on is caused largely by today's higher engine operating temperatures and wider throttle plate openings that are necessary for emission controls. Ordinarily, when the

ignition is shut off, the loss of spark is enough to stop the engine. If the engine has high enough cylinder temperatures, however, enough air-fuel mixture can pass the wide throttle plate opening and be ignited without the spark plug and the engine will continue running even after the key is turned off. The idle solenoid is attached to the carburetor to solve this problem. The solenoid has an adjustable plunger and is electrically operated. When the ignition is turned on, the plunger is extended and contacts the carburetor throttle lever, opening the throttle plate wide enough for the engine to idle properly. When the ignition is turned off, the plunger retracts and the throttle lever falls back on the lever stop. When the throttle lever is on its stop, the throttle plate opening is very small and will not allow enough air-fuel mixture to pass to run the engine with the ignition off.

The lower compression ratios reduce hydrocarbon emissions by producing better combustion shape and by leaving more heat in the exhaust to assist the aftercombustion reaction.

The distributor solenoid, on 1971 cars, is incorporated into the distributor and acts to retard the timing when the throttle is closed. A set of electrical contacts energize the solenoid when they are closed by the throttle lever. The solenoid on 1972 cars is a start-only solenoid. The solenoid is energized only when the ignition switch is in the "start" position. The solenoid supplies additional distributor advance when the engine is started and is de-energized when the engine is running.

Service

The service procedure for the CAP and CAS systems is limited to a very careful tune-up. A tune-up should be performed every 12 months. Refer to the decal containing information pertinent to the specific engine/vehicle application for the proper specifications. This decal is posted in a conspicuous location in the engine compartment of each vehicle.

HEATED AIR INTAKE

1. Run the engine until it is completely warmed up. Look into the air cleaner air intake tube and see if the tube is open all the way into the air cleaner element. If the system is operating properly, there will be

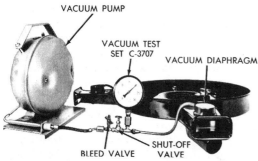

Testing the vacuum diaphragm (Courtesy of Chrysler Corp.)

no obstruction in the tube after the engine is warmed up. If it is blocked off, continue to the next step.

2. Remove the air cleaner from the carburetor and allow it to cool to 90° F. Connect a vacuum source to the sensor as well as a vacuum gauge.

3. Apply 20 in. of Hg to the sensor. (The door should be in the heat on or up position, blocking the air inlet tube.) If it remains in the off or down position, test the vacuum motor.

4. Connect the motor to a vacuum source. In addition to the vacuum gauge, a hose clamp and a bleed valve are necessary. Connect them in the following order: vacuum source, hose clamp or shut-off valve, bleed valve, vacuum gauge, and vacuum motor.

5. Apply 20 in. of Hg vacuum to the motor. Use the hose clamp to block the line, so that the motor will retain the vacuum. The door operating motor should retain this amount of vacuum for five minutes. Release the hose clamp.

NOTE: *If the vacuum cannot be built up to the specified amount, the diaphragm has a leak and the valve will require replacement.*

6. Check the operation of the door by slowly closing the bleed valve. The door should start to raise at not less than 5 in. Hg and should be fully raised at no more than 9 in. Hg.

7. If the vacuum motor fails any of the tests in steps 3–5, it is defective. Replace it with a new unit.

8. If the door works properly but fails to pass step 2, the sensor is at fault and should be replaced.

1973

The name CAS was dropped, but all the elements of the CAS were retained, and a new device was added. The Orifice Spark Advance Control system (OSAC) is used on all engines to help control NOₓ emissions. Vacuum for the distributor advance unit is routed through a small valve mounted on the firewall. The valve has a tiny port through which the vacuum must pass. This causes a 17-second delay before the distributor advance unit receives a signal when going from idle to part throttle. When decelerating, the vacuum change will be instantaneous. The valve works only when the temperature is 60° or above.

Service

ORIFICE SPARK ADVANCE CONTROL VALVE

NOTE: *Air temperature around the car must be above 68° F for this test because the OSAC valve contains a temperature sensor.*

1. Check the vacuum hoses and connections for any signs of leaks or plugging.

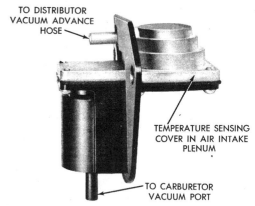

Orifice spark advance control valve (Courtesy of Chrysler Corp.)

2. Detach the vacuum line which runs from the distributor to the OSAC valve at the distributor end. Connect a vacuum gauge to this line.

3. Connect a tachometer to the engine. Rapidly open the throttle and then stabilize the engine speed at 2,000 rpm in neutral. When the throttle is rapidly opened, the vacuum gauge reading should drop to zero.

4. With the engine speed at a steady 2,000 rpm, it should take about 15 seconds for the vacuum level to rise and stabilize.

5. If the vacuum level rises immediately,

the valve is defective and must be replaced.

6. If there is no increase in vacuum at all, disconnect the hose which runs from the carburetor to the OSAC valve at the valve and connect a vacuum gauge to this hose. Speed the engine up to 2,000 rpm.

7. If there is no vacuum reading on the gauge, check for a clogged carburetor port, filters, or hoses.

8. If there is a vacuum reading, the valve is defective and must be replaced.

9. Reconnect the vacuum hoses, after disconnecting the vacuum gauge. Disconnect the tachometer.

A careful tune-up is the only additional service required.

EVAPORATION CONTROL SYSTEMS

All 1970 vehicles sold in California and all post-1970 vehicles have an Evaporation Control System (ECS) to reduce evaporation losses from the fuel system. The system has an expansion tank in the main fuel tank. This prevents spillage due to expansion of warm fuel. A special filler cap with a two-way relief valve is used. An internal pressure differential, caused by thermal expansion, opens the valve, as does an external pressure differential, caused by fuel usage. Fuel vapors from the carburetor and fuel tank are routed to the crankcase ventilation system. A separator is installed to prevent liquid fuel from entering the crankcase ventilation system.

ECS systems used on 1972 vehicles also include a charcoal canister and an overflow-limiting valve.

The limiting valve prevents the fuel tank from being overfilled by trapping fuel in the filler when the tank is full. When pressure in the tank becomes greater than the valve operating pressure, the valve opens and allows the gasoline vapors to flow into the charcoal canister. The charcoal canister is mounted in the engine compartment. It absorbs vapors and retains them until clean air is drawn through a line from it that runs to the PCV valve. Absorption occurs while the car is parked; cleaning occurs while the engine is running.

Service

The only routine service required to the evaporation control system is replacement of the filter that is located in the bottom of the charcoal canister. This should be done every 12 months / 12,000 miles, or more frequently in dusty areas. If any of the hoses in the system require replacement, use only fuel-resistant hoses.

If the fuel tank has collapsed, it may be the fault of clogged or pinched vent lines, a defective vapor separator, or a plugged or incorrect fuel filler cap.

To test the filler cap, clean it and blow into the relief valve housing. If the cap passes pressure with light blowing or if it fails to release with hard blowing, it is defective and must be replaced.

NO_x CONTROL SYSTEM

All 1973 and 1972 vehicles sold in California have a NOx system to control the emission of oxides of nitrogen. These engines have a special camshaft and a 185° F thermostat.

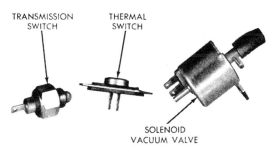

Manual transmission NOx components (Courtesy of Chrysler Corp.)

The manual transmission NOx system uses a transmission switch, a thermal switch, and a solenoid vacuum valve. The transmission switch is screwed into the transmission housing and is closed, except in high gear. The thermal switch, mounted on the firewall, is open whenever the ambient temperature is above 70° F. With the transmission in any gear except high and the temperature above 70° F, the solenoid vacuum valve is energized. This shuts off the distributor vacuum advance line preventing vacuum advance. Below 70° F, the vacuum advance functions normally.

The NO_x system for automatic transmissions is more complex than the manual transmission system. It prevents vacuum advance when the ambient temperature is above 70° F, and speed is below 30 mph, or the car is accelerating. The solenoid vacuum valve is interchangeable with that used in the manual system. The speed switch senses vehicle speed and is driven

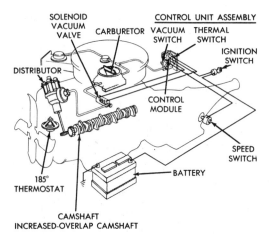

Automatic Transmission NOx components (Courtesy of Chrysler Corp.)

by the speedometer cable. The control unit is mounted on the firewall. It contains a control module, thermal switch, and a vacuum switch. The control unit senses ambient temperature and manifold vacuum.

Service

MANUAL TRANSMISSIONS

1. Be sure that the ambient temperature is above 70° F.
2. Switch on the ignition. Shift the transmission into neutral.
3. Disconnect the wire from the B+ connector of the ballast resistor while holding the solenoid vacuum valve. The valve solenoid should be felt to de-energize.
4. Reconnect the wire. The valve solenoid should be felt to energize.
5. Shift into high. Repeat steps 3 and 4. The system should be inoperative.
6. To test the solenoid vacuum valve, remove the connector on the valve. Connect the piggyback connector on the ballast resistor to one of the solenoid vacuum valve terminals. Ground the other terminal. The solenoid should energize with the ignition switch in the on position.
7. To test the thermal switch, disconnect and replace it with a length of wire. The solenoid should energize.
8. To test the transmission switch, turn on the ignition switch and shift into neutral. Remove and ground the wire from the transmission switch. The solenoid should energize. Switch installation torque must be 180 in. lbs.

AUTOMATIC TRANSMISSION

1. Warm the engine to normal operating temperature. Be sure that the ambient temperature is above 70° F.
2. Using a tee connector, connect a vacuum gauge between the distributor and the solenoid vacuum valve.
3. Raise the car on a lift with the wheels hanging free.
4. Disconnect the vacuum line at the vacuum switch on the control unit.
5. Start the engine and run at a speed above 850 rpm. The vacuum gauge should read zero.
6. Disconnect the wire from the control unit. The vacuum gauge should read normal operating vacuum. Reconnect the wire. The gauge should drop to zero.
7. Unplug and reconnect the vacuum line to the vacuum switch. Disconnect the wire from the control unit to the speed switch. The gauge should read normal operating vacuum.
8. Place the transmission in Drive. Sharp acceleration should cause the gauge reading to drop sharply to zero. Do not exceed 40 mph.
9. Accelerate above 30 mph. The gauge should read normal operating vacuum. If the solenoid valve did not operate during the tests, replace the control unit.

EXHAUST GAS RECIRCULATION

Exhaust Gas Recirculation (EGR) was introduced in 1972 on California cars and is found on all cars in 1973. It is used to reduce nitrogen oxide emissions. There are several systems used to control the rate of exhaust gas recirculation depending on the engine.

EGR reduces the peak flame temperature of the burning gases in the combustion chamber by introducing a small amount of exhaust gases into the intake manifold. An EGR valve opens and closes the EGR passages to the intake manifold. This valve, then, controls the rate of exhaust gas recirculation.

The EGR valve is operated by vacuum on all 1973 engines except those 340 and 400 cu in. V8s with four-barrel carburetors. In the venturi vacuum control system for EGR valve control, vacuum is supplied by an orifice in the carburetor venturi. In the ported vacuum control system, a slot type port in the carburetor throttle body is

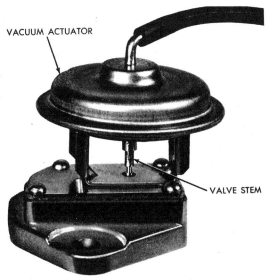

EGR control valve (Courtesy of Chrysler Corp.)

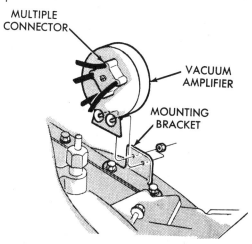

EGR vacuum amplifier (Courtesy of Chrysler Corp.)

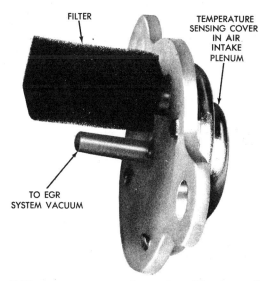

EGR temperature sensing valve (Courtesy of Chrysler Corp.)

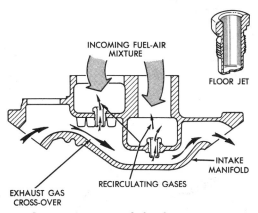

EGR floor jets (Courtesy of Chrysler Corp.)

used. The port is exposed to an increasing percentage of manifold vacuum as the throttle blade opens. Both control systems eliminate EGR at idle and cruising speeds, EGR is operating during acceleration when engine temperature is above 70° F.

The vacuum signal for these systems is amplified by a vacuum amplifier found on the top of the engine. At low speeds, the vacuum signal is too low to operate the EGR valve properly, making the vacuum amplifer necessary.

On 1972 California cars, the EGR system was much simpler. There was no EGR valve and metering was accomplished by floor jets found in the manifold directly below the carburetor. These jets were always open to the exhaust gas passages in the manifold. This meant that the EGR system was constantly functioning.

Floor Jet Service

All six-cylinder engines have one floor jet, while all V8s have two.

1. Turn off the engine. Remove the air cleaner assembly from the carburetor.

2. Hold the choke and throttle valves open. Shine a flashlight through the carburetor to inspect the floor jet(s). The jet(s) is/are in satisfactory condition if the passage shows an open path to the orifice.

3. If the jet(s) is/are clogged, completely remove the carburetor. Withdraw the jet and clean it.

CAUTION: *Use care when handling the*

jets. They have very thin walls and are, therefore, easily damaged. Because they are made out of stainless steel, they are not magnetic and cannot be retrieved readily if dropped into the manifold.

4. Install the jet(s) and tighten them to 25 ft lbs. Install the carburetor and attach the air cleaner.

NOTE: *"Shorting out" cylinders on engines equipped with floor jets is not a reliable test procedure. The unburned mixture is circulated to the other cylinders, causing the engine speed to fluctuate. Because of this, false test results may be obtained.*

1973 Proportional EGR System Tests

NOTE: *Air temperature should be above 68° F for this test.*

1. Check all of the vacuum hoses which run between the carburetor, intake manifold, EGR valve, and the vacuum amplifier (if so equipped). Replace the hoses and tighten the connections, as required.

2. Allow the engine to warm up. Connect a tachometer. Start with the engine idling in neutral and rapidly increase the engine speed to 2,000 rpm.

3. If the EGR valve stem moves (watch the groove on the stem), the valve and the rest of the system are functioning properly. If the stem does not move, proceed with the rest of the EGR system tests.

4. Disconnect the vacuum supply hose from the EGR valve. Apply a vacuum of at least 10 in. Hg to the valve with the engine warmed up and idling, and the transmission in neutral.

NOTE: *The intake manifold vacuum connection is a source of more than adequate vacuum. Run a hose from the EGR valve directly to the connection.*

5. When vacuum is applied to the EGR valve, the engine speed should drop at least 50 rpm. The engine may even stall in some cases. If the engine does not slow down and the EGR valve does not operate, the valve is defective or dirty. Replace it or remove the deposits from it.

NOTE: *Always replace the EGR valve gasket with a new one when the valve is removed for service, even if the valve itself is not replaced.*

6. If the EGR valve is functioning properly, reconnect its vacuum line and test the temperature control valve.

7. Disconnect the vacuum hose which runs to the temperature control valve and plug it. Repeat steps 2 and 3. If the EGR valve now functions, the temperature control valve is defective and must be replaced.

8. If everything else is functioning properly, the EGR system does not work, and the engine is equipped with a vacuum amplifier (see the chart below), the amplifier is at fault. Replace it and repeat the system test.

AIR INJECTION SYSTEM

Air Injection System is used on all 225, 400, and 440 1972–73 California engines. This system injects a controlled amount of air, through special passages in the cylinder head or external tubing, into the exhaust manifold at the exhaust port. This causes further oxidation of the gases and thereby reduces the carbon monoxide and hydrocarbon emissions to the required levels.

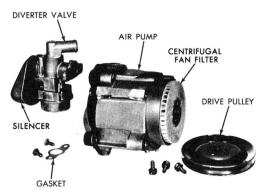

AIR injection components (Courtesy of Chrysler Corp.)

The air injection system consists of a belt-driven air pump, a check valve, injection tubes, and a combination diverter/pressure relief valve assembly.

Air Pump Tests

Belt Tension and Air Leaks

1. Before proceeding with the tests, check the tension of the pump drive belt to see if it is within specifications.

2. Turn the pump by hand. If it has seized, the belt will slip, producing noise. Disregard any chirping, squealing, or rolling sounds from inside the pump; these are normal when it is turned by hand.

3. Check the hoses and connections for leaks. Hissing or a blast of air is indicative of a leak. Soapy water, applied lightly around the area in question, is a good method for detecting leaks.

AIR OUTPUT TESTS

1. Disconnect the air supply hose at the antibackfire valve.
2. Connect a vacuum gauge to the air supply hose with a suitable adaptor.
NOTE: *If there are two hoses, plug the second one.*
3. With the engine at normal operating temperature, increase the idle speed and watch the vacuum gauge.
4. The air flow from the pump should be steady and fall between 2 and 6 psi. If it is unsteady or falls below this, the pump is defective and must be replaced.

PUMP NOISE DIAGNOSIS

The air pump is normally noisy; as engine speed increases, the noise of the pump will rise in pitch. The rolling sound the pump bearings make is normal, however if this sound becomes objectionable at certain speeds, the pump is defective and will have to be replaced.

A continual hissing sound from the air pump pressure relief valve at idle indicates a defective valve. Replace the relief valve.

If the pump rear bearing fails, a continual knocking sound will be heard. Since the rear bearing cannot be replaced separately, the pump will have to be replaced as an assembly.

ANTIBACKFIRE VALVE TESTS, BY-PASS (DIVERTER) TYPE

1. Detach the hose which runs from the by-pass valve to the check valve, at the by-pass valve hose connection.
2. Connect a tachometer to the engine. With the engine running at normal idle speed, check to see that air is flowing from the by-pass valve hose connection.
3. Speed up the engine so it is running at 1,500–2,000 rpm. Allow the throttle to snap shut. The flow of air from the by-pass valve at the check valve hose connection should stop momentarily and air should then flow from the exhaust port on the valve body or the silencer assembly.
4. Repeat step 3 several times. If the flow of air is not diverted into the atmosphere from the valve exhaust port or if it

fails to stop flowing from the hose connection, check the vacuum lines and connections. If these are tight, the valve is defective and requires replacement.
5. A leaking diaphragm will cause the air to flow out both the hose connection and the exhaust port at the same time. If this happens, replace the valve.

CHECK VALVE TEST

1. Before starting the test, check all of the hoses and connections for leaks.
2. Detach the air supply hose or hoses from the check valve.
3. Insert a suitable probe into the check valve and depress the plate. Release it; the plate should return to its original position against the valve seat. If binding is evident, replace the valve.
4. Repeat step three if two valves are used.
5. With the engine running at normal operating temperature, gradually increase its speed to 1,500 rpm. Check for exhaust gas leakage. If any is present, replace the valve assembly.
NOTE: *Vibration and flutter of the check valve at idle speed is a normal condition and does not mean that the valve should be replaced.*

CRANKCASE VENTILATION SYSTEM

This system is used on all 1968–73 engines.

Crankcase vapors are generated by piston blow-by (i.e., vapors that get past the piston and rings during combustion). These vapors are drawn out of the engine through a crankcase ventilation valve and into the carburetor to be reburned.

Service

See the "Tune-Up" chapter for service procedures of the crankcase ventilation system.

TEMPERATURE OPERATED VACUUM BY-PASS VALVE

A vacuum by-pass valve is used on some engines to reduce the possibility of the engine overheating under extremely high-temperature operating conditions. When the temperature of the engine coolant reaches 225° F, the valve opens automatically and applies intake manifold vacuum directly to the distributor, by-passing the emission control system into which the

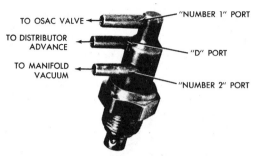

TO OSAC VALVE

TO DISTRIBUTOR ADVANCE

TO MANIFOLD VACUUM

"NUMBER 1" PORT

"D" PORT

"NUMBER 2" PORT

Temperature operated by-pass valve (Courtesy of Chrysler Corp.)

valve is incorporated. The Air Injection System, NOx control system, and the EGR venturi vacuum control system use this by-pass valve.

Service

NOTE: *On some cars with distributor control systems, this valve also is used to override the control system under overheating conditions. If a malfunction of the distributor control system occurs, remember to check the vacuum valve.*

1. Check all of the vacuum hoses for proper installation and routing.

2. Connect a tachometer to the engine.

3. Run the engine until it reaches normal operating temperature but do not allow it to overheat. Be sure that the choke is open.

4. Detach the distributor solenoid ground lead at the carburetor (if so equipped).

5. Check engine rpm with the carburetor at curb idle.

6. Detach the vacuum line from the intake manifold at the valve end. Plug this hose.

7. Check the idle speed; there should be no change. If the idle speed drops 100 rpm or more, the valve is defective and must be replaced.

8. Check the coolant level and radiator cap. Reconnect the intake manifold hose to the temperature valve.

9. Cover the radiator to increase the coolant temperatre. Then, do one of the following:

a. If the car is equipped with a temperature gauge, run the engine until the gauge registers near the top of the "normal" range.

b. On cars equipped with warning lights, run the engine until the red temperature light comes on.

CAUTION: *Do not run the engine at an abnormally high temperature for any longer than is required to test the valve. It is neither necessary, nor desirable, to overheat an engine when the car uses a temperature gauge (i.e., the gauge should never be allowed to register "H" (hot) when testing the valve).*

10. If the engine speed has increased by at least 100 rpm, the valve is functioning properly. If there is little or no increase in engine speed, the valve is faulty and must be replaced.

11. Uncover the radiator and allow the car to cool by running the engine at idle.

12. Remember to connect the distributor solenoid wire.

Fuel System

MECHANICAL FUEL PUMP

Removal and Installation

1. Remove the fuel inlet and outlet lines. Plug the fuel inlet line to prevent emptying the fuel tank.

3. Remove the two fuel pump securing bolts.

3. Remove the fuel pump from the car.

4. Reverse the above steps to install.

THROTTLE LINKAGE ADJUSTMENTS

1968–73 Automatic Transmission V8 Except Hemi Three-Section Throttle Rod

1. Apply a thin film of grease to the friction points of the throttle linkage.

2. Disconnect the choke and make sure the fast idle cam is not holding the throttle open.

3. Insert a 3/16 in. rod into the holes provided in the upper bellcrank and lever. Adjust the length of the intermediate transmission rod by means of the threaded adjustment at the upper end of the rod. The ball socket must line up with the ball end when the rod is held up and the transmission lever is forward against its stop.

4. Assemble the ball socket to the ball end and remove the 3/16 in. rod.

5. Disconnect the return spring. Adjust the length of the carburetor rod by pulling forward on the rod and turning the

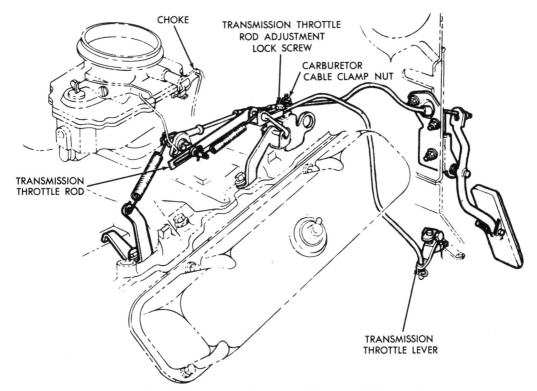

V8 automatic linkage single section throttle rod (Courtesy of Chrysler Corp.)

threaded adjuster link until the rear end of the slot just contacts the carburetor lever pin. Lengthen the rod by two full turns of the link and reinstall the link on the lever pin.

6. Loosen the cable clamp nut. Adjust the position of the cable mounting ferrule in the clamp so that all slack is removed from the cable. To remove the slack, move the ferrule in the clamp away from the carburetor lever. Leave ¼ in. free-play.

1968–73 Automatic V8 Except Hemi, Single-section Throttle Rod

1. Lubricate the friction points in the throttle linkage.

2. Disconnect the choke at the carburetor and block it open. Make sure the throttle is off the fast idle cam.

3. Loosen the transmission throttle rod adjustment lockscrew.

4. Hold the transmission lever forward against its stop while adjusting the linkage.

5. Adjust the transmission rod at the carburetor by pushing forward on the re-

tainer and rearward on the rod to remove all slack. Tighten the transmission rod adjustment locking screw. The rear edge of the link slot must be against the carburetor lever pin during this adjustment. Reconnect the choke.

1968–71 Hemi Automatic Transmission

1. Lubricate the friction points of the throttle linkage.

2. Disconnect the choke linkage and block the choke open.

3. Make sure the throttle is off the fast idle cam.

4. Make sure the transmission throttle lever is against its stop while adjusting the linkage.

5. Insert a 3/16 in. rod into the holes provided in the upper bellcrank and lever. Adjust the length of the intermediate transmission rod by means of the threaded adjustment at the upper end of the rod. The ball socket must line up with the ball end.

6. Assemble the ball socket to the ball end and remove the pin.

7. Remove the transmission linkage re-

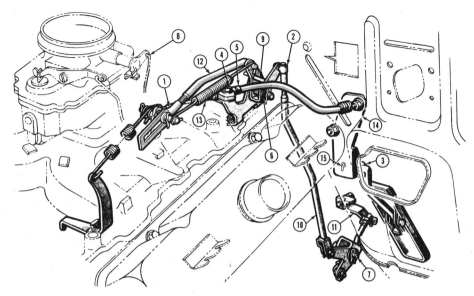

V8 automatic linkage three section throttle rod (Courtesy of Chrysler Corp.)

1. Rod adjusting slot	6. Upper bellcrank	11. Transmission bellcrank
2. Transmission linkage adjusting slot	7. Transmission linkage bellcrank	12. Carburetor rod
3. Pedal link	8. Choke link	13. Return spring
4. Cable adjusting nut	9. $\frac{3}{16}$ in. adjusting rod	14. Cable housing ferrule
5. Cable	10. Transmission linkage rod	

turn spring from the slotted adjuster link. Remove the slotted adjuster link from the carburetor lever stud. Adjust the slotted adjuster link by turning it so that the rear end of the slot just contacts the lever stud. There should be no force exerted on the lever stud when the adjuster link is in its normal operating position.

8. Reinstall the transmission linkage return spring.

9. Check for freedom of movement.

10. Reinstall the choke linkage.

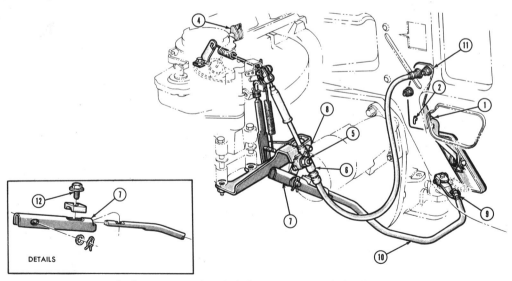

6 cylinder automatic throttle linkage (Courtesy of Chrysler Corp.)

1. Pedal link	6. Cable	10. Transmission linkage rod
2. Spring	7. Transmission rod adjusting link	11. Cable bracket
4. Choke link	8. Pivot pin	12. Adjusting screw
5. Cable adjusting nut	9. Transmission bellcrank	

1968–73 6 Cylinder Automatic

1. Lubricate the friction points of the throttle linkage.

2. Disconnect the choke at the carburetor and make sure the throttle is off the fast idle cam.

3. The transmission lever must remain firmly against its stop while adjusting the throttle linkage.

4. Loosen the slotted link lockbolt to adjust the length of the transmission rod. Pull forward on the slotted adjuster link to maintain pressure against the carburetor lever pin and remove all slack in the linkage.

5. Tighten the transmission rod adjustment lockbolt.

6. To adjust the throttle cable, loosen the cable clamp nut and position the cable up or down to obtain 1/4 in. of slack and then tighten the nut.

7. Reconnect the choke linkage and check the linkage for freedom of operation.

1968–73 6 Cylinder and V8 Manual Transmission

1. Lubricate the friction points of the throttle linkage.

2. Disconnect the choke at the carburetor and make sure the throttle is off the fast idle cam.

3. Loosen the cable clamp nut. Adjust the cable by moving the cable housing so that there is about 1/4 in. of slack in the cable at idle.

4. Tighten the cable clamp nut.

5. Reconnect the choke and check the linkage for free movement.

CARBURETOR REMOVAL AND INSTALLATION

1. Remove the air cleaner and disconnect the throttle linkage.

2. Note the position of all vacuum lines attached to the carburetor and disconnect the lines.

3. Disconnect the choke linkage.

4. Remove the carburetor attaching nuts and remove the carburetor.

5. Reverse the above steps to install. Use a new gasket. Tighten the carburetor nuts evenly and make sure the carburetor is not cocked on the intake manifold.

GENERAL OVERHAUL PRECAUTIONS

Generally, when a carburetor requires major service, a rebuilt carburetor may be purchased or a kit may be used.

The kit contains the necessary parts and instructions for carburetor rebuilding.

There are some general overhaul procedures which should be observed:

1. All parts, except for those made of plastic and the choke diaphragm assembly, should be cleaned. Carburetor cleaning solution is available in many auto parts stores.

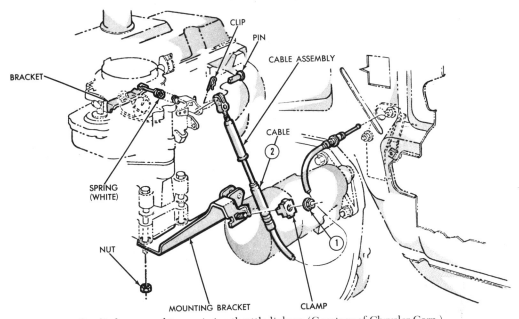

6 cylinder manual transmission throttle linkage (Courtesy of Chrysler Corp.)

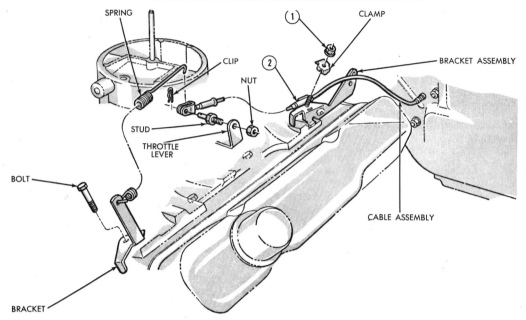

V8 manual transmission throttle linkage (Courtesy of Chrysler Corp.)

2. Make sure all parts are rinsed clean of solvent.

3. High-pressure air is useful for cleaning carburetor passages.

4. All rebuilding must be done under the cleanest conditions possible; even the smallest particles of dirt will clog carburetor passages.

5. Never use a drill or wire to clean jets and passages. This may enlarge the orifices and render the part useless.

AFB CARBURETOR 1968–71

This carburetor is used on the Hemi.

Float Level Adjustment and Air Horn Removal and Installation

1. Remove the air horn from the carburetor. To remove the air horn, disconnect the fast idle connector rod from the choke lever. Remove the rod from the accelerator pump lever. Remove the screws

attaching the step-up piston and rod cover plates. Hold down the cover to prevent the piston and rod from flying out. Slowly remove the cover and remove the rod and piston. Remove the ten screws that attach the air horn to the main body. Lift the air horn straight up.

2. Invert the air horn and, leaving the gasket in place, measure the distance between the gasket and the top of the float.

3. If the distance does not meet the specifications, bend the float arm until the correct clearance is obtained.

4. Reverse steps 1 and 2 to install.

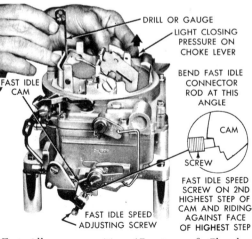

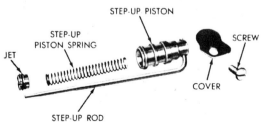

Carter carburetor step up jet, rod and piston (Courtesy of Chrysler Corp.)

Fast idle cam position (Courtesy of Chrysler Corp.)

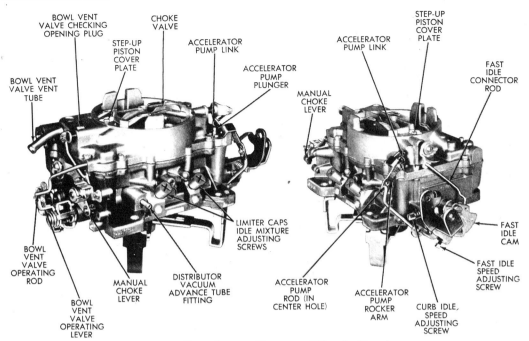

Carter AFB carburetor (Courtesy of Chrysler Corp.)

Fast Idle Speed Adjustment

1. Thoroughly warm up the engine.

2. Turn off the engine and place the transmission in Park or neutral.

3. Close the choke until the fast idle screw is on the second highest speed step of the fast idle cam.

4. Start the engine without touching the throttle. Adjust the fast idle screw until the engine idles at the specified speed.

AVS CARBURETOR 1968–71

Float Level Adjustment and Air Horn Removal and Installation

1. Remove the fast idle connector rod from the fast idle cam.

2. Remove the connector rod from the accelerator pump arm.

3. Remove the screws attaching the step-up piston and rod cover plates. Hold

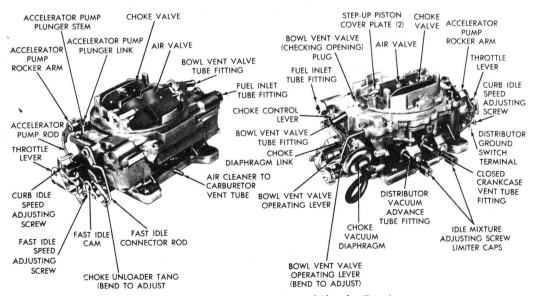

Carter AVS carburetor (Courtesy of Chrysler Corp.)

down the plates with your finger to keep them from flying out. Remove the piston and rod.

4. Disconnect the vacuum hose between the vacuum diaphragm and the throttle body.

5. Disconnect the choke linkage.

6. Remove the idle solenoid, if so equipped.

7. Remove the eight screws holding the air horn to the throttle body. Lift the air horn away from the throttle body. Be careful not to bend the floats.

8. Invert the air horn and leave the air horn gasket in place.

9. Check the float level by measuring the distance between the gasket and the top of the float at the outer end.

10. If the float level is incorrect, bend the float arm until the proper specification is reached.

11. Reverse steps 1–7 to install.

Fast Idle Speed Adjustment

Use the same procedure as given in the AFB carburetor section.

Choke Vacuum Kick Adjustment

The choke diaphragm, adjusted in this procedure, regulates the choke valve under part-throttle conditions while the engine is cold.

1. Start the engine and allow the choke to close to kick position with the engine at idle.

2. Insert a drill of the proper size between the choke valve and the air horn body.

3. Apply a slight amount of pressure to

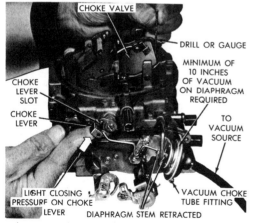

Choke vacuum kick adjustment (Courtesy of Chrysler Corp.)

the choke valve lever to take up any clearance between the choke valve and the drill. Release the pressure and allow the springs in the linkage to hold the choke valve shut.

4. Slowly remove the drill. If there is a slight drag, no adjustment is necessary. Excessive drag or no drag indicates that the length of the choke diaphragm link must be changed.

5. Adjust the link by opening or closing the U-bend in the middle link until a slight drag is felt.

6. After the adjustment is completed, check the linkage for freedom of movement with the engine turned off.

Choke Unloader Adjustment

The choke unloader is used to open the choke valve under full throttle operating conditions.

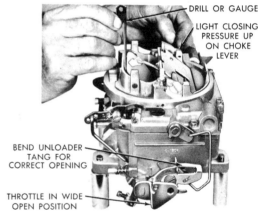

Choke Unloader adjustment (Courtesy of Chrysler Corp.)

1. Insert a drill of the proper size between the throttle valve and the air horn body.

2. Close the valve on the drill. Slowly pull out the drill. A slight drag should be felt.

3. If there is excessively heavy drag or no drag at all, it is necessary to bend the unloader tang on the fast idle cam until the proper opening is obtained.

BBD CARBURETOR 1968–73

This is a two-barrel carburetor with a 1¼ in. bore.

Float Level Adjustment and
Air Horn R & R

1. Disconnect the accelerator pump operating rod.

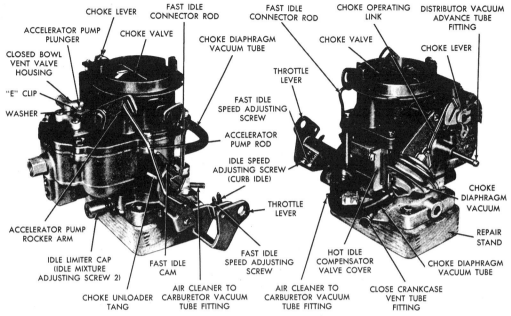

Ball and Ball BBD carburetor (Courtesy of Chrysler Corp.)

2. Disconnect the fast idle connector rod from the fast idle cam and the choke lever.

3. Disconnect the vacuum hose between the choke vacuum diaphragm and the main body.

4. Remove the choke vacuum diaphragm.

5. Remove the air horn retaining screws and lift the air horn straight up. Be careful not to damage the float.

6. Invert the main body. Be careful not to drop the pump intake check ball when inverting the air horn.

7. Check the float level by measuring the distance between the fuel bowl gasket surface and the top of each float at the center.

8. If adjustment is necessary, hold the float to the bottom of the float bowl and bend the float lip toward or away from the needle valve to obtain the proper adjustment.

9. Reverse steps 1–5 to install.

Fast Idle Adjustment

Use the same procedure as given in the AFB carburetor section.

Choke Unloader

See the AVS carburetor section for the proper procedure.

Choke Vacuum Kick Adjustment

See the AVS carburetor section for the proper procedure.

Dashpot Adjustment, Manual Transmission Only

1. Set the curb idle speed and mixture.

2. Start the engine and position the throttle lever so that the actuating tab on the lever is just touching, but not depressing, the dashpot stem.

3. Release the lever and measure the time the engine takes to stabilize. It should take about 30 seconds.

4. To adjust the dashpot, loosen the locknut and turn the dashpot in or out as required.

HOLLEY 1920 CARBURETOR (1971)

This is a single-throat carburetor used on the 225 cu in. 6-cylinder engine.

Float Level Adjustment and Air Horn Removal and Installation

1. Remove the four fuel bowl retaining screws and remove the bowl.

2. Measure the float level height with the factory gauge and adjust the float level accordingly. Measure the wet fuel level as described in the following section if you cannot find a gauge.

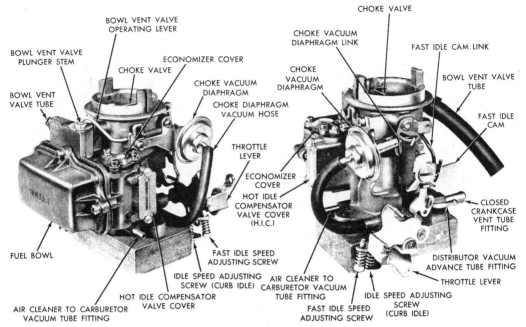

Holley 1920 carburetor (Courtesy of Chrysler Corp.)

Wet Fuel Level Checking and Adjustment

1. Remove the economizer retaining screws.

2. Lift the economizer cover, diaphragm, and stem out of the carburetor.

3. Start the engine. Make sure the car is on a level floor.

4. Insert the 6 in. rule and measure the distance from the machined surface of the economizer opening to the exact fuel surface. The distance should be $^{27}/_{32}$ in.

5. If the measurement indicates that the fuel level is wrong, remove the fuel bowl and adjust the float up or down to give the proper level.

Fast Idle Speed Adjustment

Use the same procedure as given under the AFB carburetor section.

Vacuum Kick Adjustment

See the AVS carburetor section for the proper procedure.

HOLLEY 2210 CARBURETOR (1972–73)

This is a two-barrel carburetor used on 400 cu in. engines with automatic transmissions.

Float Level Adjustment and Air Horn Removal and Installation

1. Remove the nut and washer attaching the accelerator pump rocker arm to the accelerator pump shaft. Remove the arm from the shaft.

2. Remove the accelerator pump rod from the arm.

3. Remove the choke diaphragm and hose.

4. Remove the choke lever from the choke valve shaft.

5. Remove the eight air horn attaching screws and lift the air horn straight up and away from the carburetor body. Be careful

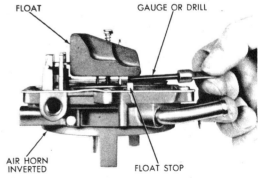

Float level adjustment, Holley 2210 (Courtesy of Chrysler Corp.)

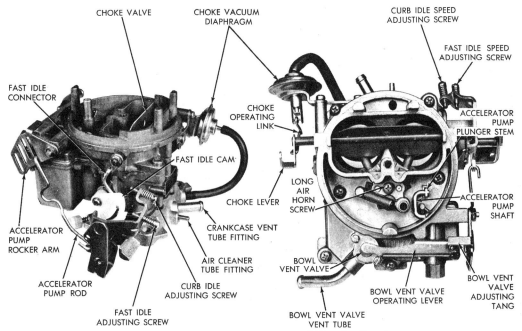

Holley 2210 carburetor (Courtesy of Chrysler Corp.)

not to damage the float and main well tubes attached to the bottom of the air horn.

6. Invert the air horn and measure the clearance between the top of the float and the float stop.

7. Bend the tang on the float arm until the float is properly adjusted.

8. Reverse steps 1–5 to install.

Fast Idle Adjustment

Use the same procedure as given under the AFB carburetor section.

Choke Unloader

See the AVS carburetor section for the proper procedure.

Vacuum Kick Adjustment

See the AVS carburetor section for the proper procedure.

HOLLEY 2300 CARBURETOR (1971–72)

This carburetor is used on the high-performance 340 and 440 engines, with the Six Pack option. The center carburetor has a choke and all the normal fuel and vacuum circuits. The two outboard carburetors are missing a choke, power enrichment, accelerator pump, an idle circuit, and spark advance. Aside from the above-mentioned

differences, the three carburetors are the same.

Float Level Adjustment

1. Remove the four fuel bowl attaching screws and remove the fuel bowl.

2. Center the float in the bowl with the bowl inverted.

It is possible to use the wet fuel level procedure to set the float level as described in the following section.

Checking the Wet Fuel Level

1. Start the engine and remove the sight plug from the fuel bowl.

2. Loosen the adjusting screw locknut and turn the fuel level adjusting screw until fuel just starts to dribble out of the sight hole. Use a rag to catch any fuel that comes out of the sight hole.

3. Reinstall the sight hole plug and tighten the locknut.

Fast Idle Speed Adjustment

1. Warm up the engine.

2. Turn off the engine and poisition the throttle on the second highest speed step on the fast idle cam.

3. Without touching the throttle, start the engine.

4. Bend the fast idle tang by use of a

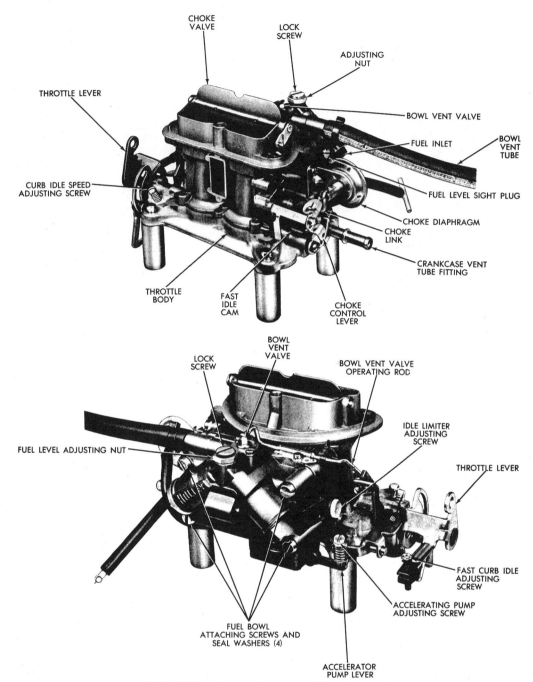

Holley 2300 carburetor (Courtesy of Chrysler Corp.)

screwdriver placed in the tang slot to adjust the speed.

Choke Unloader

See the AVS carburetor section for the proper procedure.

Vacuum Kick Adjustment

See the AVS carburetor section for the proper procedure.

HOLLEY 4160 CARBURETOR (1971–72)

Float Level Adjustment

1. Remove the fuel bowl attaching screws and slide the bowl off the fuel transfer tube.

2. Invert the fuel bowl. Measure the clearance between the toe of the float and the surface of the fuel bowl. The measure-

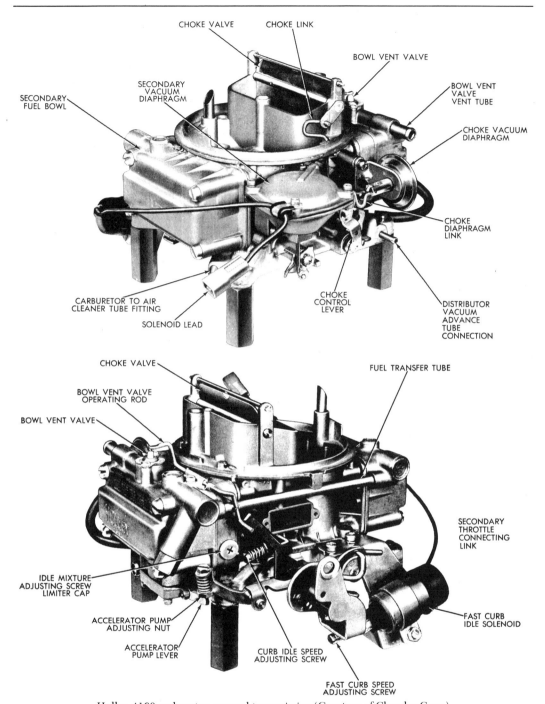

Holley 4160 carburetor, manual transmission (Courtesy of Chrysler Corp.)

ment for the primary fuel bowl is 0.110 in. and the secondary fuel bowl is 0.204 in. Bend the float tang to obtain the correct clearance.

3. Reinstall the fuel bowl.

Fast Idle Adjustment

Use the same procedure as given in the AFB carburetor section.

Vacuum Kick Adjustment

Use the same procedure as given in the AVS carburetor section.

Choke Unloader Adjustment

Use the same procedure as given in the AVS carburetor section.

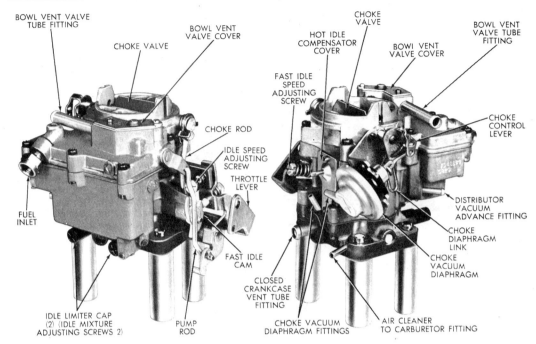

BOWL VENT VALVE
TUBE FITTING
CHOKE VALVE
BOWL VENT
VALVE COVER
CHOKE ROD
IDLE SPEED
ADJUSTING
SCREW
THROTTLE
LEVER
FUEL
INLET
FAST IDLE
CAM
IDLE LIMITER CAP
(2) (IDLE MIXTURE
ADJUSTING SCREWS 2)
PUMP
ROD
CLOSED
CRANKCASE
VENT TUBE
FITTING
CHOKE VACUUM
DIAPHRAGM FITTINGS

CHOKE
VALVE
HOT IDLE
COMPENSATOR
COVER
BOWL VENT
VALVE COVER
FAST IDLE
SPEED
ADJUSTING
SCREW
BOWL VENT
VALVE TUBE
FITTING
CHOKE
CONTROL
LEVER
DISTRIBUTOR
VACUUM
ADVANCE FITTING
CHOKE
DIAPHRAGM
LINK
CHOKE
VACUUM
DIAPHRAGM
AIR CLEANER
TO CARBURETOR FITTING

Rochester 2GV carburetor (Courtesy of Chrysler Corp.)

ROCHESTER 2GV

Float Level Adjustment and Air Horn Removal and Installation

1. Remove the fuel inlet fitting.
2. Disconnect the accelerator pump rod.
3. Remove the idle adjusting screw from the body casting.
4. Remove the fast idle cam attaching screw and remove the fast idle cam and rod assembly.
5. Remove the choke control lever from the end of the choke shaft.
6. Remove the vacuum hose from the choke vacuum diaphragm and throttle body. Remove the vacuum diaphragm.
7. Remove the eight air horn attaching screws and lift the air horn straight up and away from the throttle body.
8. Invert the air horn. Measure the distance from the air horn gasket to the lip at the toe of the float. To obtain the proper adjustment bend the float tang at the rear of the float next to the needle valve.
9. Reverse steps 1–7 to install.

Fast Idle Adjustment

Use the same procedure as given in the AFB carburetor section.

Choke Unloader Adjustment

Use the same procedure as given in the AVS carburetor section.

Vacuum Kick Adjustment

Use the same procedure as given in the AVS carburetor section.

CARTER THERMO-QUAD

Float Level Adjustment and Air Horn Removal and Installation

1. Remove the retainers which secure the throttle connector rod to the accelerator pump arm and throttle lever. Remove the rod from the carburetor.
2. Unfasten the accelerator pump arm screw and disengage the pump rod S-link (leave the S-link connected to the pump rod). Remove the lever.
3. Remove the choke countershaft fast idle lever attachment screw while holding the lever. Disengage the lever from the countershaft and then swing the fast idle connector rod in an arc until it can be disengaged from the fast idle operating lever.
4. Remove the retainers and washer which secure the choke diaphragm

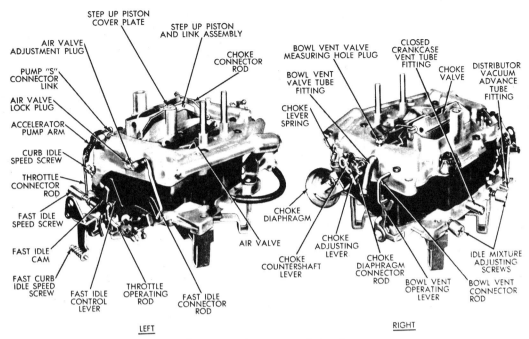

Carter Thermo-Quad (Courtesy of Chrysler Corp.)

connector rod to the choke vacuum diaphragm and air valve lever. Remove the lever.

5. Remove the retainer which attaches the choke connector rod to the choke countershaft. Disengage and swing the rod in an arc to remove the choke shaft lever assembly.

6. Withdraw the step-up piston cover plate securing screw and cover plate. Remove the step-up piston and link assembly with the step-up rods. Remove the step-up piston spring.

7. Remove the pump jet housing screw, housing, and gasket. Invert the carburetor and remove the discharge check needle.

8. Withdraw the bowl cover retaining screws and remove the bowl cover.

9. Invert the bowl cover. With the bowl cover gasket in place and the float needle seated, use a depth gauge to measure the distance from the bowl cover gasket to the bottom side of the float. This dimension should be 1.00 in.

10. If an adjustment is necessary, bend the float lever until the correct distance is obtained.

11. Reverse steps 1–9 to install.

Vacuum Kick Adjustment

Before the vacuum kick adjustment can be performed, the choke control lever and the choke diaphragm connector rod must be correctly set. These settings can be made on or off the vehicle.

1. If the setting is to be made on the engine, remove the choke assembly, stainless steel cup, and gasket. If the setting is to be made off the vehicle, place the carburetor on a clean, flat surface, such as a table top or workbench, so that the carburetor flange is flush against the work surface.

2. Close the choke valve by pushing on the choke lever with the throttle partly open.

3. Measure the verticle distance from the top of the rod hole in the choke control lever down to the clean choke pad surface (on the engine), or down to the work surface (off the engine). This measurement should be 5.641 in. on the engine or 3.422 in. off the engine.

4. If an adjustment is necessary, bend the link which connects the two choke shafts until the correct measurement is obtained.

5. Refit the choke assembly, if removed.

After the choke control lever has been properly set, continue this procedure to adjust the choke diaphragm connector rod and the vacuum kick. The choke diaphragm must be energized during both of these adjustments.

1. If the adjustment is to be made on

the engine (with the engine running at curb idle), measure the clearance between the air valve and its stop. The clearance should be 0.040 in. with the air valve closed. If necessary, adjust the connector rod until the correct clearance is obtained. Back off the fast idle screw until the choke can be closed to the kick position. Note the number of screw turns required so that the fast idle can be returned to the original adjustment.

2. If the adjustment is to be made off the engine, disconnect the vacuum hose from the carburetor body and connect it to the auxiliary vacuum source. Apply a vacuum of at least 10 in. Hg and measure the clearance between the air valve and its stop. The clearance should be 0.040 in. with the air valve closed. If necessary, adjust the connector rod until the correct clearance is obtained. Disconnect the vacuum line from the auxiliary source, open the throttle valves, and move the choke valve to its closed position with the control lever. Release the throttle before releasing the choke to trap the fast idle cam in the closed choke position. Reconnect the vacuum line to the auxiliary vacuum source and again apply a vacuum of at least 10 in. Hg.

3. Insert the specified size drill or gauge between the long side (lower edge) of the choke valve and the air horn wall.

4. Apply sufficient closing pressure to the choke control lever to provide a minimum choke valve opening without distorting the choke linkage. Note that only this carburetor extends a spring connecting the control lever to the adjustment lever. This spring must be fully extended for the proper measurement of the vacuum kick adjustment.

5. Remove the drill or gauge. If a slight drag is not felt as the drill or gauge is removed, an adjustment of the adjusting lever is necessary. Bend the adjusting lever tang to change the contact with the end of the diaphragm rod.

6. Refit the vacuum hose to the carburetor body and return the fast idle screw to its original position.

7. With no vacuum applied to the diaphragm, the choke valve should move freely between its open and closed positions.

Choke Unloader

Use the same procedure as under the AVS carburetor section.

Fast Idle Adjustment

Use the same procedure as under the AVS carburetor section.

Curb Idle Speed Solenoid Adjustment

1. Warm up the engine.

2. Using a tachometer and with the solenoid energized (engine running), turn the curb idle solenoid adjusting screw against the solenoid plunger to obtain the specified rpm.

3. With the engine still running, adjust the engine-off throttle stopscrew until the end of the screw just touches the stop. Back off the screw one turn to obtain the low-speed setting. Test the setting by disconnecting the solenoid wire at the connector. The solenoid should de-energize and give the low-speed idle setting.

Carter AFB

	1968	1969	1970	1971
Fast Idle Speed (rpm)	1800	2000	2000	2300
Float Setting (in.)	$\frac{7}{32}$	$\frac{7}{32}$	$\frac{7}{32}$	$\frac{7}{32}$
Float Drop (in.)	$\frac{3}{4}$	$\frac{3}{4}$	$\frac{3}{4}$	$\frac{3}{4}$
Idle Mixture Screws (turns out)	1–2	1–2	1–2	1–2

Carter AVS

	1968	1969	1970	1971
Fast Idle Speed (rpm)	Auto. 1400 Man. 1600	1700	1800	①
Float Setting (in.)	$\frac{5}{16}$	340 engine $\frac{7}{32}$ 383 engine $\frac{5}{16}$	$\frac{7}{32}$	$\frac{7}{32}$
Float Drop (in.)	$\frac{1}{2}$	$\frac{1}{2}$	$\frac{1}{2}$	$\frac{1}{2}$
Choke Unloader (in.)	$\frac{1}{4}$	$\frac{1}{4}$	$\frac{1}{4}$	$\frac{1}{4}$
Vacuum Kick (in.)	Auto. 0.15 Man. 0.2	Auto. 0.11 Man. 0.07	0.16	0.09
Idle Mixture Screws (turns out)	1–2	1–2	—	—

Auto.—Automatic transmission
Man.—Manual transmission
① 383 engine, auto.—1700
    440 engine, auto.—1800
    440 engine, man.—2100

Ball and Ball BBD

	1968	1969	1970	1971	1972	1973
Fast Idle Speed (rpm)	1600	1600	1700	Auto. 1700 Man. 1900	Auto. 1700 Man. 1800 ②	1700
Float Setting (in.)	$\frac{5}{16}$	$\frac{5}{16}$	$\frac{5}{16}$	$\frac{5}{16}$	$\frac{1}{4}$	$\frac{1}{4}$
Choke Unloader (in.)	$\frac{1}{4}$	$\frac{1}{4}$	$\frac{1}{4}$	$\frac{1}{4}$	$\frac{1}{4}$	$\frac{1}{4}$
Vacuum Kick	Auto. 0.18 Man. 0.23	$\frac{5}{16}$	0.16	Auto. 0.14 Man. 0.16	0.15	0.15①
Idle Speed Screws (turns out)	$1\frac{1}{2}$	$1\frac{1}{2}$	$1\frac{1}{2}$	$1\frac{1}{2}$	—	—

Auto.—Automatic transmission
Man.—Manual transmission
① 318 engine, Auto., Non-California, 0.13
② California cars—Auto.—1800
                Man.—2000

Holley 1920

	1969	1970	1971
Fast Idle Speed (rpm)	Auto. 1800 Man. 1600	Auto. 700 Man. 650	Auto. 1900 Man. 1600
Float Setting	Use gauge	Use gauge	Use gauge
Choke Unloader (in.)	9/32	9/32	9/32
Vacuum Kick	Auto. 0.07 Man. 0.10	0.10	0.10
Idle Mixture Screws (turns out)	2	—	—

Auto.—Automatic transmission
Man.—Manual transmission

Holley 2210

	1972	1973
Fast Idle Speed (rpm)	Auto. 1900 Man. 2000	1800
Dry Float Setting (in.)	0.18	0.18
Choke Unloader (in.)	0.17	0.17
Vacuum Kick (in.)	0.11	0.15

Auto.—Atuomatic transmission
Man.—Manual transmission

Holley 2300

	1970	1971	1972
Fast Idle Speed (rpm)	2200	①	1800
Float Setting	Center float in bowl	Center float in bowl	Center float in bowl
Choke Unloader (in.)	5/32	5/32	0.15
Vacuum Kick (in.)	0.07	②	0.07

Auto.—Automatic transmission
Man.—Manual transmission
① 340 engine, auto.—2600
   340 engine, man.—2800
   440 engine, 1800

② 340 engine, auto.—0.10
   340 engine, man.—0.14
   440 engine, auto.—0.07
   440 engine, man.—0.14

Holley 4160

	1968	1969	1970	1971	1972
Fast Idle Speed (rpm)	700①	1400①	1600	1700	Auto. 1600 ③ Man. 1800
Dry Float Setting (in.)	Primary $\frac{7}{64}$ Secondary $\frac{15}{64}$	$\frac{15}{64}$ $\frac{17}{64}$	$\frac{15}{64}$ $\frac{17}{64}$	$\frac{15}{64}$ $\frac{17}{64}$	0.110 0.204
Wet Float Setting (in.)	Primary $\frac{9}{16}$ Secondary $\frac{13}{16}$	$\frac{9}{16}$ $\frac{13}{16}$	$\frac{9}{16}$ $\frac{13}{16}$	$\frac{9}{16}$ $\frac{13}{16}$	$\frac{9}{16}$ $\frac{13}{16}$
Choke Unloader (in.)	$\frac{5}{32}$	$\frac{5}{32}$	0.15	0.15	0.15
Vacuum Kick	0.06	0.08	0.14	②	Auto. 0.08 Man. 0.14
Idle Mixture Screws (turns out)	1–1¼	1–1¼	—	—	—

① On step no. 5
② Fresh air, auto.—0.14
    Fresh air, man.—0.08
    Heated air, auto.—0.08
    Heated air, man.—0.14
③ California cars, auto.—1800
             man.—2000
Auto.—Automatic transmission
Man.—Manual transmission

Rochester 2 GV

	1971
Fast Idle Speed (rpm)	1800
Float Setting (in.)	$\frac{21}{32}$
Float Drop (in.)	1¾
Choke Unloader (in.)	0.136
Vacuum Kick (in.)	0.096

Thermo Quad (Carter)

	1971	1972	1973
Fast Idle Speed (rpm)	900	Auto. 750 ② Man. 900	1700①
Float Setting (in.)	1	1	$1\frac{1}{16}$
Choke Unloader (in.)	0.190	0.190	0.190
Vacuum Kick (in.)	0.110	Auto. 0.140 Man. 0.160	0.160

Auto.—Automatic transmission
Man.—Manual transmission
① 400 engine, Auto.—1800
② California cars, Auto.—750
               Man.—800

5 · Chassis Electrical

Heater

NOTE: *On models equipped with a console it is necessary to loosen the console and move it rearward to get enough clearance to remove the heater.*

CORE

Removal and Installation (Non-Air Conditioned Cars)

1968–70

1. Disconnect the ground cable from the battery and drain the radiator.

2. Remove the upper half of the glove compartment.

3. Working inside the engine compartment, disconnect the heater hoses at the firewall. Plug the heater core hose fittings to prevent spilling coolant in the interior.

4. Working in the interior, remove the heater to cowl support bracket located under the dashboard.

5. Remove the defroster hoses and disconnect the blower motor resistor wiring.

6. Disconnect the shut-off door and fresh air vent control cables at the heater. Reaching through the glove compartment, disconnect the temperature control door cable.

7. Working in the engine compartment, remove the three nuts which secure the heater to the firewall.

8. Pull the heater away from the firewall and rotate it until the mounting studs are facing up. Carefully withdraw the heater from under the instrument panel.

9. Remove the heater cover to expose the heater core.

10. Remove the heater core securing screws and remove the core.

11. Reverse the above steps to install.

1971–73

1. Drain the coolant and disconnect the battery ground cable.

2. Disconnect the heater hoses from the heater core at the firewall. Plug the heater core hose fittings to prevent spillage of coolant in the interior.

3. Remove the three blower mounting nuts around the blower and the nut near the center of the firewall.

4. Unplug the antenna wire from the radio and move it out of the way.

5. Remove the screw from the housing to plenum support rod on the right side of the housing above the outside air opening.

6. Disconnect the air door cables.

7. Disconnect the wires from the blower motor resistor.

8. Rotate the unit down and pull it out from under the instrument panel.

CHILTON'S
FUEL ECONOMY
& TUNE-UP TIPS

Tune-Up • Spark Plug Diagnosis • Emission Controls

Fuel System • Cooling System • Tires and Wheels

General Maintenance

CHILTON'S FUEL ECONOMY & TUNE-UP TIPS

Fuel economy is important to everyone, no matter what kind of vehicle you drive. The maintenance-minded motorist can save both money and fuel using these tips and the periodic maintenance and tune-up procedures in this Repair and Tune-Up Guide.

There are more than 130,000,000 cars and trucks registered for private use in the United States. Each travels an average of 10-12,000 miles per year, and, in total they consume close to 70 billion gallons of fuel each year. This represents nearly ⅔ of the oil imported by the United States each year. The Federal government's goal is to reduce consumption 10% by 1985. A variety of methods are either already in use or under serious consideration, and they all affect your driving and the cars you will drive. In addition to "down-sizing", the auto industry is using or investigating the use of electronic fuel delivery, electronic engine controls and alternative engines for use in smaller and lighter vehicles, among other alternatives to meet the federally mandated Corporate Average Fuel Economy (CAFE) of 27.5 mpg by 1985. The government, for its part, is considering rationing, mandatory driving curtailments and tax increases on motor vehicle fuel in an effort to reduce consumption. The government's goal of a 10% reduction could be realized — and further government regulation avoided — if every private vehicle could use just 1 less gallon of fuel per week.

How Much Can You Save?

Tests have proven that almost anyone can make at least a 10% reduction in fuel consumption through regular maintenance and tune-ups. When a major manufacturer of spark plugs sur-

TUNE-UP

1. Check the cylinder compression to be sure the engine will really benefit from a tune-up and that it is capable of producing good fuel economy. A tune-up will be wasted on an engine in poor mechanical condition.

2. Replace spark plugs regularly. New spark plugs alone can increase fuel economy 3%.

3. Be sure the spark plugs are the correct type (heat range) for your vehicle. See the Tune-Up Specifications.

Heat range refers to the spark plug's ability to conduct heat away from the firing end. It must conduct the heat away in an even pattern to avoid becoming a source of pre-ignition, yet it must also operate hot enough to burn off conductive deposits that could cause misfiring.

The heat range is usually indicated by a number on the spark plug, part of the manufacturer's designation for each individual spark plug. The numbers in bold-face indicate the heat range in each manufacturer's identification system.

Manufacturer	Typical Designation
AC	R **45** TS
Bosch (old)	WA **145** T30
Bosch (new)	HR **8** Y
Champion	RBL **15** Y
Fram/Autolite	**415**
Mopar	P-**62** PR
Motorcraft	BRF-**42**
NGK	BP **5** ES-15
Nippondenso	W **16** EP
Prestolite	14GR **5** 2A

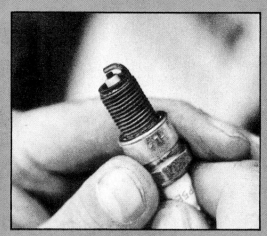

Periodically, check the spark plugs to be sure they are firing efficiently. They are excellent indicators of the internal condition of your engine.

On AC, Bosch (new), Champion, Fram/Autolite, Mopar, Motorcraft and Prestolite, a higher number indicates a hotter plug. On Bosch (old), NGK and Nippondenso, a higher number indicates a colder plug.

4. Make sure the spark plugs are properly gapped. See the Tune-Up Specifications in this book.

5. Be sure the spark plugs are firing efficiently. The illustrations on the next 2 pages show you how to "read" the firing end of the spark plug.

6. Check the ignition timing and set it to specifications. Tests show that almost all cars

veyed over 6,000 cars nationwide, they found that a tune-up, on cars that needed one, increased fuel economy over 11%. Replacing worn plugs alone, accounted for a 3% increase. The same test also revealed that 8 out of every 10 vehicles will have some maintenance deficiency that will directly affect fuel economy, emissions or performance. Most of this mileage-robbing neglect could be prevented with regular maintenance.

Modern engines require that all of the functioning systems operate properly for maximum efficiency. A malfunction anywhere wastes fuel. You can keep your vehicle running as efficiently and economically as possible, by being aware of your vehicles operating and performance characteristics. If your vehicle suddenly develops performance or fuel economy problems it could be due to one or more of the following:

PROBLEM	POSSIBLE CAUSE
Engine Idles Rough	Ignition timing, idle mixture, vacuum leak or something amiss in the emission control system.
Hesitates on Acceleration	Dirty carburetor or fuel filter, improper accelerator pump setting, ignition timing or fouled spark plugs.
Starts Hard or Fails to Start	Worn spark plugs, improperly set automatic choke, ice (or water) in fuel system.
Stalls Frequently	Automatic choke improperly adjusted and possible dirty air filter or fuel filter.
Performs Sluggishly	Worn spark plugs, dirty fuel or air filter, ignition timing or automatic choke out of adjustment.

Check spark plug wires on conventional point type ignition for cracks by bending them in a loop around your finger.

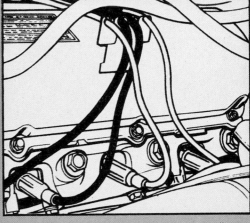

Be sure that spark plug wires leading to adjacent cylinders do not run too close together. (Photo courtesy Champion Spark Plug Co.)

have incorrect ignition timing by more than 2°.

7. If your vehicle does not have electronic ignition, check the points, rotor and cap as specified.

8. Check the spark plug wires (used with conventional point-type ignitions) for cracks and burned or broken insulation by bending them in a loop around your finger. Cracked wires decrease fuel efficiency by failing to deliver full voltage to the spark plugs. One misfiring spark plug can cost you as much as 2 mpg.

9. Check the routing of the plug wires. Misfiring can be the result of spark plug leads to adjacent cylinders running parallel to each other and too close together. One wire tends to pick up voltage from the other causing it to fire "out of time".

10. Check all electrical and ignition circuits for voltage drop and resistance.

11. Check the distributor mechanical and/or vacuum advance mechanisms for proper functioning. The vacuum advance can be checked by twisting the distributor plate in the opposite direction of rotation. It should spring back when released.

12. Check and adjust the valve clearance on engines with mechanical lifters. The clearance should be slightly loose rather than too tight.

SPARK PLUG DIAGNOSIS

Normal

APPEARANCE: This plug is typical of one operating normally. The insulator nose varies from a light tan to grayish color with slight electrode wear. The presence of slight deposits is normal on used plugs and will have no adverse effect on engine performance. The spark plug heat range is correct for the engine and the engine is running normally.

CAUSE: Properly running engine.

RECOMMENDATION: Before reinstalling this plug, the electrodes should be cleaned and filed square. Set the gap to specifications. If the plug has been in service for more than 10-12,000 miles, the entire set should probably be replaced with a fresh set of the same heat range.

Oil Deposits

APPEARANCE: The firing end of the plug is covered with a wet, oily coating.

CAUSE: The problem is poor oil control. On high mileage engines, oil is leaking past the rings or valve guides into the combustion chamber. A common cause is also a plugged PCV valve, and a ruptured fuel pump diaphragm can also cause this condition. Oil fouled plugs such as these are often found in new or recently overhauled engines, before normal oil control is achieved, and can be cleaned and reinstalled.

RECOMMENDATION: A hotter spark plug may temporarily relieve the problem, but the engine is probably in need of work.

Incorrect Heat Range

APPEARANCE: The effects of high temperature on a spark plug are indicated by clean white, often blistered insulator. This can also be accompanied by excessive wear of the electrode, and the absence of deposits.

CAUSE: Check for the correct spark plug heat range. A plug which is too hot for the engine can result in overheating. A car operated mostly at high speeds can require a colder plug. Also check ignition timing, cooling system level, fuel mixture and leaking intake manifold.

RECOMMENDATION: If all ignition and engine adjustments are known to be correct, and no other malfunction exists, install spark plugs one heat range colder.

Photos Courtesy Champion Spark Plug Co.

Carbon Deposits

APPEARANCE: Carbon fouling is easily identified by the presence of dry, soft, black, sooty deposits.

CAUSE: Changing the heat range can often lead to carbon fouling, as can prolonged slow, stop-and-start driving. If the heat range is correct, carbon fouling can be attributed to a rich fuel mixture, sticking choke, clogged air cleaner, worn breaker points, retarded timing or low compression. If only one or two plugs are carbon fouled, check for corroded or cracked wires on the affected plugs. Also look for cracks in the distributor cap between the towers of affected cylinders.

RECOMMENDATION: After the problem is corrected, these plugs can be cleaned and reinstalled if not worn severely.

MMT Fouled

APPEARANCE: Spark plugs fouled by MMT (Methycyclopentadienyl Maganese Tricarbonyl) have reddish, rusty appearance on the insulator and side electrode.

CAUSE: MMT is an anti-knock additive in gasoline used to replace lead. During the combustion process, the MMT leaves a reddish deposit on the insulator and side electrode.

RECOMMENDATION: No engine malfunction is indicated and the deposits will not affect plug performance any more than lead deposits (see Ash Deposits). MMT fouled plugs can be cleaned, regapped and reinstalled.

High Speed Glazing

APPEARANCE: Glazing appears as shiny coating on the plug, either yellow or tan in color.

CAUSE: During hard, fast acceleration, plug temperatures rise suddenly. Deposits from normal combustion have no chance to fluff-off; instead, they melt on the insulator forming an electrically conductive coating which causes misfiring.

RECOMMENDATION: Glazed plugs are not easily cleaned. They should be replaced with a fresh set of plugs of the correct heat range. If the condition recurs, using plugs with a heat range one step colder may cure the problem.

Ash (Lead) Deposits

APPEARANCE: Ash deposits are characterized by light brown or white colored deposits crusted on the side or center electrodes. In some cases it may give the plug a rusty appearance.

CAUSE: Ash deposits are normally derived from oil or fuel additives burned during normal combustion. Normally they are harmless, though excessive amounts can cause misfiring. If deposits are excessive in short mileage, the valve guides may be worn.

RECOMMENDATION: Ash-fouled plugs can be cleaned, gapped and reinstalled.

Detonation

APPEARANCE: Detonation is usually characterized by a broken plug insulator.

CAUSE: A portion of the fuel charge will begin to burn spontaneously, from the increased heat following ignition. The explosion that results applies extreme pressure to engine components, frequently damaging spark plugs and pistons.

Detonation can result by over-advanced ignition timing, inferior gasoline (low octane) lean air/fuel mixture, poor carburetion, engine lugging or an increase in compression ratio due to combustion chamber deposits or engine modification.

RECOMMENDATION: Replace the plugs after correcting the problem.

Photos Courtesy Fram Corporation

EMISSION CONTROLS

13. Be aware of the general condition of the emission control system. It contributes to reduced pollution and should be serviced regularly to maintain efficient engine operation.

14. Check all vacuum lines for dried, cracked or brittle conditions. Something as simple as a leaking vacuum hose can cause poor performance and loss of economy.

15. Avoid tampering with the emission control system. Attempting to improve fuel econ-

---

FUEL SYSTEM

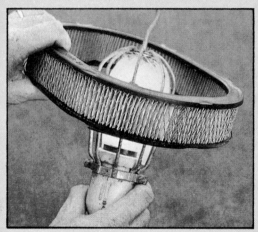

Check the air filter with a light behind it. If you can see light through the filter it can be reused.

Extremely clogged filters should be discarded and replaced with a new one.

18. Replace the air filter regularly. A dirty air filter richens the air/fuel mixture and can increase fuel consumption as much as 10%. Tests show that ⅓ of all vehicles have air filters in need of replacement.

19. Replace the fuel filter at least as often as recommended.

20. Set the idle speed and carburetor mixture to specifications.

21. Check the automatic choke. A sticking or malfunctioning choke wastes gas.

22. During the summer months, adjust the automatic choke for a leaner mixture which will produce faster engine warm-ups.

COOLING SYSTEM

29. Be sure all accessory drive belts are in good condition. Check for cracks or wear.

30. Adjust all accessory drive belts to proper tension.

31. Check all hoses for swollen areas, worn spots, or loose clamps.

32. Check coolant level in the radiator or expansion tank.

33. Be sure the thermostat is operating properly. A stuck thermostat delays engine warm-up and a cold engine uses nearly twice as much fuel as a warm engine.

34. Drain and replace the engine coolant at least as often as recommended. Rust and scale

---

TIRES & WHEELS

38. Check the tire pressure often with a pencil type gauge. Tests by a major tire manufacturer show that 90% of all vehicles have at least 1 tire improperly inflated. Better mileage can be achieved by over-inflating tires, but never exceed the maximum inflation pressure on the side of the tire.

39. If possible, install radial tires. Radial tires deliver as much as ½ mpg more than bias belted tires.

40. Avoid installing super-wide tires. They only create extra rolling resistance and decrease fuel mileage. Stick to the manufacturer's recommendations.

41. Have the wheels properly balanced.

omy by tampering with emission controls is more likely to worsen fuel economy than improve it. Emission control changes on modern engines are not readily reversible.

16. Clean (or replace) the EGR valve and lines as recommended.

17. Be sure that all vacuum lines and hoses are reconnected properly after working under the hood. An unconnected or misrouted vacuum line can wreak havoc with engine performance.

23. Check for fuel leaks at the carburetor, fuel pump, fuel lines and fuel tank. Be sure all lines and connections are tight.

24. Periodically check the tightness of the carburetor and intake manifold attaching nuts and bolts. These are a common place for vacuum leaks to occur.

25. Clean the carburetor periodically and lubricate the linkage.

26. The condition of the tailpipe can be an excellent indicator of proper engine combustion. After a long drive at highway speeds, the inside of the tailpipe should be a light grey in color. Black or soot on the insides indicates an overly rich mixture.

27. Check the fuel pump pressure. The fuel pump may be supplying more fuel than the engine needs.

28. Use the proper grade of gasoline for your engine. Don't try to compensate for knocking or "pinging" by advancing the ignition timing. This practice will only increase plug temperature and the chances of detonation or pre-ignition with relatively little performance gain.

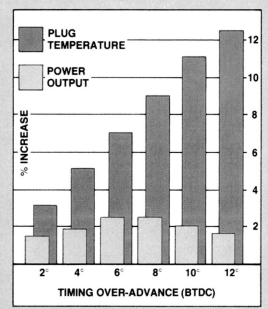

Increasing ignition timing past the specified setting results in a drastic increase in spark plug temperature with increased chance of detonation or preignition. Performance increase is considerably less. (Photo courtesy Champion Spark Plug Co.)

that form in the engine should be flushed out to allow the engine to operate at peak efficiency.

35. Clean the radiator of debris that can decrease cooling efficiency.

36. Install a flex-type or electric cooling fan, if you don't have a clutch type fan. Flex fans use curved plastic blades to push more air at low speeds when more cooling is needed; at high speeds the blades flatten out for less resistance. Electric fans only run when the engine temperature reaches a predetermined level.

37. Check the radiator cap for a worn or cracked gasket. If the cap does not seal properly, the cooling system will not function properly.

42. Be sure the front end is correctly aligned. A misaligned front end actually has wheels going in different directions. The increased drag can reduce fuel economy by .3 mpg.

43. Correctly adjust the wheel bearings. Wheel bearings that are adjusted too tight increase rolling resistance.

Check tire pressures regularly with a reliable pocket type gauge. Be sure to check the pressure on a cold tire.

GENERAL MAINTENANCE

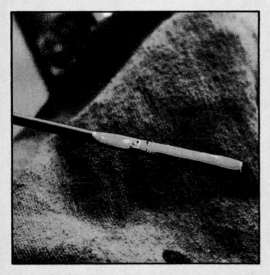

Check the fluid levels (particularly engine oil) on a regular basis. Be sure to check the oil for grit, water or other contamination.

A vacuum gauge is another excellent indicator of internal engine condition and can also be installed in the dash as a mileage indicator.

44. Periodically check the fluid levels in the engine, power steering pump, master cylinder, automatic transmission and drive axle.

45. Change the oil at the recommended interval and change the filter at every oil change. Dirty oil is thick and causes extra friction between moving parts, cutting efficiency and increasing wear. A worn engine requires more frequent tune-ups and gets progressively worse fuel economy. In general, use the lightest viscosity oil for the driving conditions you will encounter.

46. Use the recommended viscosity fluids in the transmission and axle.

47. Be sure the battery is fully charged for fast starts. A slow starting engine wastes fuel.

48. Be sure battery terminals are clean and tight.

49. Check the battery electrolyte level and add distilled water if necessary.

50. Check the exhaust system for crushed pipes, blockages and leaks.

51. Adjust the brakes. Dragging brakes or brakes that are not releasing create increased drag on the engine.

52. Install a vacuum gauge or miles-per-gallon gauge. These gauges visually indicate engine vacuum in the intake manifold. High vacuum = good mileage and low vacuum = poorer mileage. The gauge can also be an excellent indicator of internal engine conditions.

53. Be sure the clutch is properly adjusted. A slipping clutch wastes fuel.

54. Check and periodically lubricate the heat control valve in the exhaust manifold. A sticking or inoperative valve prevents engine warm-up and wastes gas.

55. Keep accurate records to check fuel economy over a period of time. A sudden drop in fuel economy may signal a need for tune-up or other maintenance.

9. Remove the heater core from the heater.

10. Reverse the above steps to install.

BLOWER MOTOR

Removal and Installation (Non-Air Conditioned Cars)

1968, 1971–73

1. Remove the heater as described above.

2. Remove the blower motor wiring.

3. Remove the six screws and retaining clips and separate the mounting plate and blower motor from the housing.

4. Remove the blower fan from the blower motor shaft.

5. Remove the mounting plate retaining nuts and separate the motor from the plate.

6. Reverse the above steps to install.

1969–70

1. Remove the heater as described above.

2. Disconnect the blower motor wiring.

3. Remove the blower motor cooling tube.

4. Remove the fan from the blower motor shaft.

5. Remove the blower motor from the backplate.

6. Reverse the above steps to install.

HEATER CORE

Removal and Installation (Air Conditioned Cars)

CAUTION: *Never attempt to disconnect any air conditioning lines. They contain high pressure refrigerant and serious injury may result if the lines are disconnected improperly. Always take the car to a properly trained mechanic if the lines must be disconnected.*

1968–70

NOTE: *The heater core is located behind a separate cover attached to the evaporator case forward of the instrument panel. The heater core may be removed separately without disconnecting any air conditioning hoses.*

1. Disconnect the negative ground cable, drain the cooling system, remove the air cleaner, and disconnect the heater hoses.

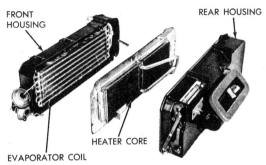

Heater assembly, air conditioned cars (Courtesy of Chrysler Corp.)

2. Remove the distribution housing glove box and heater core inlet-outlet tube assembly.

3. Remove the fresh air recirculating air inlet hose.

4. Disconnect the floor air actuator rod from the linkage.

5. Disconnect the actuator vacuum hoses and remove the fresh air recirculating door housing.

6. Remove the defroster hoses. Disconnect the electrical connections from the resistor.

7. Remove the screws which attach the water bypass valve to the heater cover and remove the operating link attaching screw.

8. Disconnect the air conditioning door actuator from the mounting bracket and remove the support braces.

9. Remove the retainer spring clips and screws which hold the cover to the case.

10. To remove the cover and heater core it will be necessary to pull the lower edge rearward, then lift the assembly ⅜ in. to unhook the cover lip from the case. Carefully lower the assembly out to the right side.

11. Reverse the above steps to install.

1971–73

The heater core can not be removed without disconnecting the air conditioning lines. Take the car to a properly trained mechanic for service.

BLOWER MOTOR

Removal and Installation (Air Conditioned Cars)

1968–73

1. Working inside the engine compartment, disconnect the blower wiring and remove the blower air tube.

MOUNTING STUDS

Blower motor, air conditioned cars (Courtesy of Chrysler Corp.)

2. Remove the mounting plate, blower motor, and fan as an assembly.

3. Reverse the above steps to install.

Radio

Removal and Installation

1968

1. Disconnect the battery ground cable.

2. If equipped with air conditioning, remove the spot cooler hoses and distribution duct.

3. Remove the control knobs, two mounting nuts, and the bezel.

4. Disconnect the speaker, power, and antenna wires from the rear of the radio.

5. Remove the radio support bracket.

6. Remove the radio from under the instrument panel.

7. Reverse the above steps to install.

1969–70

1. Disconnect the battery ground cable.

2. Remove the radio trim panel.

3. Remove the radio finish plate.

4. Remove the rear mounting nut from the mounting bracket.

5. Support the radio and remove the two mounting screws from the front of the instrument panel. Remove the radio from under the instrument panel.

6. Reverse the above steps to install.

1971

1. Disconnect the battery ground cable.

2. Remove the ash tray.

3. Remove the radio knobs and mounting nuts. Disconnect the radio antenna and wiring.

4. Remove the radio from under the instrument panel.

5. Reverse the above steps to install.

1972–73

1. Disconnect the battery ground cable.

2. Remove the radio knobs and mounting nuts.

3. Disconnect the antenna, speaker, and power wires.

4. Remove the rear support bracket.

5. Remove the radio from under the instrument panel.

Windshield Wipers

WINDSHIELD WIPER MOTOR

Removal and Installation

1968 WITHOUT AIR CONDITIONING

1. Disconnect the battery ground cable.

2. Disconnect the wiper motor wiring.

3. Working under the instrument panel, remove the crank-arm nut and remove the crank arm from the wiper motor shaft. Remove the motor mounting nuts and remove the motor.

4. Be sure all three spacers are inserted in the wiper motor mounting holes. Note the position of the flats on the motor shaft and install the motor so that the flats index with the flats in the crank arm.

5. Tighten the motor mounting nuts and reverse steps 1 and 2 to complete the installation.

1968 WITH AIR CONDITIONING

1. Perform steps 1 and 2 in the above procedure.

2. Remove the motor mounting nuts and the motor wiring.

3. Remove the instrument cluster.

4. Remove the drive link from the left pivot arm.

5. Slip the motor off the mounting studs enough to gain access to the crank arm securing nut. Remove the nut and carefully remove the arm.

6. Remove the motor from the studs.

7. Make sure all three spacers are in the motor mounting holes.

8. Index the flats on the motor shaft with the flats in the crank arm and just start the nut on the motor shaft. Place the motor on the lower right mounting stud, tighten the nut and rotate the motor upward until all the holes are aligned with the mounting studs.

9. Reverse steps 1 through 4 to complete the installation.

1969–70

This procedure is the same as the "1968 Without Air Conditioning" procedure.

1970–73 WITH NON-CONCEALED WIPERS

1. Disconnect the battery ground cable.
2. Disconnect the wiper motor wiring.
3. Remove the wiper motor mounting nuts. On cars equipped with air conditioning, remove the crank arm securing nut and crank arm while working the instrument panel, and omit the next step.
4. Slip the motor off the mounting studs enough to gain clearance to remove the crank arm and crank arm nut.
5. Remove the wiper motor.
6. To install the motor, index the flats on the motor shaft with the flats in the crank arm and tighten the nut. Reverse steps 1 through 5 to complete installation.

1970–73 WITH CONCEALED WIPERS

1. Disconnect the battery ground cable.
2. Remove the wiper arm and blade assemblies.
3. Remove the cowl screen. Disconnect the motor wiring.
4. Holding the motor crank with a wrench, remove the crank arm nut and then the crank arm.
5. Remove the motor securing nuts and remove the motor.
6. To install, index the flats on the motor shaft with the flats in the crank arm and tighten the nut.
7. Reverse steps 1 through 5 to install.

LINKAGE AND PIVOT

Removal and Installation

1968–70 NON-CONCEALED WIPERS

1. Disconnect the battery ground cable.
2. On air conditioned models, remove the left supply duct for the spot cooler for easier access to the left wiper pivot.
3. Using a wide blade screwdriver in-

serted between the plastic link bushing and the pivot crank arm, force the link and bushing from the pivot pin.

4. Remove the wiper motor.
5. After the crank arm has been removed from the motor, remove the drive link assembly from under the left side of the panel.
6. To remove the connecting link from the pivots, remove the glove box.
7. Reaching through the glove box opening, pry the link and bushing from the right pivot crank arm. Repeat the operation at the left pivot. Withdraw the link from under the left side of the instrument panel.
8. Reverse the above steps to install.

Instrument Panel

Removal and Installation

1968–70

1. Disconnect the battery and remove the four screws which secure the steering column trim cover.
2. Roll the carpet out of the way and remove the lower mounting plate.
3. Remove the steering column clamp and support the column.
CAUTION: *The steering column must be supported at all times or the column will bend.*
4. If equipped, remove the six upper trim moulding screws and remove the trim.
5. If equipped, remove the left side trim moulding.
6. If equipped, remove the left side trim plate.
7. Remove the radio trim plate.
8. Remove the four switch bezel screws and remove the bezel.
9. Remove the ignition switch.
10. Remove the center air conditioning opening cover, if so equipped.
11. Remove the lower trim pad securing screws and remove the pad from under the panel.
12. Disconnect the speedometer cable.
13. Remove the six cluster securing screws and carefully slide the cluster out. Disconnect the wiring and remove the cluster from the car.
14. Reverse the above steps to install.

1971-72

1. Disconnect the negative battery cable.

2. Remove the ash tray.

3. Remove the radio knobs and mounting nuts.

4. Remove the radio.

5. Remove the heater control panel.

6. Remove the upper steering column clamp and lower the steering column. The column must be supported at all times or the column will bend.

7. Remove the instrument cluster mounting screws.

8. Disconnect the speedometer cable from the back of the cluster.

9. Disconnect the wiring and remove the cluster.

10. Reverse the above steps to install.

1973

Removal of the instrument cluster requires disturbing the steering column which is extremely sensitive to bending. Lowering the column to provide clearance for removal of the cluster is excessively complicated and extreme caution must be exercised to keep from damaging the column. Take the car to the dealer for removal of the cluster.

Headlight Switch

Removal and Installation

1968

1. Remove the fuse box attaching screw and position the fuse box out of the way.

2. Disconnect the connector from the rear of the switch.

3. Press the release button on the body of the switch and pull the control knob and shaft from the switch.

4. Remove the bezel nut which secures the switch to the dash and remove the switch.

5. Reverse the above steps to install.

1969-73

1. Disconnect the wiring from the rear of the switch. On air conditioned models, it may be necessary to disconnect air ducts to gain clearance to the rear of the switch.

2. Remove the two screws (1973 cars, remove the bezel nut) which secures the switch to the dash and remove the switch.

3. Reverse the above steps to install.

Ignition Switch

Removal and Installation

1968-69

1. Disconnect the multiple connector from the rear of the switch.

2. Remove the bezel nut which secures the switch to the dash and remove the switch.

3. Reverse the above steps to install.

Lock Cylinder

Removal and Installation

1968-69

1. Disconnect the battery.

2. Remove the cylinder by placing the switch so that a stiff wire may be inserted into the small hole to depress the plunger that holds the cylinder in place.

3. With the key and wire in place rotate the cylinder until it can be withdrawn from its housing.

4. Reverse the above steps to install.

Ignition Switch and Lock Cylinder 1970-73

Removal and Installation

Lock Cylinder—Tilt Steering Column

1. Disconnect the battery ground cable.

2. Remove the steering wheel with a puller.

3. Remove the turn signal lever.

4. Remove the gearshift lever pivot pin and lever, the tilt release lever, and the turn signal switch lever.

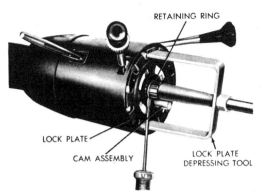

RETAINING RING

LOCK PLATE

CAM ASSEMBLY

LOCK PLATE DEPRESSING TOOL

Removing the lock plate snap ring, tilt wheel (Courtesy of Chrylser Corp.)

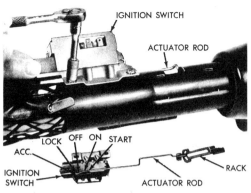

IGNITION SWITCH

ACTUATOR ROD

LOCK OFF ON START

ACC.

IGNITION SWITCH

RACK

ACTUATOR ROD

SLIDER DETENT POSITIONS IN SWITCH

Ignition switch, tilt wheel, 1970–73 (Courtesy of Chrysler Corp.)

5. Press down on the lock plate and carrier and remove the snap ring. Remove the lock plate, carrier, and spring.

6. Remove the three turn signal switch attaching screws, place the shiftbowl in the low position, and remove the switch and wiring. The shiftbowl is the section to which the shift lever is attached.

7. Remove the buzzer switch.

8. Lock the switch and remove the key.

9. Insert a small screwdriver into the slot next to the switch mounting screw

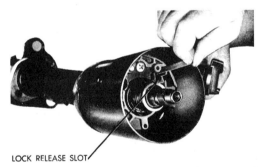

LOCK RELEASE SLOT

Removing the lock cylinder, 1970–73 (Courtesy of Chrysler Corp.)

boss (right hand slot) and depress the spring latch at the bottom of the slot. Slide the lock cylinder from its housing.

IGNITION SWITCH—TILT STEERING WHEEL

1. Remove the ignition switch securing screws. It may be necessary to lower the steering column to obtain clearance. The switch is located at the lower end of the column.

2. Disconnect the switch wiring.

3. Remove the switch from the car.

4. Reverse the above steps to install. Make sure the switch is properly adjusted.

The switch has elongated mounting holes and the switch may be moved up and down to obtain the proper adjustment.

IGNITION SWITCH AND LOCK CYLINDER— STANDARD STEERING COLUMN

1. Disconnect the battery ground cable.

2. Remove the steering wheel.

3. Remove the turn signal lever.

4. Remove the turn signal switch and upper bearing retainer.

5. Remove the ignition key lamp assembly.

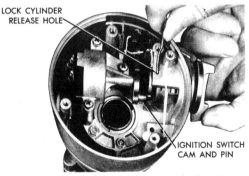

LOCK CYLINDER RELEASE HOLE

IGNITION SWITCH CAM AND PIN

Removing the lock cylinder, standard column 1970–73 (Courtesy of Chrysler Corp.)

6. Remove the snap ring from the upper end of the steering shaft.

7. Remove the three bearing housing-to-lock housing screws.

8. Pull the bearing housing from the shaft. Remove the bearing lower snap ring.

9. Pry the sleeve off the steering shaft lock plate hub to expose the pin.

10. Press, do not hammer, the pin from the shaft.

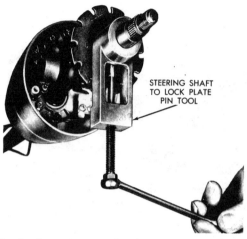

Lock plate pin removal and installation, standard column (Courtesy of Chrysler Corp.)

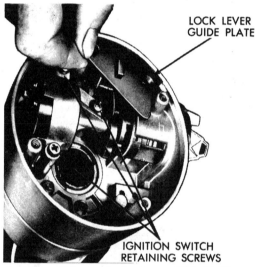

Ignition switch, standard column, 1970–73 (Courtesy of Chrysler Corp.)

11. Remove the lock plate from the steering shaft.

12. Remove the buzzer switch and the lock lever guide plate.

13. Lock the ignition switch and remove the key.

14. Insert a stiff wire into the lock cylinder release hole, push in to release the lock retainer and pull the lock cylinder out.

15. Remove the three retaining screws and ignition switch assembly.

16. Reverse the above steps to install.

Turn Signal Switch

Removal and Installation

1968–69

1. Lower the steering column and support it. Remove the turn signal wire shielding from the steering column. The steering column is extremely easy to bend.

2. Remove the steering wheel.

3. Disconnect the turn signal switch at the base of the column. Tape the wire connector end to the wires so that the wires can be drawn up through the column. It is necessary to remove the wires from the connector.

4. Tie a piece of string to the wire connector so that the new turn signal switch wires may be pulled back through the column during installation.

5. Remove the turn signal switch securing screws and remove the switch.

6. Reverse the above steps to install.

1970–73

1. Remove the steering wheel.

2. Remove the turn signal switch securing screws.

3. Unplug the switch wiring from the back of the switch.

4. Remove the switch.

5. Reverse the above steps to install.

Lighting

Sealed Beam Removal and Installation

1. Remove the screws from the headlight panel and remove the panel.

2. Remove the screws from the interior retaining ring and remove the ring. Do not confuse the retaining ring screws with the adjusting screws. There are two adjusting screws and three retaining ring screws.

3. Remove the sealed beam from the car and disconnect the wiring at the back of the beam.

4. Reverse the above steps to install. It may be necessary to re-aim the headlight.

Wiring Diagrams

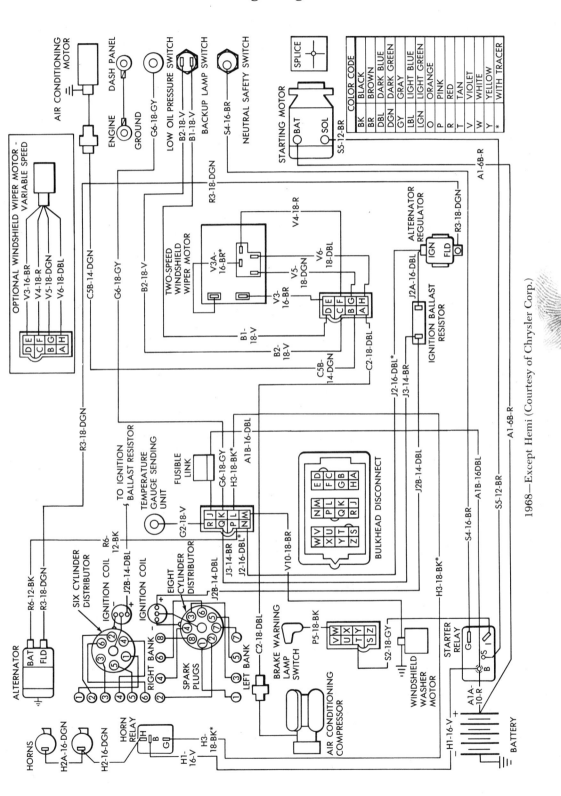

1968—Except Hemi (Courtesy of Chrysler Corp.)

COLOR CODE	
BK	BLACK
BR	BROWN
DBL	DARK BLUE
DGN	DARK GREEN
GY	GRAY
LBL	LIGHT BLUE
LGN	LIGHT GREEN
O	ORANGE
P	PINK
R	RED
T	TAN
V	VIOLET
W	WHITE
Y	YELLOW
*	WITH TRACER

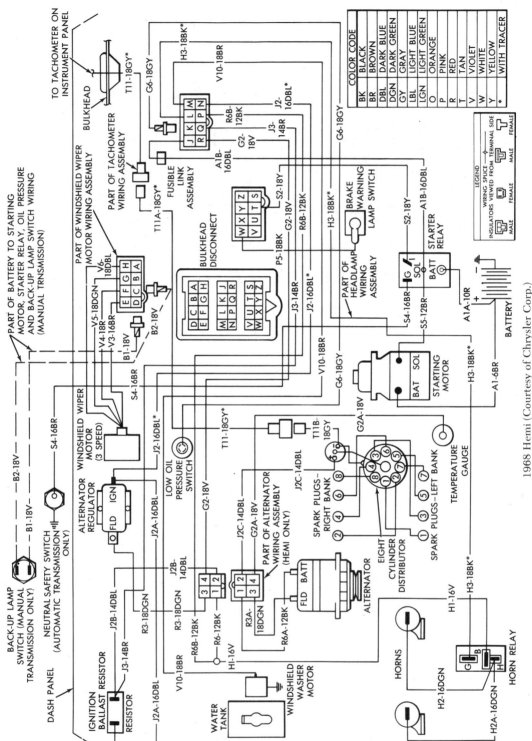

1968 Hemi (Courtesy of Chrysler Corp.)

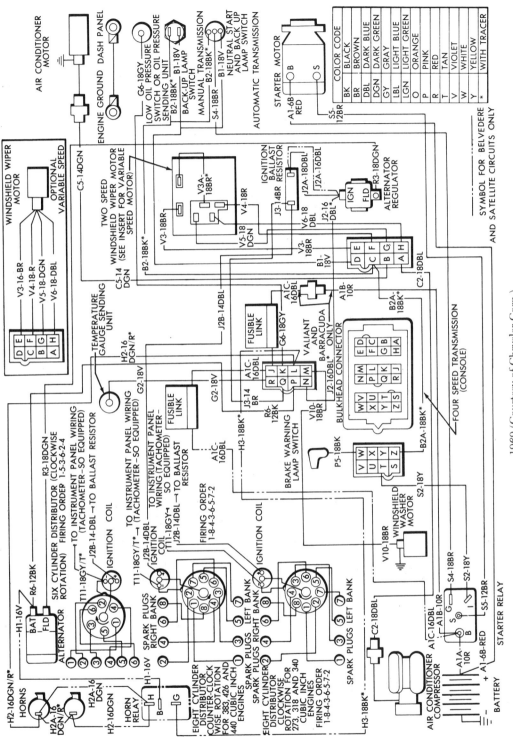

1969 (Courtesy of Chrysler Corp.)

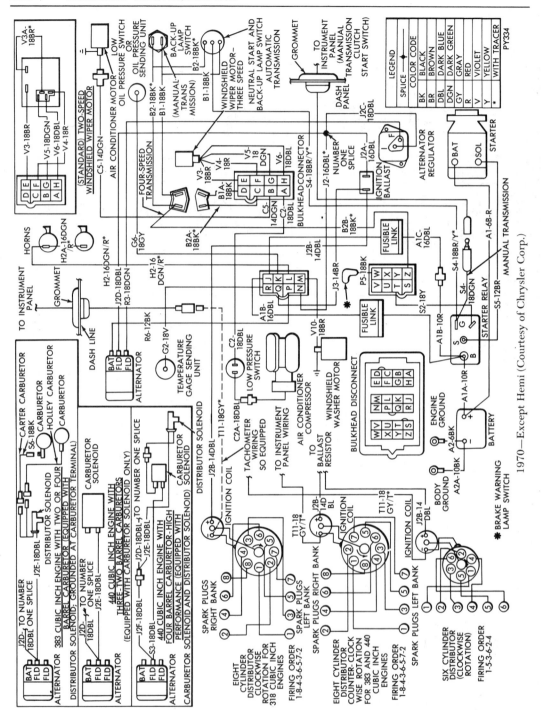

1970—Except Hemi (Courtesy of Chrysler Corp.)

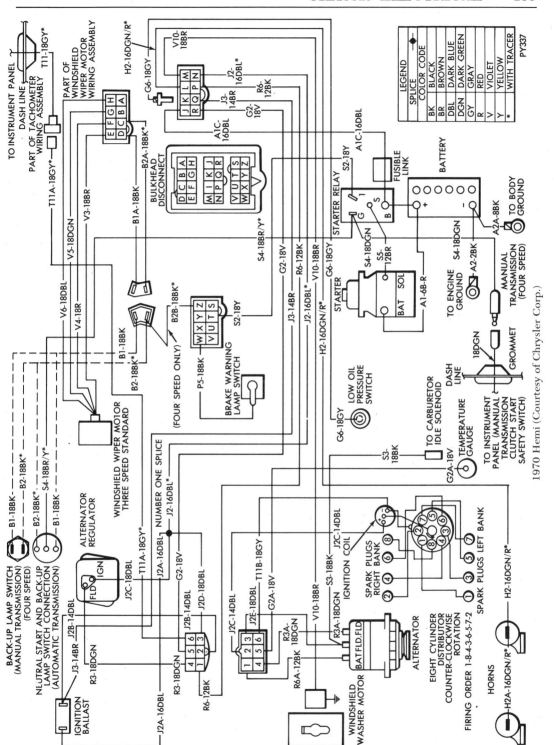

1970 Hemi (Courtesy of Chrysler Corp.)

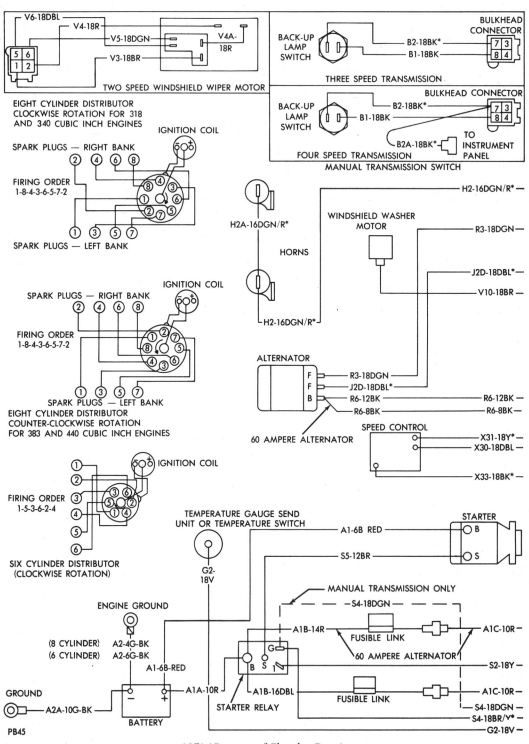

V6-18DBL
V4-18R
V5-18DGN
V4A-18R
V3-18BR

5 6
1 2

TWO SPEED WINDSHIELD WIPER MOTOR

EIGHT CYLINDER DISTRIBUTOR
CLOCKWISE ROTATION FOR 318
AND 340 CUBIC INCH ENGINES

IGNITION COIL

SPARK PLUGS — RIGHT BANK

2 4 6 8

FIRING ORDER
1-8-4-3-6-5-7-2

8 4
1
2 7
6
3 5 7

SPARK PLUGS — LEFT BANK

IGNITION COIL

SPARK PLUGS — RIGHT BANK

2 4 6 8

FIRING ORDER
1-8-4-3-6-5-7-2

1 7
8 5
4 3 6

SPARK PLUGS — LEFT BANK

EIGHT CYLINDER DISTRIBUTOR
COUNTER-CLOCKWISE ROTATION
FOR 383 AND 440 CUBIC INCH ENGINES

IGNITION COIL

1
2
3 6
5 4
4
5
6

FIRING ORDER
1-5-3-6-2-4

SIX CYLINDER DISTRIBUTOR
(CLOCKWISE ROTATION)

BACK-UP
LAMP
SWITCH

B2-18BK*
B1-18BK

BULKHEAD
CONNECTOR
7 3
8 4

THREE SPEED TRANSMISSION

BACK-UP
LAMP
SWITCH

B2-18BK*
B1-18BK

BULKHEAD CONNECTOR
7 3
8 4

B2A-18BK*

TO
INSTRUMENT
PANEL

FOUR SPEED TRANSMISSION

MANUAL TRANSMISSION SWITCH

H2A-16DGN/R*

HORNS

H2-16DGN/R*

H2-16DGN/R*

WINDSHIELD WASHER
MOTOR

R3-18DGN

J2D-18DBL*
V10-18BR

ALTERNATOR

F   R3-18DGN
F   J2D-18DBL*
B   R6-12BK   R6-12BK
     R6-8BK   R6-8BK

60 AMPERE ALTERNATOR

SPEED CONTROL

X31-18Y*
X30-18DBL

X33-18BK*

TEMPERATURE GAUGE SEND
UNIT OR TEMPERATURE SWITCH

A1-6B RED

STARTER
B

S5-12BR

S

G2-18V

ENGINE GROUND

(8 CYLINDER) A2-4G-BK
(6 CYLINDER) A2-6G-BK

A1-6B-RED

GROUND

A2A-10G-BK

A1A-10R

BATTERY

STARTER RELAY

A1B-14R

B S

G

MANUAL TRANSMISSION ONLY

S4-18DGN

FUSIBLE LINK

A1C-10R

60 AMPERE ALTERNATOR

S2-18Y

A1B-16DBL

FUSIBLE LINK

A1C-10R

S4-18DGN
S4-18BR/Y*
G2-18V

PB45

1971 (Courtesy of Chrysler Corp.)

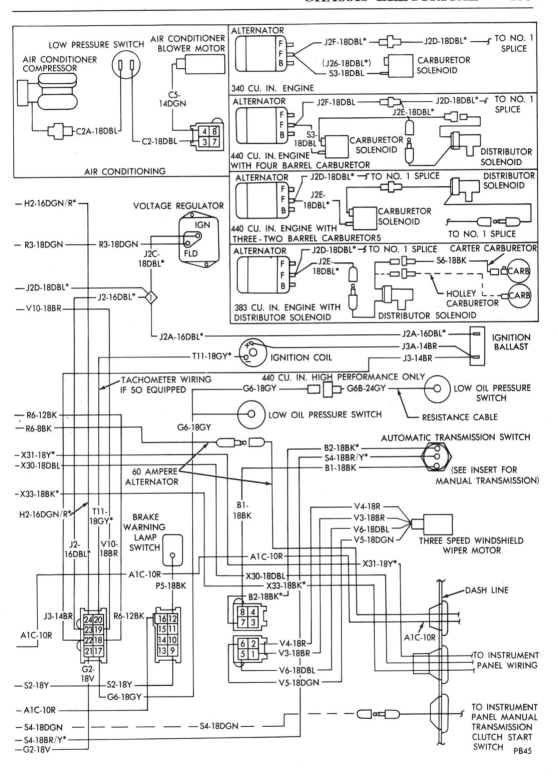

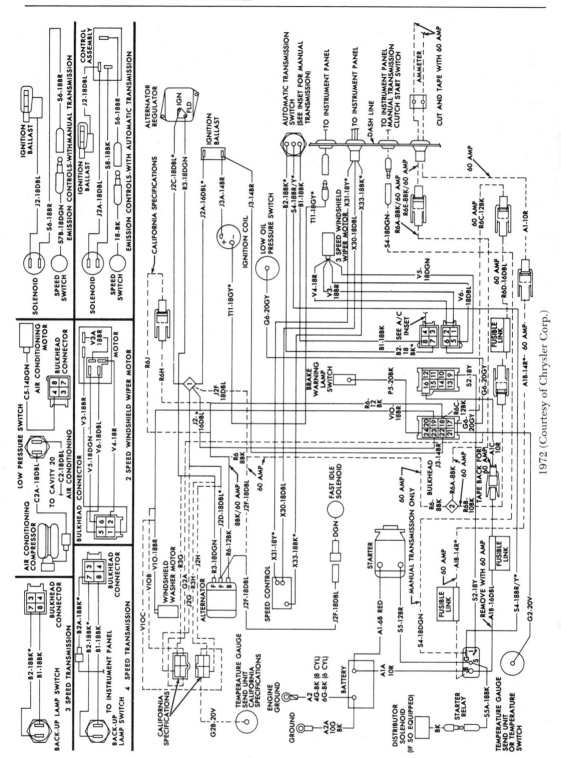

1972 (Courtesy of Chrysler Corp.)

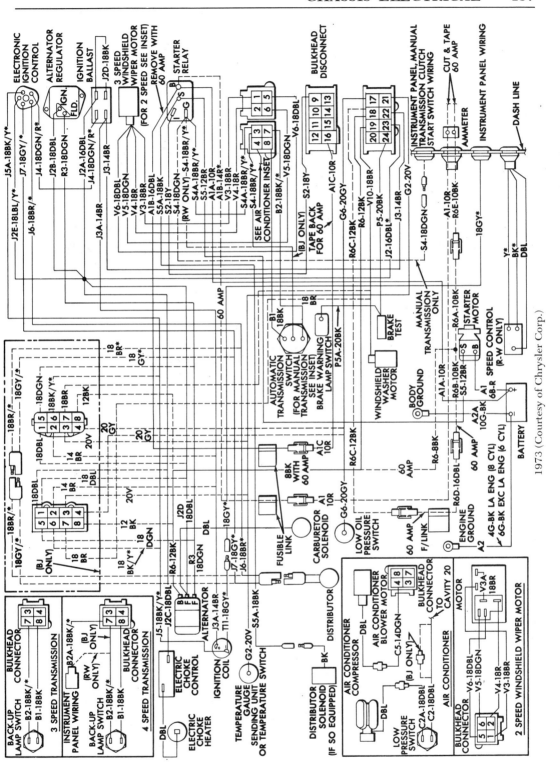

1973 (Courtesy of Chrysler Corp.)

6 · Clutch and Transmission

Manual

There are three types of manual transmission offered these models. The A-250 is a three-speed transmission with a non-synchronized first gear and is used only on six-cylinder engines. The A-230 is a fully synchronized three-speed transmission and is an option on the six-cylinder engines and standard on all other engines. The A-833 transmission is a fully synchronized four-speed gear box.

REMOVAL AND INSTALLATION

3 Speed and 4 Speed

1. Jack up the car.
2. Drain the transmission. Remove the shift rods from the transmission levers.
3. After marking both parts for reassembly, detach the driveshaft and the rear universal joint.
4. Remove the speedometer cable and back-up light switch. Unbolt the shifter from the extension housing on V8 floor shift models.
5. Unfasten the transmission extension housing from the center crossmember and jack up the engine and transmission about 1 in.
6. Remove the center crossmember.
7. On some models it may be necessary to disconnect or loosen the exhaust system

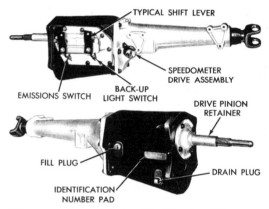

Three speed transmission identification (Courtesy of Chrysler Corp.)

and position it to one side to gain clearance in order to remove the transmission.
8. Remove the bolts which secure the transmission to the bellhousing. Support the transmission on a jack.
9. Slide the transmission toward the rear until the pinion shaft clears the clutch disc. Lower the transmission and remove it from the car.
10. Installation is the reverse of removal. Lubricate the pinion shaft pilot bearing. Do not lubricate the clutch splines or the clutch release levers.

Floor Shifter Removal and Installation

1. Disconnect the battery.
2. Remove the gearshift lever knob.

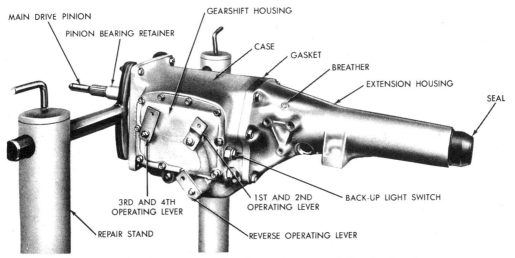

MAIN DRIVE PINION
PINION BEARING RETAINER
GEARSHIFT HOUSING
CASE
GASKET
BREATHER
EXTENSION HOUSING
SEAL
3RD AND 4TH OPERATING LEVER
1ST AND 2ND OPERATING LEVER
BACK-UP LIGHT SWITCH
REPAIR STAND
REVERSE OPERATING LEVER

Four speed transmission identification (Courtesy of Chrysler Corp.)

FLOOR SHIFT ASSEMBLY

HAND LEVER

.010" FEELER GAGE DRIVER'S SIDE

Removing gearshift lever (Courtesy of Chrysler Corp.)

3. If a console is fitted, withdraw the console mounting screws and label the electrical leads after disconnecting them. Remove the console.

4. Remove the floor pan boot retaining screws and slide the boot off from the shift lever.

5. Slide a knife blade, or feeler gauge, down along the driver's side of the shift lever to release the spring clip which retains the shift lever, and then withdraw the lever.

6. Remove the retaining clips, washers, and control rods from the transmission shift levers.

7. Remove the bolts and washers which hold the shifter assembly to its transmission mounting plate and withdraw the shifter assembly.

8. Installation is the reverse of the above.

Linkage Adjustment, 3 Speed

1968–73, COLUMN SHIFT

1. Remove the second and third swivels from the steering column lever and the first reverse swivel from the transmission lever.

2. The transmission must be in neutral. Both shift levers are in the middle detent when the transmission is in neutral.

3. Adjust the second/third swivels so that the gearshift lever is 12° above horizontal.

4. Place a screwdriver between the crossover blade and the second/third lever at the steering column. Both lever pins should be engaged by the crossover blade.

CROSS-OVER BLADE IN NEUTRAL

SCREWDRIVER

Holding the crossover in the neutral position (Courtesy of Chrysler Corp.)

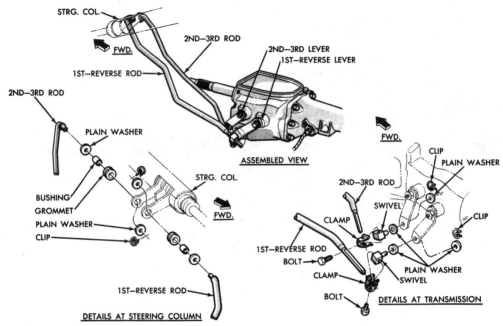

1968–73 manual column shift linkage (Courtesy of Chrysler Corp.)

5. Adjust the first/reverse rod swivel by loosening the clamp bolt and sliding the swivel along the rod so it will enter the first/reverse lever at the transmission. Tighten the clamp bolt.

6. Check the adjustment.

1970–73 FLOOR SHIFT

1. Make a lever alignment tool from $1/16$ in. sheet metal to the dimensions shown.

2. Insert the tool into the slots in the levers and shifter frame. This will hold the

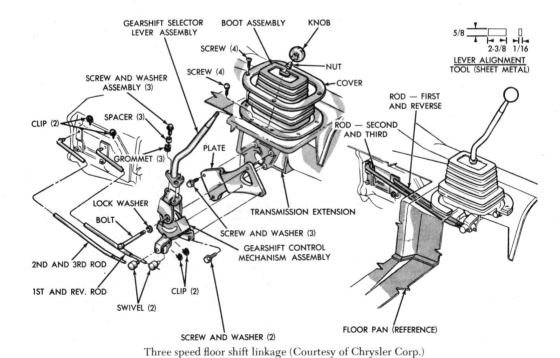

Three speed floor shift linkage (Courtesy of Chrysler Corp.)

levers in the neutral crossover position.

3. Place the transmission levers in the middle detent or the neutral position. Adjust the shift rod swivels so that the rods will slip in and out of the levers easily.

4. Remove the alignment tool and check the shift pattern.

Linkage Adjustment, 4 Speed

1968, FLOOR

1. Disconnect the negative cable from the battery. Unscrew the shift lever knob.

2. Raise the console lid, if so equipped, and remove the two screws from the rear end of the finish plate. Working the plate rearward, disengage it from the front of the console.

3. Disconnect any wiring connected to the finish plate. Work the rubber boot off from the shift lever and remove the plate and boot.

4. If so equipped, remove the four screws securing the console to the floor brackets. Disconnect any wiring and remove the console.

5. Remove the four upper boot securing screws and slide the boot up the shift lever.

6. Raise the car and place the transmission in neutral. Disconnect the shift rods from the transmission.

7. Work the lower boot down and insert the lever alignment tool. This tool holds all three levers in the neutral position.

8. Adjust the length of the rods so that they enter the transmission levers freely without any rearward or forward movement.

9. Reverse the above steps for reassembly.

1969–73, FLOOR

1. Working under the car, insert the factory alignment tool. This tool holds the levers in the neutral position while the adjustment is being performed.

2. Remove the shift rods from the transmission shift levers. Place the transmission shift levers in the neutral position.

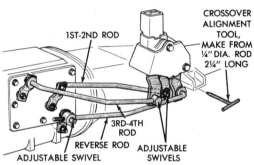

Four speed crossover alignment tool (Courtesy of Chrysler Corp.)

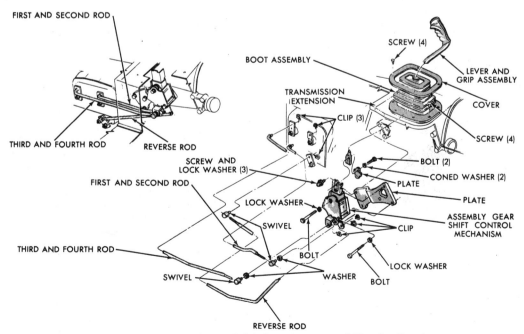

1969–73 Four speed floor shift linkage (Courtesy of Chrysler Corp.)

3. Adjust the length of the shift rods, using the threaded swivels, so that the length of the rods is exactly the right length to fit into the transmission levers.

4. Reinstall the shift rods, remove the alignment tool, and test the shift pattern.

Floor-Mounted 4 Speed Hurst Shifter

This shifter uses three shift rods and levers. The adjustment should be made with the aid of a neutral alignment rod, which is supplied with the shift linkage kit, or by using a piece of ¼ in. rod.

1. Place the shifter unit in neutral.

2. Back both shifter stop-bolts out of the shifter frame until only a few threads remain engaged.

3. Remove the shifting rods and the rod adjusting buttons from the shifter unit.

4. Align the levers with the shifter frame and insert the neutral alignment rod through the notches in the frame and the holes in the levers.

5. Rotate the transmission arms backward and forward. The neutral position for each arm can be felt at the middle position of full travel toward the front.

6. Adjust the positions of the buttons on each rod to permit each button to slip easily into the nylon bushing of its corresponding lever.

NOTE: *The transmission arms must remain in their neutral positions during this step.*

7. Remove the neutral alignment rod. Test the shifter unit. The shifter stick should move freely from side to side in Neutral. If the shifter functions properly, proceed to step 10.

8. If the stick cannot be moved freely between First and Second, Third and Fourth, or Reverse, one or more of the rod button adjustments must be corrected. Move the stick forward into Third gear, then back into Fourth and then into Neutral. Insert the neutral alignment rod. If the rod cannot be inserted freely, the Third-Fourth shifter rod button is incorrectly adjusted. A similar test of the First-Second shift will show the alignment of the First-Second adjustment.

9. To check the Reverse rod button adjustment, place the stick in neutral and disconnect the Reverse rod adjusting button from the reverse lever. Grasp the rod and push it toward the front of the car. Adjust the rod button so that it easily slips into its bushing. Reassemble and fasten it with a spring clip.

10. Push the stick firmly into Third gear and hold it in this position. Screw the Third gear stop-bolt in, until contact is felt. Back out the bolt one full turn and tighten the locknut. Pull the stick firmly back into Fourth gear, screw the Fourth gear stop-bolt in until contact is felt. Back the stop-bolt out one full turn and tighten the locknut.

Clutch

All cars equipped with manual transmissions use a single-plate clutch. While the

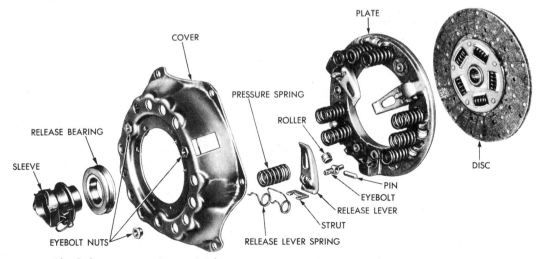

Clutch disc, pressure plate, and throwout bearing exploded view (Courtesy of Chrysler Corp.)

clutch assembly lacks a wear adjustment, the excessive free pedal play may be adjusted out by means of an adjustable rod in the clutch linkage. The clutch is removed through the bottom of the bellhousing.

Removal and Installation

1. Remove the transmission as described in the "Removal and Installation" procedures for manual transmissions.

2. Remove the clutch housing pan.

3. Remove the spring washer which secures the clutch fork rod to the torque shaft lever and remove the fork rod.

4. Disconnect the fork return spring at the fork. Disconnect the torque shaft return spring, if so equipped, at the torque shaft assembly.

5. Remove the clip and plain washer which secure the interlock rod to the torque shaft lever and remove the spring and plain washers and the rod from the torque shaft.

6. Remove the clutch release (throwout) bearing from the clutch release fork. Remove the release fork and boot from the clutch housing.

7. Using a metal punch, mark the clutch cover (pressure plate) and the flywheel to indicate their correct positions for reassembly.

8. Loosen the clutch cover (pressure plate) securing bolts one or two turns at a time in succession to prevent warping the clutch cover.

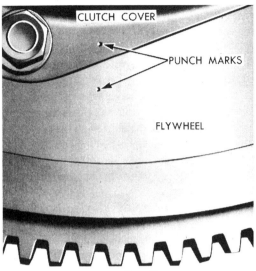

Punch marks (Courtesy of Chrysler Corp.)

9. Remove the securing bolts and withdraw the clutch disc and pressure plate through the bottom of the bellhousing. Do not get any grease or oil on the pressure plate or the clutch disc.

10. Lightly lubricate the pilot bearing in the end of the crankshaft.

11. Clean the surfaces of the flywheel and pressure plate with fine sandpaper.

12. Place the clutch disc and pressure plate in position and insert a clutch disc aligning tool or spare transmission driveshaft through the clutch disc hub and into the pilot bearing.

NOTE: *The springs on the clutch disc*

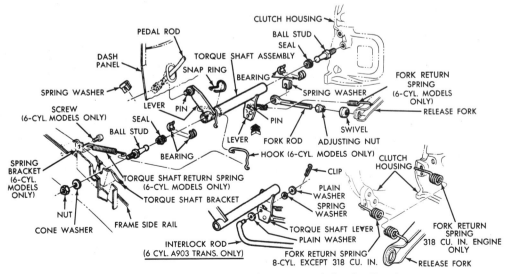

Clutch linkage and torque shaft (Courtesy of Chrysler Corp.)

Clutch aligning tool (Courtesy of Chrysler Corp.)

should be facing away from the flywheel when the disc is properly installed.

13. Align the punch marks, that were made before removal, in the flywheel and the pressure plate.

14. Install the pressure plate securing bolts and tighten them one to two turns at a time in an alternating sequence. Remove the clutch alignment tool.

15. Pack the throwout bearing cavity and the release fork pads with grease.

16. Insert the throwout bearing bell-housing and place the fork fingers under the throwout bearing retaining springs.

17. Reverse steps 1–6 to finish installation.

18. Adjust clutch pedal free-play.

Clutch Linkage Adjustment—Pedal Height and Free-play

1. Disconnect the gearshift interlock by loosening the interlock rod swivel clamp screw.

2. Adjust the fork rod by rotating the nut to provide 5/32 in. of free-play at the fork end. This adjustment will give the proper 1 in. of free-play at the clutch pedal.

3. Readjust the interlock as described below, if equipped.

Gear Shift Interlock Adjustment

1. Disconnect the interlock pawl from the clutch rod swivel.

2. Adjust the clutch linkage as described above.

3. With the first reverse lever on the transmission in the Neutral (middle de-

tent) position, the interlock pawl should enter the slot in the First/Reverse lever.

4. Loosen the swivel clamp bolt and move the swivel on the rod so that it will enter the pawl. The clutch pedal must be in the fully returned position during this adjustment. The clutch rod should never be pulled rearward to engage the pawl swivel.

5. Check the adjustment by making a normal shift from Neutral to First, disengaging and engaging the clutch. Check again by shifting from Neutral to reverse. The clutch action should be normal.

6. Disengage the clutch and shift halfway to First or Reverse. The clutch should be held down by the interlock to within 1–2 in. off the floor. If necessary, readjust the interlock and repeat steps 5 and 6.

Automatic Transmission

There are two Chrysler Torqueflite transmissions. The A-904 is standard on the 225 and 318. The A-727 is the heavy-duty version Torqueflite and is an option on the 225 and 318 and is standard on all other engines.

Pan Removal

1. Loosen the pan bolts. Loosen the bolts at one corner of the pan a little more than the rest.

2. Tap the pan to loosen it and let the fluid drain out at that corner of the pan with extra clearance.

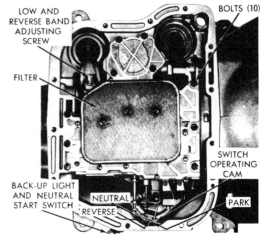

Bottom view of transmission with the pan removed (Courtesy of Chrysler Corp.)

3. Remove the rest of the bolts and lower the pan away from the bottom of the transmission.

4. To install the pan, reverse the above steps. Always use a new gasket and do not overtighten the pan bolts.

5. Start the engine and check for leaks.

Filter Service

1. Remove the pan as described above.

2. Remove the three filter attaching bolts and remove the old filter.

3. Install a new filter, making sure all gaskets are in place.

4. Install the pan using a new gasket.

Band Adjustments

KICK-DOWN BAND

The kick-down band adjusting screw is located on the left-hand side of the transmission case near the throttle lever shaft.

1. Loosen the locknut and back it off about five turns. Be sure that the adjusting screw is free in the case.

2. Using a torque wrench and, if necessary, an adapter, torque the adjusting screw to 50 in. lbs (if an adapter is used) or to 72 in. lbs (if an adapter is not used).

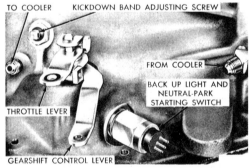

Kickdown band adjusting screw (Courtesy of Chrysler Corp.)

3. Back off the adjusting screw the exact number of turns specified below. Keep the screw from turning and torque the locknut.

LOW AND REVERSE BAND

The oil pan must be removed from the transmission to gain access to the Low/Reverse band adjusting screw. See the bottom view of the transmission.

1. Drain the transmission and remove the oil pan.

2. Loosen the band adjusting screw locknut and back it off about five turns. Be

sure that the adjusting screw turns freely in the lever.

3. Using a torque wrench and, if necessary, an adapter, torque the adjusting screw to 47–50 in. lbs (if an adapter is used) or to 72 in. lbs (if an adapter is not used).

4. Back off the adjusting screw the exact number of turns specified below. Keep the screw from turning and torque the locknut.

5. Install the pan and use a new gasket. Torque the bolts to 150 in. lbs. Refill the transmission with the correct type of transmission fluid.

Band Adjustment Specifications

KICK-DOWN BAND

Year	Engine/Trans	Turns
1968–73	All engines/A-904	2
1968–70	All engines except 426/A-727 transmission	2
1968–70	426 engine/A-727 transmission	1½
1971–72	All engines/A-904 transmission	2
1971–72	All engines except 426 and 440 Six Pack/A-727 transmission	2½
1971–72	426 and 440 Six Pack/A-727	1½
1973	All engines/A-904 transmission	2
1973	All engines/A-727 transmission	2½

LOW AND REVERSE BAND

Year	Engine/Trans	Turns
1968–73	All engines except 318/A-904 transmission	3¼
1968–73	318/A-904 transmission	4
1968–70	All engines/A-727 transmission	4
1971–73	All engines/A-727 transmission	2

Neutral Safety Switch Adjustment

The neutral safety switch is mounted in the transmission case on all models. When the gearshift lever is placed in either the Park or Neutral position, a cam, which is attached to the transmission throttle lever inside the transmission, contacts the neutral safety switch and provides a ground to complete the starter solenoid circuit.

The back-up lamp switch has been incorporated into the neutral safety switch. This combination switch can be identified

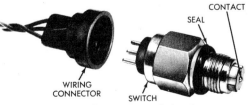

Neutral safety switch (Courtesy of Chrysler Corp.)

by the three electrical terminals on the rear of the switch. On this type of switch, the center terminal is for the neutral safety switch and the two outer terminals are for the back-up lamps.

There is no adjustment provided for the neutral safety switch. If a malfunction occurs, first check to make sure that the transmission gearshift linkage is properly adjusted and that the actuator cam is centered in the switch mounting hole in the transmission. If the malfunction continues, the switch must be removed and replaced.

To remove the switch, disconnect the electrical leads and unscrew the switch from the transmission. Use a drain pan to catch the transmission fluid that drains out of the mounting hole. Install a new switch using a new gasket and refill the transmission to the proper level.

Shift Linkage Adjustment

1968–69 CONSOLE SHIFT AND COLUMN SHIFT

1. Place the gearshift lever in the Park position.
2. Loosen the lower rod swivel clamp screw several turns.
3. Move the transmission control lever to the rearmost, or Park, detent.
4. With the gearshift lever in the Park position and the transmission lever in the Park position, tighten the swivel clamp screw and test the linkage.
5. The shift effort must be free and the detents should feel crisp. All gate stops must be positive. It should be possible to start the car in the Park and Neutral positions only.

1970–73 CONSOLE SHIFT

1. Loosen the clamping screw in the adjustable rod swivel clamp.
2. Line up the locating slots in the bottom of the shift housing and the bearing housing, found at the upper end of the steering column.
3. Install the tool to keep the slots aligned and lock the column with the ignition key.
4. Put the console gearshift lever in Park.
5. Put the transmission lever in the rearmost, or Park, position.
6. Set the adjustable rods to the proper length with no load applied in either

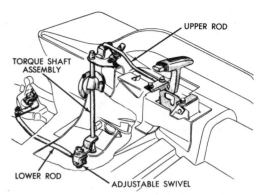

1970–73 Automatic transmission console shift linkage (Courtesy of Chrysler Corp.)

direction on the linkage and tighten the clamp bolts.
7. The shift effort must be free and the detents should feel crisp. All gate stops must be positive. It should be possible to start the car in the Park and Neutral positions only.

1970–73 COLUMN SHIFT

1. Loosen the clamping screw in the adjustable rod swivel clamp.
2. Put the gearshift selector lever in the Park position and lock the steering column with the key.

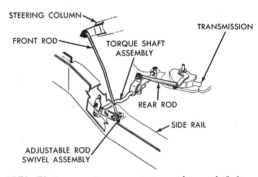

1970–73 Automatic transmission column shift linkage (Courtesy of Chrysler Corp.)

3. Put the transmission shift control lever in the rearmost, or Park, detent.
4. Set the adjustable rod to the proper length and install the rod with no load in either direction on the linkage.
5. Check the linkage as in step 7 above.

Removal and Installation

CAUTION: *Remove the transmission and torque converter as an assembly, in order to avoid damaging the converter drive plate and the converter oil seal.*

When removing the transmission from the car, make sure the converter does not slip off the transmission input shaft. Do not allow the transmission to hang on the engine unsupported. Do not allow the engine to hang unsupported.

1. Disconnect the negative battery terminal and the coil wire.

2. Remove the cover plate from in front of the converter to provide access to the converter drain plug and mounting bolts.

3. Rotate the engine to bring the converter to the six o'clock position. Drain the torque converter and transmission.

4. Match-mark the converter and drive plate to aid reassembly. There are offset holes in the crankshaft flange bolt circle, in the inner and outer circle of holes in the drive plate, and in the front face of the converter. These offset holes should be used as reference marks for reassembly.

5. On some models, the exhaust system must be lowered for clearance.

6. Remove the bolts securing the torque converter to the drive plate. They are accessible through the cover plate and it will be necessary to rotate the converter to remove all of the bolts.

7. Remove the starter motor.

8. Disconnect the wire from the neutral safety switch.

9. Disconnect the gearshift rod from the transmission lever. Remove the gearshift torque shaft from the transmission housing and the left frame member.

10. On cars equipped with console shifters; withdraw the two bolts which secure the gearshift torque shaft lower bracket to the extension housing and swing the bracket out of the way.

11. Disconnect the throttle rod from the bellcrank at the left side of the transmission bellhousing.

12. Disconnect the fluid cooler lines at the transmission and remove the fluid filler tube. Disconnect the speedometer cable at the transmission.

13. Disconnect the driveshaft at the rear universal joint. Carefully pull the driveshaft from the end of the transmission.

14. Withdraw the transmission mount-to-extension housing bolts.

15. Loosen the engine mount bolts and raise the engine slightly. Block the engine in place.

16. Remove the crossmember bolts and remove the crossmember.

17. Support the transmission with a jack.

18. Attach a small C-clamp to the edge of the converter housing to hold the converter in place while the transmission is being removed.

19. Withdraw the converter housing retaining bolts. Carefully work the transmission to the rear of the engine-to-transmission locating dowels. This should disengage the converter hub from the end of the crankshaft.

20. Lower and remove the transmission. The converter may be removed at this time.

21. Installation is the reverse of the above. Torque the drive plate-to-torque converter bolts to 55 ft lbs.

7 · Drive Train

Driveline

According to engine usage, Plymouths are equipped with one of five different rear axles. These are designated by the diameter of the ring e.g. 7¼, 8¼, 8¾, 9¼, and 9¾ in.

The 7¼ through the 8¾ rear axles are used for the 6 cylinder and small V8 engines. The 9¼ and 9¾ in. rear axles are used on the 440 standard and Power Pak engines as well as the 426 Hemi. The 9¼ in. rear axle was dropped in 1969. All 440 Power Pak and 426 Hemi four speed cars are equipped with Sure Grip rear axles. The 9¾ in. axle was dropped in 1973. The Sure Grip differential is optional on the 7¼ and the 8¾ axles.

DRIVESHAFT

Removal and Installation

1. Match mark the driveshaft, U-joint and pinion flange before disassembly. These marks must be realigned during reassembly to maintain the balance of the driveline. Failure to align them may result in excessive vibration.

2. Remove both of the clamps from the differential pinion yoke and slide the driveshaft forward slightly to disengage the U-joint from the pinion yoke. Tape the two loose U-joint bearings together to prevent them from falling off.

CAUTION: *Do not disturb the bearing assembly retaining strap. Never allow the driveshaft to hang from either of the U-joints. Always support the unattached end of the shaft to prevent damage to the joints.*

3. Lower the rear end of the driveshaft and gently slide the front yoke/driveshaft assembly rearward disengaging the assembly from the transmission output shaft. Be careful not to damage the splines or the surface which the output shaft seal rides on.

4. Check the transmission output shaft seal for signs of leakage.

5. Installation is the reverse of removal. Be sure to align the match marks.

U-JOINTS

Removal and Installation

1. Remove the driveshaft.

2. To remove the bearings from the yoke, first remove the bearing retainer snap rings located at the base or open end of each bearing cap.

3. Pressing on one of the bearings, drive the bearing in toward the center of the joint. This will force the cross to push the opposite bearing out of the universal joint. This step may be performed using a hammer and suitable drift or a vise and sockets or pieces of pipe. However installation of bearing must be done using the vise or a press.

4. After the bearing has been pushed all

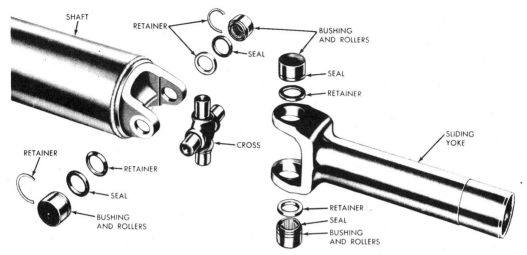

Front universal joint assembly (Courtesy of Chrysler Corp.)

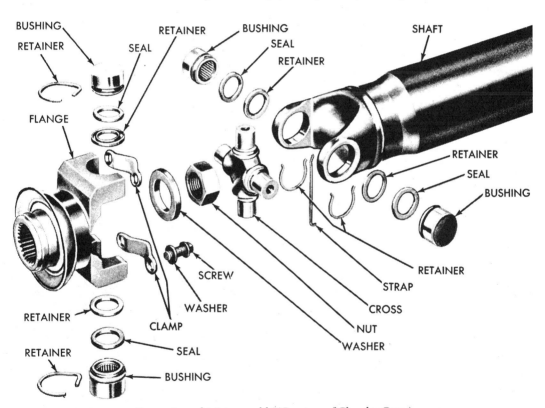

Rear universal joint assembly (Courtesy of Chrysler Corp.)

the way out of the yoke, pull up the cross slightly and pack some washers under it. Then press on the end of the cross from which the bearing was just removed to force the first bearing out of the yoke. Repeat steps 3 and 4 to remove the remaining two bearings.

5. If a grease fitting is supplied with the new U-joint assembly, install it. If no fitting is supplied, make sure that the joint is amply greased. Pack grease in the recesses in the end of the cross.

6. To reassemble start both bearing cups into the yoke at the same time and hold the cross carefully in the fingers in its installed position. Be careful not to knock any rollers out of position.

7. Squeeze both bearings in a vise or

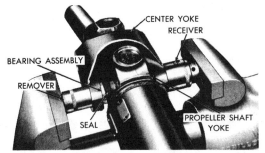

Removing universal bearings using a vise (Courtesy of Chrysler Corp.)

press, moving the bearings into place. Continually check for free movement of the cross in the bearings as they are pressed into the yoke. If there is a sudden increase in the force needed to press the bearings into place, or the cross starts to bind, the bearings are cocked in the yoke. They must be removed and restarted in the yoke. Failure to do so will greatly reduce the life of the bearing. Repeat steps 6 and 7 to reinstall the remaining two bearings.

Rear Axle

Rear Axle Identification

Axle Size	Filler Plug Location	Cover Bolts
7¼	Cover	9 Bolts
8¼	Carrier Right Side	10 Bolts
8¾	Carrier Right Side	Welded
9¼	Cover [1]	10 Bolts
9¾	Cover [1]	10 Bolts

[1] Service procedures for these axles are the same.

There are two types of Chrysler rear axles, the C type and the non-C type. The axle shafts on the C type are retained by C-shaped locks, which fit in grooves at the inner end of the axle shaft. Axle shafts of the non-C type are retained by a plate located at the brake drum end of the axle or by the backing plate itself. However, visual inspection is necessary to determine the type as the 8¼ and sometimes the 7¼ axles are the C type.

"C" shaped lock, 8¼ in. axle (Courtesy of Chrysler Corp.)

AXLE SHAFT

Removal and Installation

7¼ AND 8¼ AXLES-C TYPE

To visually determine the axle type, remove the differential cover.

1. Raise the vehicle and remove the wheels. Drain the oil from the rear axle.

2. Remove the differential cover, if not already removed.

Pinion shaft lockscrew (Courtesy of Chrysler Corp.)

3. Remove the differential pinion shaft lockscrew and the differential pinon shaft.

4. Push the flanged end of the axle shaft toward the center of the vehicle and remove the C lock from the end of the shaft.

5. Remove the axle shaft from the hous-

ing, being careful not to damage the oil seal. The axle shaft may not slide easily out of the housing. If so, obtain an axle puller.

6. The axle bearing will come out with the axle and will have to be replaced at an automotive repair shop.

7. Pry the axle seal loose from the bore and tap a new seal into place.

8. Installation is the reverse of removal. Use new gaskets for reassembly.

7¼ and 8¼-Non-C Type

1. Jack the car up so the rear wheels are off the ground. Remove the wheel and brake drum from the axle being removed.

2. Remove the nuts holding the retainer plate to the backing plate. Disconnect the brake line, if necessary.

3. Remove the retainer and reinstall the nuts fingertight to prevent the backing plate from being dislodged.

4. Using a slide hammer, pull out the axle shaft and bearing assembly.

5. Pry the old seal from its bore and install a new seal.

6. You will have to take the axle assembly to a machine shop to have the bearing removed.

7. Reverse the above steps to install. Bleed the brakes if the brake line has been disconnected.

8¾, 9¼, and 9¾ Axles

These axles are all of the non-C type. They also have both inner and outer axle seals and adjustable end play.

1. Remove the wheel and brake drum.

2. If the backing plate must be removed, disconnect the brake line at the wheel cylinder.

3. Working through the hole in the flange, remove the five nuts from the retainer plate. The right hand shaft, with the

end play adjuster in the retainer plate, will also have a lock on one of the studs that will have to be removed at this time.

4. Remove the axle and bearing assembly with an axle puller.

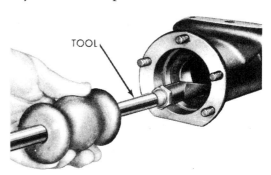

Removing inner axle seal (Courtesy of Chrysler Corp.)

5. Pry the inner axle seal from its bore and tap a new seal in place.

6. If the outer axle seal is located in the axle retainer it will have to be replaced along with the axle bearing at a machine shop. If the seal is located in the backing plate, tap the seal from the plate and install a new one.

7. Install the left hand axle. Install the retaining plate using a new gasket.

8. Install the right hand backing plate using a new gasket.

9. Back off the adjuster on the right axle shaft assembly until the inner face of the adjuster is flush with the inner face of the retainer.

10. Slide the right axle assembly into the housing and install the retaining plate.

11. With a dial indicator mounted on the brake support, tighten the adjuster

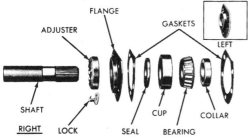

Axle shaft components, 8¾, 9¼, 9¾ axles (Courtesy of Chrysler Corp.)

Measuring axle shaft end play (Courtesy of Chrysler Corp.)

until there is zero end play. Then, back off approximately four notches to get 0.013–0.023 in. end play.

12. Install the adjuster lock and recheck the end play adjustment. Make sure both axles are fully seated.

13. Reinstall the brake drums and wheels.

Rear Axle Housing

Removal and Installation

1. Raise the car and support the car in front of the springs.

2. Remove the rear wheels.

3. Disconnect the hydraulic brake hose at the left side of the axle.

4. Disconnect the parking brake cable.

5. Disconnect the drive shaft at the differential yoke.

6. Remove the shock absorber lower mounts from the axle.

7. Remove the U-bolts and plates which secure the axle to the springs.

8. Remove the axle from the vehicle.

9. Installation is the reverse of removal. Bleed the brakes after installing the axle.

Determining Axle Ratio

The rear axle ratio may be determined by noting the code number that is stamped on the front face of the pad at the bottom of the axle housing and checking it at an authorized dealership. The ratio may be approximated by jacking up one of the rear wheels, placing a mark on the driveshaft, then rotating the tire one revolution. As the tire is rotated count the number of revolutions the driveshaft turns, this number will be the approximate rear axle ratio.

8 · Suspension and Steering

All models have torsion bar front suspension and semi-elliptical, leaf-type rear springs with a solid rear axle.

Steering arm assemblies and lower ball joints on all models may have a considerable amount of play before they wear out. Play in these joints is taken up when the weight of the car is on the wheels and will not affect the front wheel alignment or vehicle stability. All the ball joints have rubber boots for dust and moisture protection. Should these boots become damaged, rapid failure of the joint will take place. Be careful when lubricating the front end with a high pressure grease gun as the gun can easily rupture the boots. All suspension components containing rubber, such as rubber bushings, should be tightened while the suspension is at the specified height and with the full weight of the car on its wheels.

The rear springs are semi-elliptical leaf type. When lightly loaded, these springs have very little camber or are almost flat. A flat spring gives better stability and reduces side sway.

All models use double acting shock absorbers. Replace a shock absorber when it is broken or leaking. A shock that has lost its resistance in one or both directions should also be replaced. A slight fluid seepage, especially in cold weather, is normal and does not affect the performance of the shock.

Rear Suspension

SPRINGS

Removal and Installation

1. Jack up the car and remove the wheels. Position jack stands under the axle to remove the weight of the rear axle from the springs.

2. Disconnect the rear shock absorbers at the bottom attaching bolts. Lower the axle assembly to allow the rear springs to hang free.

3. Remove the U-bolt nuts and remove the U-bolts and plate. Remove the nuts

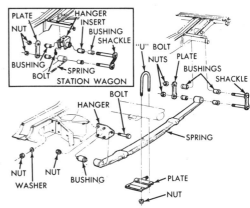

Rear spring and mounting assembly (Courtesy of Chrysler Corp.)

153

which secure the front spring hanger to the body mounting bracket.

4. Remove the rear spring hanger bolts and let the spring drop far enough to allow the front spring hanger bolts to be removed.

5. Remove the front pivot bolt from the front spring hanger.

6. Remove the shackle nuts and remove the shackle from the rear spring.

7. To start installation, assemble the shackle and bushings in the rear of the spring and hanger. Start the shackle bolt nut. Do not lubricate the rubber bushings to ease installation and do not tighten the bolt nut.

8. Install the front spring hanger to the front spring eye and insert the pivot bolt and nut but do not tighten them.

9. Install the rear spring hanger to the body bracket and tighten the bolts.

10. Raise the spring and insert the bolts in the spring hanger mounting bracket holes. Tighten the bracket nuts.

11. Position the axle assembly so it is correctly aligned with the spring center bolt.

12. Position the center bolt over the lower spring plate. Insert the U-bolt and nut and tighten the nuts.

13. Install the shock absorbers.

14. Lower the car. Tighten the pivot bolts and shackle nuts.

15. Test drive the car. Check the front suspension height and adjust if necessary.

SHOCK ABSORBER

Removal and Installation

1. Jack up the car and support it under the rear axle. It is necessary to support the car under the rear axle to relieve the load from the shock absorber.

2. Remove the nut which attaches the shock to the spring mounting plate stud and then pull the shock from the stud.

3. At the upper mount, remove the shock attaching bolt and remove the shock from the car.

4. To install the shock, position it so the upper bolt may be inserted. Hand tighten the nut and bolt.

5. Align the shock with the spring mounting plate stud, install the nut and washer, and hand tighten the nut.

6. Lower the car and tighten the upper and lower nuts.

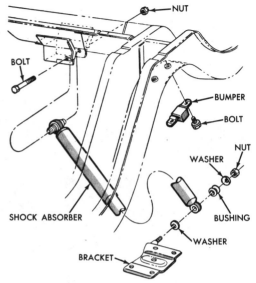

Rear shock absorber and mounting assembly (Courtesy of Chrysler Corp.)

Front Suspension

TORSION BARS

Removal and Installation

NOTE: *Left and right torsion bars are not interchangeable.*

1. Remove the upper control arm rebound bumper.

2. Raise the car and support it so that there is no weight on the suspension.

3. Remove all load from the torsion bars by rotating the anchor adjusting bolts counterclockwise.

4. Remove the lockring at the torsion bar rear anchor.

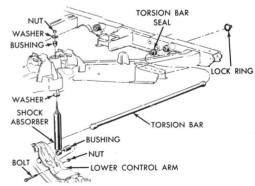

Left front torsion bar assembly (Courtesy of Chrysler Corp.)

5. Remove the torsion bar from its mounts. A special tool is available for this job.

CAUTION: *The torsion bar may be under some load so be careful when removing it. Never use heat to ease removal of the bar as this will destroy the temper of the bar.*

6. It may be necessary to move the rear balloon seal out of the way to ease removal, if the car is so equipped. Slide the torsion bar out through the rear mounting. Be careful not to damage the balloon seal.

7. Inspect the torsion bar and lightly dress any sharp edges. Coat the dressed area with a rust preventive. Clean and lightly lubricate the bar.

8. Start replacement by sliding the bar into the rear anchor. Slide the balloon seal over the bar with the cupped end toward the rear of the bar.

9. Insert the torsion bar through the hex opening of the lower control arm. Replace the lockring in the rear anchor.

10. Fully pack the ring opening in the rear anchor with grease.

11. Install the balloon seal on the rear anchor so the seal lip engages the anchor groove.

12. Rotate the adjusting bolt clockwise to load the torsion bar. Lower the vehicle and adjust the front suspension height. Replace the upper control arm rebound bumper and tighten the nut.

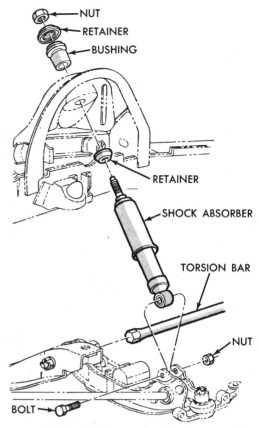

Front shock absorber and mounting assembly (Courtesy of Chrysler Corp.)

SHOCK ABSORBERS

Testing

Shock absorber action may be tested by bouncing the front or rear of the car by hand. If the car continues to bounce after it is released, the shock absorbers are worn.

Handling problems will arise if shock absorbers are worn. After hitting a bump the car will oscillate two or three times instead of recovering from the bump with a single bounce. The car may also be more susceptible to side winds or it may lean excessively in corners.

Removal and Installation

1. Remove the washer and nut from the upper end of the shock absorber. Be sure to note the positions of all the washers and rubber grommets.

2. Raise the car and remove the lower attaching bolt from the shock absorber.

3. Fully compress the shock absorber and remove the shock from the car.

4. Compress the new shock and insert it through the upper bushing and install the washers, rubber grommets, and nut. Be sure that all of the washers are installed with the concave side in contact with the rubber grommets.

5. Position and align the lower mount of the shock absorber. Install the bolt and nut fingertight. Lower the car and tighten the nut.

FRONT SUSPENSION HEIGHT

Checking and Adjusting

1. Make sure that the fuel tank is full, the tire pressures are correct, and that the car is parked on a level floor.

2. Clean road dirt from the bottom of both steering knuckles. Clean the lowest area of the height adjusting blades directly below the center of the lower control arm inner pivot assembly.

3. Bounce the car several times and release the car on the downward motion.

4. Check the distance from the bottom of one adjusting blade to the floor and from the lowest point of the steering knuckle arm at the centerline. Measure one side at a time.

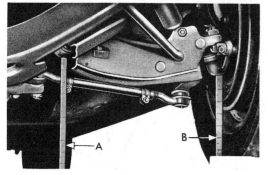

Measuring points for checking front suspension height (Courtesy of Chrysler Corp.)

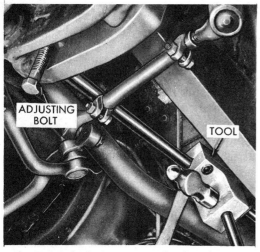

Adjusting bolt for suspension height adjustment (Courtesy of Chrysler Corp.)

5. The difference between the two measurements is the front suspension height.

6. Adjustment is performed by rotating the torsion bar adjusting bolt clockwise to increase height and counterclockwise to decrease height. After each adjustment, bounce the vehicle before checking the height. Both sides must be measured even though only one side may have to be adjusted. Be sure that the height does not vary more than $1/8$ in. from side to side.

Front Suspension Height

Side to side variation is + or − $1/8$ in.
The height variation is + or − $1/8$ in.

Year	Height
1968	$1\frac{7}{8}$ in.
1969	$1\frac{7}{8}$ in.
1970	$1\frac{7}{8}$ in.
1971	$1\frac{5}{8}$ in.
1972	$1\frac{5}{8}$ in.
1973	$1\frac{7}{8}$ in.

BALL JOINTS

Removal and Installation

UPPER BALL JOINT

1. Raise the car by placing a floor jack under the lower control arm.

2. Remove the wheel and tire. Remove the brake drum, if so equipped. On models with disc brakes, remove the caliper and disc from the steering knuckle. Position the caliper out of the way with the brake line attached.

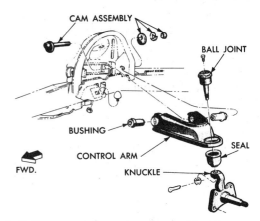

Left front upper control arm assembly (Courtesy of Chrysler Corp.)

3. Remove the nut that attaches the upper ball joint to the steering knuckle. Loosen the ball joint stud from the steering knuckle. Ball joint removal tools are available at auto parts stores and large mail order houses. These press the ball joint out. Follow the manufacturer's directions for operating the tool. An alternate method for stud removal is hammering firmly on the side of the steering knuckle until the stud pops out of the steering knuckle. Never strike the ball joint stud. Brace the knuckle with another hammer.

4. Unscrew the upper ball joint from the upper control arm and remove it from the vehicle.

5. Position a new ball joint on the upper control arm and screw the joint into the

arm. Be careful not to cross thread the joint in the arm.

6. Position a new seal on the ball joint stud and install the seal in the ball joint making sure the seal is fully seated on the ball joint housing.

7. Position the ball joint stud in the steering knuckle and install the retaining nut.

8. Lubricate the ball joint if equipped with a fitting.

9. Install the brakes and wheels. Lower the car and adjust the front suspension height.

LOWER BALL JOINT

The lower ball joint is integral with the steering arm and is not serviced separately.

1. Raise the car so the front suspension will drop to the downward limit of its travel.

2. Remove the upper control arm rebound bumper.

3. Turn the torsion bar adjusting bolt in a counterclockwise direction to remove any load on the torsion bar.

4. Remove the wheel and tire. Remove the brake drum, if so equipped. On models with disc brakes, remove the caliper and disc from the steering knuckle as described in chapter 9. Position the caliper out of the way with the brake line attached.

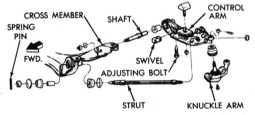

Left front lower control arm (Courtesy of Chrysler Corp.)

5. Remove the two lower bolts that attach the steering arm ball joint assembly to the brake assembly mounting plate.

6. Remove the ball joint stud retaining nut and cotter pin. Disconnect the tie rod end from the steering arm. Ball joint removal tools are available at auto parts stores and mail order houses. These press the ball joint out. Follow the manufacturer's directions for operating the tool. An alternate method for stud removal is hammering very firmly on the side of the steer-

ing arm where the stud attaches to the arm until the stud pops out of the arm. Never strike the ball joint stud itself. Brace the knuckle with another hammer.

7. Remove the ball joint stud retaining nut and cotter pin and separate the ball joint stud from the lower control arm. Remove the stud as described in the above step.

8. Remove the steering arm and ball joint assembly from the car.

9. To install the ball joint, position the ball joint assembly on the steering knuckle and install the two retaining bolts.

10. Insert the ball joint stud in the lower control arm and install the retaining nut and cotter pin.

11. Position the tie rod end in the steering knuckle and install the retaining nut and cotter pin.

12. Place a load on the torsion bar by turning the adjusting bolt in a clockwise direction.

13. Install the brake, wheels, and tires.

14. Lower the car and install the upper control arm rebound bumper. Check the alignment of the front end.

Ball Joint Inspection

NOTE: *Before performing the inspection, make sure the wheel bearings are adjusted correctly and that the control arm bushings are in good condition.*

1. Place a jack under the front lower control arm.

2. Raise the car until there is 1–2 in. of clearance under the wheel.

3. Insert a bar under the wheel and pry upward. If the wheel raises more than $1/8$ in. the ball joints are worn. Determine if the upper or lower ball joint is worn by visual inspection while prying on the wheel.

NOTE: *Due to the distribution of forces in the suspension, the lower ball joint is usually the defective joint.*

UPPER CONTROL ARM

Removal and Installation

1. Jack up the car and support it under the lower control arm.

2. Remove the tires and brake drum or if so equipped, the brake disc.

3. Remove the upper ball joint stud nut and cotter pin.

4. To remove the stud from the steering

knuckle, strike the steering knuckle sharply to loosen the stud. Do not attempt to force the stud out by striking the stud. The stud will pop out of the knuckle.

5. Remove the cam bolts, cams, nuts, and lockwashers which secure the upper control arm to its support brackets. Remove the control arm from the car.

6. Installation is the reverse of removal. It will be necessary to realign the front end and check front suspension height.

LOWER CONTROL ARM

Removal and Installation

1. Raise the car and support it under the frame. Remove the wheel, tire and brake drum or disc.

2. Remove the shock absorber at the bottom attachment and swing it up out of the way. Remove the torsion bar from its mounting at the lower control arm.

3. Remove the tie rod end from the steering knuckle arm. Be careful not to damage the seal.

4. Remove the sway bar link from the lower control arm. Remove the knuckle arm-to-brake support bolts and remove the knuckle arm from the lower control arm, as outlined in the "Lower Ball Joint Removal" section.

5. At the forward end of the crossmember, remove the strut spring pin, nut, and bushings, taking note of their positions. Remove the nut and washer from the lower control arm shaft.

6. Using a brass hammer, tap the end of the lower control arm shaft and remove it from the crossmember.

7. Remove the lower control arm, strut and shaft as an assembly.

8. To install the control arm, insert a new strut bushing into the crossmember with a twisting motion. Lubricate the bushing with soapy water.

9. Position the strut bushing inner retainer on the strut and install the control arm, strut, and shaft assembly. Replace the shaft bushing outer retainer and finger tighten the nut.

10. Replace the lower control arm shaft washer and finger tighten the nut.

11. Replace the lower ball joint stud into the lower control arm and tighten it.

12. Install the brake support to steering knuckle and replace the two upper bolts and finger tighten them.

13. Install the steering knuckle on the steering knuckle arm and insert the two lower bolts. Tighten all four bolts.

14. Install the tie rod end to the steering knuckle arm.

15. Connect the shock absorber and finger tighten the bolt.

16. Replace the torsion bar assembly.

17. Install brakes and tires.

18. Lower the car. Tighten the strut nut, lower control arm shaft nut, and shock absorber. Readjust the front suspension height and realign the front end.

FRONT END ALIGNMENT

Because of the special equipment necessary to perform these adjustments, it is not possible to give exact procedures to accomplish these operations. In all cases, follow the alignment equipment manufacturer's recommendations. Set the front end to specifications. Some general notes on this operation follow.

Before attempting wheel alignment, the following points should be checked and corrected as necessary.

1. Front wheel bearing adjustment.

2. Check front wheel and tire for both radial and lateral run out.

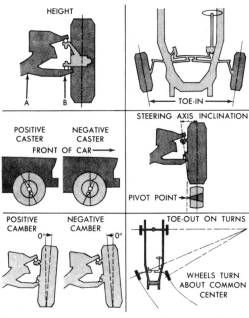

Illustrations of caster, camber, and toe-in (Courtesy of Chrysler Corp.)

3. Wheel and tire balance.

4. Ball joints and steering linkage pivots.

5. Check tire wear, size, and inflation for uniformity and proper specifications.
6. Shock absorbers.
7. Steering gear operation.
8. Rear springs.
9. Front suspension height.

Caster and Camber

Camber is the inward or outward tilt of the wheel. Camber is measured in degrees. A wheel that is tilted outward at the top has positive (+) camber. A wheel that is tilted inward at the top has negative (−) camber. Caster is the backward or forward tilt of the top of the steering knuckle. If the steering knuckle is tilted forward, it has negative caster. If the steering knuckle is tilted backward it has positive caster. Caster is also measured in degrees.

Caster and camber are adjusted by rotating the adjusting cams and locking them into position. Caster should be as nearly equal as possible on both wheels. Camber sometimes differs slightly from side to side if the car is driven where the roads are crowned.

Toe-In

Toe-in is the amount by which the wheels are closer together at the front compared to the rear. This is measured in inches, between the edges of the wheel rims or between the centers of the tire treads.

Toe-in is adjusted by rotating the tie rod sleeves. The front wheels must be in the straight ahead position when adjusting toe-in. Be sure to turn both sleeves an equal amount. Be sure the steering wheel is centered in its travel and on its shaft.

Front End Height

Year	*Model*	*Front End Height ▲*
'67–'69	M.S.—Belvedere, Satellite	1⅞ ± ⅛
	P.S.—Belvedere, Satellite	1⅞ ± ⅛
'70–'73	M.S.—Belvedere, Satellite	1⅞ ± ⅛①
	P.S.—Belvedere, Satellite	1⅞ ± ⅛①

① '71–'73—1⅝ ± ⅛
▲ See text for procedure

Wheel Alignment Specifications

		CASTER		*CAMBER*				*WHEEL PIVOT RATIO (deg)*	
Year	*Model*	*Range (deg)*	*Pref Setting (deg)*	*Range (deg)*	*Pref Setting (deg)*	*Toe-in (in.)*	*Steering Axis Inclin.*	*Inner Wheel*	*Outer Wheel*
'67–'69	M.S.—Belvedere, Satellite	0 to 1N	½N	①	①	3/32 to 5/32	7½	20	17.8
	P.S.—Belvedere, Satellite	¼P to 1¼P	¾P	①	①	3/32 to 5/32	7½	20	17.8
'70–'72	M.S.—Belvedere, Satellite	½N ± ½	½N	①	①	3/32 to 5/32	7½	20	17.8
	P.S.—Belvedere, Satellite	¾P ± ½	¾P	①	①	3/32 to 5/32	7½	20	17.8
'73	M.S.—Satellite	1 5/16N to 1/16P	⅝N	③	③	⅛ ± 3/32	7½	20	17.8
	P.S.—Satellite	1/16N to 1 5/16P	⅝P	③	③	⅛ ± 3/32	7½	20	17.8

M.S. Manual steering
P.S. Power steering
N Negative
P Positive

① Left—¼P to ¾P; ½P preferred
Right 0 to ½P; ¼P preferred
② Heavy duty—2⅛ ± ⅛

③ Left—⅛P to ⅞P; ½P preferred
Right—⅛N to ⅝P; ¼P preferred

Steering

A worm and recirculating ball type steering gear is used with the manual steering system.

Constant Control power steering is an option on all models. Hydraulic power is provided by a vane type, belt driven pump.

The studs on all the tie rod ends are secured by a nut and cotter pin. The studs also fit in a tapered hole. The studs are removed by the use of a ball joint removal tool available at auto parts stores or by the following method: Remove the securing nut and cotter pin. Using a large hammer, strike the side of the tapered hole very firmly while holding an equally heavy hammer against the opposite side of the hole. Never strike the ball joint stud itself. It may take many hard blows but the stud will eventually pop out of the tapered hole.

STEERING WHEEL

Removal and Installation

NOTE: *All models are equipped with collapsible steering columns. A sharp blow or excessive pressure on the column will cause it to collapse. The column will then have to be replaced with a new unit.*

1. Disconnect the ground cable from the battery.

2. Remove the padded center assembly. This center assembly is often held on only by spring clips. However, on deluxe interiors it is held on by screws behind the arms of the wheel.

3. Remove the large center nut. Mark the steering wheel and steering shaft so that the wheel may be replaced in its original position.

4. Using a puller, pull the steering wheel from the steering shaft. It is possible to make a puller by drilling two holes in a piece of steel exactly the same distance apart as the two threaded holes on either side of the large nut. Drill another hole in the center of the piece the same diameter as the steering shaft. Find a bolt of a slightly smaller diameter than the steering shaft. Place the puller over the steering shaft and thread the two bolts into the

holes in the wheel. Tighten the two bolts, and then tighten the center bolt to draw the wheel off the shaft.

5. Reverse the above procedure to install the wheel. When placing the wheel on the shaft, make sure the tires are straight ahead and the match marks are aligned.

TURN SIGNAL SWITCH

Removal and Installation

1. Disconnect the negative ground cable.

2. Disconnect the wiring connectors at the base of the steering column.

3. Remove the steering wheel as outlined above. Tie a string to the turn signal switch wires. Before proceding further, see

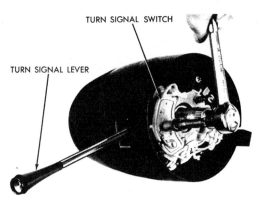

Turn signal switch location (Courtesy of Chrysler Corp.)

if the switch wiring will put out of the switch without having to remove the wiring from the column.

4. Remove the turn signal lever which is screwed into the switch.

5. It may be necessary to lower the steering column slightly to obtain working clearance. To lower the column, loosen the floor pan attaching bolts and loosen the steering column bracket to instrument panel support bolts. Save the shim pack, if equipped, found at the instrument panel support, and reinstall in its original position.

6. Remove the two screws which secure the wiring protector along the steering column and position the wiring protector out of the way.

7. Remove the switch retaining screws and remove the switch from the column.

8. Reverse the above steps to install. Tie the string to the new switch wiring and pull the wiring into position.

MANUAL STEERING GEAR

Worm Bearing Preload Adjustment

1. Remove the steering gear arm using a suitable gear puller.
2. Remove the horn button or horn ring.
3. Loosen the cross shaft adjusting screw locknut and back out the adjusting screw about two turns.

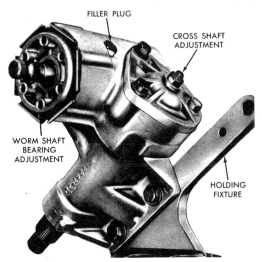

Steering gear adjustment location (Courtesy of Chrysler Corp.)

4. Turn the steering wheel two complete turns from the straight ahead position and place a torque wrench on the steering shaft nut.
5. Rotate the steering shaft at least one turn toward the straight ahead position while measuring the torque. The torque should be $1\frac{1}{2}$–$4\frac{1}{2}$ in. lbs. If the torque is not within these limits, loosen the worm shaft bearing adjuster locknut and turn the adjuster clockwise to increase the preload. Tighten the locknut when the preload is correct.

Ball Nut Rack and Sector Mesh (Cross Shaft) Adjustment

NOTE: *This adjustment can be made only after proper worm bearing preload adjustment is made.*
1. Turn the steering wheel gently from one stop to the other. Return the steering wheel to the exact center position.
2. Turn the cross shaft adjusting screw

clockwise to remove all lash. Then tighten the adjusting screw locknut.
3. Turn the steering wheel about $\frac{1}{4}$ turn away from the center or high spot. Using an in./lb torque wrench on the steering wheel nut, measure the torque required to turn the steering wheel through the high spot. The torque should be between 8 and 11 in. lbs.
4. Install the steering arm on the cross shaft.

POWER STEERING GEAR

Cross Shaft Adjustment

1. Remove the center link from the steering gear arm. Start the engine and let it idle.
2. Back off the adjusting screw until backlash is felt in the steering gear arm. Determine backlash by grasping the end of the steering gear arm. Tighten the adjusting screw until no backlash is evident, then tighten the locknut.

POWER STEERING PUMP

Removal and Installation

NOTE: *Record the exact hose routing. The hoses must be routed and installed in their original positions.*
1. Loosen the pump mounting bolts and remove the power steering belt.
2. Disconnect the hoses at the pump. Be careful not to get any dirt in the hoses.
3. Remove the pump bolts and remove the pump with the bracket.
4. To install the pump, place it in position and install the mounting bolts.
5. Install the belt and tighten the bolts.
6. Connect the pressure and return hoses. Replace the O-ring on the pressure hose, if so equipped.
7. Fill the pump with power steering fluid.
8. Start the engine and rotate the steering wheel from stop to stop several times. Check the pump oil level and fill it as required. Make certain the hoses are away from the exhaust manifold and are not kinked.

STEERING LINKAGE

Tie Rod End Removal and Installation

1. Loosen the tie rod adjuster sleeve clamp nuts.

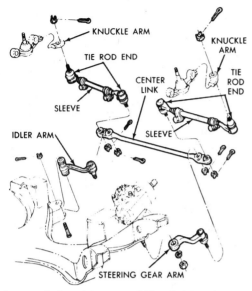

Steering linkage (Courtesy of Chrysler Corp.)

2. Remove the tie rod stud nut and cotter pin.

3. If the outer tie rod end is being removed, remove the ball joint stud from the steering knuckle. If the inner tie rod end is being removed, remove the ball joint stud from the center link.

4. Unscrew the tie rod end from the threaded sleeve. The threads may be left or right-hand threads. Count the number of turns required to remove the tie rod end.

5. To install, reverse the above. Turn the tie rod end in as many turns as was needed to remove it. This will give approximate correct alignment. Have the front end professionally realigned.

Tie Rod End Inspection

1. Raise the car under the lower control arm.

2. Make sure the control arm ball joints are good and that the wheel bearings are adjusted. Grasp the tire on either side and remove the tire from side to side. If excessive play is present (more than $1/8$ in.), visually inspect the linkage while moving the tire, in order to determine exactly where the play is.

Center Link Removal and Installation

1. Remove the left and right side inner tie rod ends from the center link.

2. Remove the idler arm stud and pitman arm stud from the center link.

3. Remove the center link from the car.

4. Reverse the above steps to install.

Idler Arm Removal and Installation

1. Remove the idler arm stud from the center link.

2. Remove the nut, cotter pin, and bolt which secure the idler arm to the frame.

3. Remove the idler arm from the car.

4. Reverse the above steps to install.

Steering Gear Arm Removal and Installation

1. Remove the steering gear arm stud from the center link.

2. Remove the nut and washer which secures the arm to the pitman shaft.

3. Using a puller, remove the arm from the pitman shaft. Do not hammer on the end of the pitman shaft.

4. Reverse the above steps to install.

9 · Brakes

Standard equipment on all models are four-wheel drum brakes. Front disc brakes and power brakes are optional.

A dual or tandem master cylinder is used on all models. This type of cylinder provides partial braking if one half of the system fails. This is possible because there are separate fluid reservoirs and pistons for the front brakes and rear brakes. If there is a failure in the line to the rear brakes, you lose only the rear brakes, the front brakes remain functional.

All the drum brakes are self adjusting. However, it is advisable to adjust the brakes manually since the self adjusters often fail to work or work at different rates on each wheel. Front disc brakes have no provision for mechanical adjustment. Disc brakes adjust themselves. As the brake pad wears the pad moves closer to the disc and stays in adjustment.

Brake System

ADJUSTMENT

It is best to adjust all four wheels at once but it is possible to adjust only the front or rear brakes. The adjustment must be equal on all wheels. The front adjustment is especially critical because a misadjusted brake will cause the car to pull or veer to one side. Remember, front disc brakes require no adjustment.

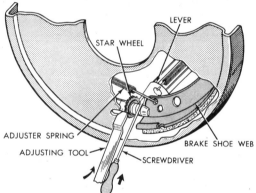

Adjusting drum brakes (Courtesy of Chrysler Corp.)

1. Raise the wheels to be adjusted so that they are free to spin.
2. Remove the rear adjusting hole cover from the backing plate.
3. Make sure the parking brake is fully released.
4. Insert an adjusting tool or screwdriver in the hole until it contacts the star wheel. Lift the handle of the tool upward, rotating the star wheel, until there is a slight drag felt when the tire is rotated.
5. Insert a piece of welding rod or a thin screwdriver into the adjustment hole. Push against the adjusting lever and hold it away from the star wheel. Back off on the star wheel until no drag is felt. Replace the adjusting hole cover.
6. Repeat the above on each wheel.

Drum brake tandem master cylinder (Courtesy of Chrysler Corp.)

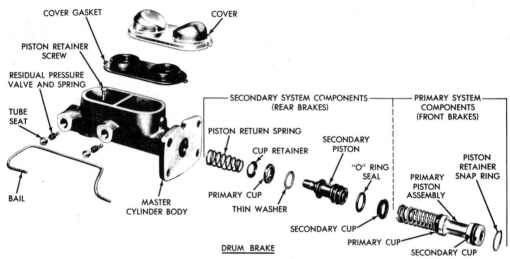

1970 to present tandem master cylinder (Courtesy of Chrysler Corp.)

Hydraulic System

MASTER CYLINDER

Removal and Installation

1. Disconnect the brake lines from the master cylinder. Use a good wrench because the connections are very tight.

2. Remove the nuts that attach the master cylinder to the fire wall or power brake booster, if so equipped.

3. On models with standard brakes, disconnect the master cylinder pushrod from the brake pedal.

4. Slide the master cylinder straight out and off the firewall or brake booster.

5. Reverse the above procedure to install the master cylinder. When reconnecting the brake lines, start the fitting with your fingers and turn the fitting in several threads before using a wrench. This will prevent cross threading. If difficulty is encountered when threading the fittings, bend the brake line slightly so that the fitting enters the hole squarely. If a fluid leak occurs tighten the fitting, check for a damaged seat or tubing end, or look for a hair line crack in the tubing.

6. Bleed the brake system after installation is complete.

Overhaul

NOTE: *Although several types of master cylinders have been used, overhaul procedures are generally the same.*

1. Clean the outside of the cylinder. Remove the cover and drain the fluid.

2. Loosen the rear piston retainer screw in the flange below the piston and flip the retainer down to release the piston assembly for removal.

3. Remove the front piston. If the piston sticks in the cylinder, air pressure may be used to remove it. Always use new rubber cups.

4. Note the position of the rubber cups and springs and remove them from the pistons and from the bore.

5. Remove the tube seats, using an easy out or a screw threaded into the seat. Unless the seat is damaged it is not absolutely necessary to remove the seats.

6. Remove the residual pressure valves and springs found under the seats.

7. Clean the inside of the master cylinder with brake fluid or denatured alcohol.

8. Closely inspect the inside of the master cylinder. Polish the inside of the bore with crocus cloth. If there is rust or pit marks it will be necessary to use a hone. Discard the master cylinder if scores or pits cannot be eliminated by honing.

9. Do not reuse old rubber parts and be sure to use all the new parts supplied in the rebuilding kit.

10. Before assembly, thoroughly lubricate all parts with clean brake fluid.

11. Replace the primary cup on the front end of the piston with the lip away from the piston.

12. Carefully slide the second seal cup over the rear of the piston and into the second land. The cup lip must face the front of the piston.

13. Slowly work the rear secondary cup over the piston and position it in the rear land. The lip must face to the rear.

14. Slide the retainer cup over the front piston stem with the beveled side facing away from the piston cup.

15. Replace the small end of the pressure spring into the retainer.

16. Position the assembly in the bore. Be sure the cups are not canted.

17. Slowly work the secondary cup over the back of the rear piston with the cup lip facing forward.

18. Position the spring retainer in the center of the rear piston assembly. It should be over the shoulder of the front piston. Position the piston assembly in the bore. Slowly work the cup lips into the bore, then seat the piston assembly.

19. Hold the pistons in the seated position. Insert the piston retaining screw with the gasket, and tighten it securely.

20. Replace the residual pressure valves and spring. Position them in the front outlet and install the tube seats.

Bleeding the Master Cylinder

Before installing a reconditioned master cylinder, it will be necessary to bleed it.

1. Insert bleeding tubes into the tube seats and fill both brake reservoirs with brake fluid.

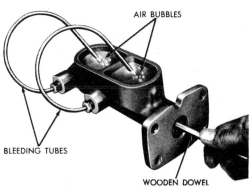

Bleeding the master cylinder (Courtesy of Chrysler Corp.)

2. Insert a dowel pin into the depression in the piston and push in and release the piston. It will return under its own spring pressure. Repeat this operation until all of the air bubbles are expelled.

3. Remove the bleeding tubes, and install the cover and the gasket.

4. Install the master cylinder on the car.

BLEEDING BRAKES

1. Fill the master cylinder with fluid.

2. Jack up the car to allow access to the bleeder valves which are located on the back side of the backing plate.

3. Attach a tube to the bleeder valve and insert the loose end into a glass jar partially filled with brake fluid.

4. With the valve closed, have an assistant pump the brake pedal several times. This will build pressure in the brake system. Then have the assistant stop pumping.

5. Slowly open the bleeder valve to release the pressure. If air is present in the system air will bubble through the fluid in the jar. When the air stops bubbling close the valve and have the assistant pump the pedal again, and release the pressure. Watch the fluid level in the master cylinder and refill as necessary during the bleeding process. Repeat this process until no air is present. Then do the same to the other three wheels.

6. Throw away the fluid in the jar because it is filled with microscopic dirt particles.

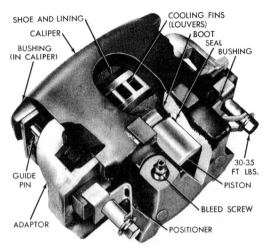

Floating caliper (Courtesy of Chrysler Corp.)

Front Disc Brakes

DISC BRAKE PADS

Removal and Installation

There are two ways to remove the brake pads, either through the caliper with the caliper left in place or by removing the caliper with the pads in place. The two types of calipers are the floating caliper and the fixed caliper.

FLOATING CALIPER

The sliding caliper is identified by a thumb sized hole in the back of the caliper. It will be obvious upon inspection that the brake pads cannot be removed without removing the caliper.

1. Jack up the car and remove the wheel and tire.

2. Remove the caliper retaining clips and anti-rattle springs.

3. Remove the caliper from the disc by slowly sliding the caliper and brake pad assembly out and away from the disc.

4. Remove the outboard pad from the caliper by prying between the pad and the caliper fingers. Remove the inboard pad

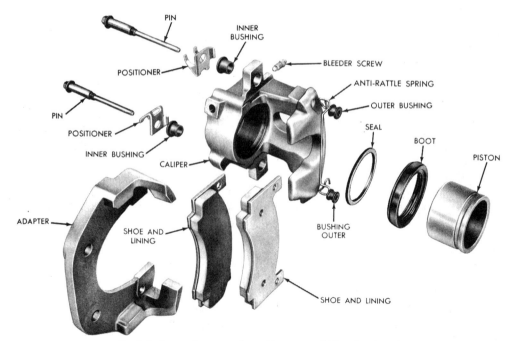

Exploded view floating caliper (Courtesy of Chrysler Corp.)

from the caliper support by the same method.

5. Push the pistons to the bottom of their bores. This may be done with a pair of large pliers or by placing a flat metal bar against the pistons and depressing the pistons with a steady force. This operation is much easier with the cover removed from the master cylinder.

6. Slide the new pads into the caliper and caliper support. The ears of the pad should rest on the bridges of the caliper.

7. Install the caliper on the disc and install the caliper retaining clips and anti-rattle springs. Pump the brake pedal until it is firm.

8. Check the fluid level in the master cylinder and add fluid as needed.

9. Install the wheel and tire.

10. Road test the car. The car may pull to one side, but the pull should disappear shortly as the pads wear in.

FIXED CALIPER

The fixed caliper is identified by a large rectangular hole in the back of the caliper. The hole may have a dust cover, but, after removing the cover, the entire length of the pads may be seen and it will not be necessary to remove the caliper in order to remove the pads.

1. Jack up the car and remove the wheel and tire.

2. Remove the pad retaining assemblies.

3. Due to a ridge of rust that may build up at the outer edge of the rotor, it will be necessary to force the pistons in the caliper to the bottom of their bores. This can be done with a large pair of pliers or by gently forcing a large screwdriver between the pad and the disc. Using a screwdriver will ruin the old pads so, use this method only if new pads are available. Be sure to take the cover off the master cylinder.

4. Using two pairs of pliers, grasp the tabs on the upper and lower ends of the pads and pull the pads from the caliper.

5. Slide the new pads into place. Be sure that the ears of the pad are resting on the bridges of the caliper.

6. Install the pad retaining assemblies.

7. Pump the brake pedal until it is firm and check the fluid level in the master cylinder.

8. Install the wheel and tire and road test the car. The car may pull to one side, but the pull should disappear shortly as the pads wear in.

DISC BRAKE CALIPERS

Removal and Installation

1. Jack up the car and remove the wheel and tire.

2. Disconnect the rubber brake hose from the tubing at the frame mount. Check the rubber hose for cracks or chafed spots.

3. On fixed calipers, remove the bolts which secure the caliper to the steering knuckle. On floating type calipers, remove

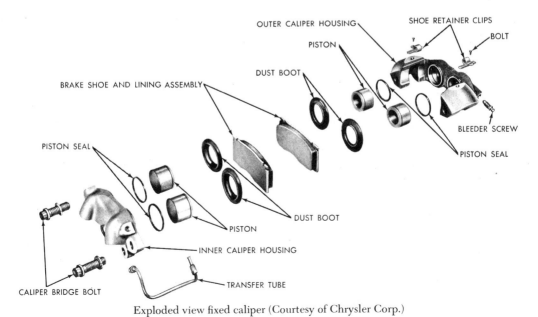

Exploded view fixed caliper (Courtesy of Chrysler Corp.)

the guide pins that attach the caliper to the adaptor.

4. Carefully slide the caliper out and away from the disc. Check the pads to be sure that they are reinstalled in the same position.

5. Installation is the reverse of removal.

Overhaul

FIXED CALIPER

1. Remove the caliper from the car as described above.

2. Remove the pad retaining clips and transfer tube from the caliper.

3. Place the caliper in a soft jawed vice, securing it by the caliper lugs.

4. Remove the pads.

5. Separe the halves of the caliper by undoing the bridge bolts.

6. Peel the dust boots off the caliper housing and piston groove. Force the pistons but their bores by applying compressed air to each transfer tube port. Be careful not to scratch the pistons or the bores. Do not pry on the pistons.

7. Using a small, pointed, wood or plastic tool, remove the piston seals from the cylinder bore groove and throw the used seals away.

8. Clean all parts with denatured alcohol or clean brake fluid.

9. Blow out all the passages and bores with compressed air. If the piston or bores are scored or pitted they must be replaced.

10. To reassemble the caliper, place the new piston seals in clean brake fluid and install them in the grooves in the caliper. Be careful not to pinch, roll, or twist the seal.

11. Coat the outside piston surface with brake fluid. Fit the pistons into the bores, with the open end and boot groove facing toward the outside of the cylinder.

12. Push the piston to the bottom of its bore with a slow steady pressure. Install a new dust boot in the caliper and piston grooves.

13. Place the two caliper halves together and install the bridge bolts. Torque the bolts to 75 ft lbs. Always use the same bolts that were removed because they are special high strength bolts.

14. Install the transfer tube.

15. Install the caliper and pads on the car. Bleed the brakes.

FLOATING CALIPER

1. Remove the caliper as described above.

2. Remove the dust boot from the piston and caliper.

3. Remove the piston from the caliper by applying air pressure to the port for the brake hose.

4. Using a small, pointed, wood or plastic tool, remove the piston seals from the cylinder bore groove and throw the used seal away.

5. If the caliper bushings are worn, they should be pressed out of their bores and replaced at this time.

6. To reassemble the caliper, coat the new piston seal in clean brake fluid and install it into its groove. Be sure the seal is not twisted, rolled, or pinched.

7. Generously coat the new dust boot and install it in its groove in the caliper.

8. Plug the brake line hole and bleeder hole. Coat the piston generously with clean brake fluid and, spreading the boot with your fingers, work the piston gently into place. The air trapped below the piston will force the boot around the piston and into its groove in the piston as the piston is depressed into its bore. Make sure the piston is not cocked.

9. Install the caliper and pads on the car. Bleed the brakes.

BRAKE DISC

Removal and Installation

The brake disc and hub are removed at the same time.

1. Jack up the car and remove the tire and wheel.

2. Remove the caliper from the disc but do not disconnect the brake line. Support the caliper.

3. Remove the grease cup, cotter pin, locknut, thrust washer, and outer wheel bearing.

4. Slide the disc off the spindle.

5. Reverse the above to install the disc. Tighten the wheel bearing nut to 70 in. lbs or finger tight.

INSPECTION

1. With the wheel removed, check to see that there is no grease or other foreign material on the disc. If the disc is badly scored replace the disc.

2. Measure the thickness of the disc

with a micrometer at 12 points around the disc, 1 in. from the disc's edge. Any variation of more than 0.0005 in. means that the disc should be replaced.

3. Using a dial indicator, check the disc run out on both sides. Run out should be no greater than 0.0025 in. If the run out exceeds this figure the disc should be replaced. Make sure the wheel bearing is tight when making this measurement.

WHEEL BEARINGS

Removal and Installation

1. Jack up the car and remove the wheel and tire.

2. Remove the caliper from the disc but not from the car.

3. Remove the brake disc from the car.

4. When removing the inner wheel bearing, remove the grease seal. This seal must be replaced with a new seal. Do not reuse an old seal.

5. Remove the wheel bearing inner race and bearing with your fingers.

6. To remove the outer race from the hub, drive the race out of the hub with a long punch and hammer. There are two notches in the shoulder against which the race is seated, to provide access for the punch.

7. Installation is the reverse of removal. The outer race must be driven in place with a non-metallic rod. Force wheel bearing grease between all the rollers of the wheel bearing and fill the hub cavity with grease.

Adjustment

1. Tighten the adjusting nut while rotating the wheel with a wrench.

2. Back off the adjusting nut to completely release any bearing preload. Then finger tighten the adjusting nut and install the locknut with a cotter pin. The resulting adjustment should yield no more than 0.003 in. of end play.

Front Drum Brakes

BRAKE DRUMS

Removal and Installation

1. Jack up the car and remove the wheel and tire.

2. Remove the wheel bearing cover, cotter pin, lock and adjusting nut, and wheel bearing.

3. Withdraw the hub, drum, and bearing assembly from the spindle. The assembly may not slip easily off the spindle either because the brake is adjusted too tight or because there is a ring of rust at the inside edge of the drum. In either case the brake adjustment must be backed off.

4. To back off on the brake adjustment, remove the rear plug from the backing plate and loosen the star wheel until the drum will slip from the spindle.

5. Reverse the above steps to install. Adjust the brakes and wheel bearings.

Inspection

1. Drum run out (out of round) and diameter should be measured. Drum diameter cannot exceed specification by more than 0.020 in. and run out can not exceed 0.006 in. Do not reface a drum more than

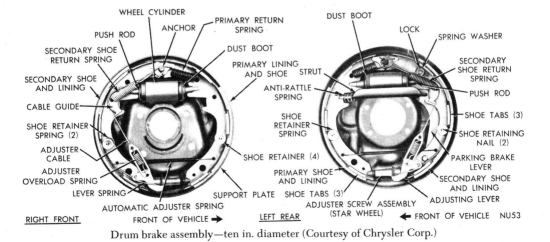

Drum brake assembly—ten in. diameter (Courtesy of Chrysler Corp.)

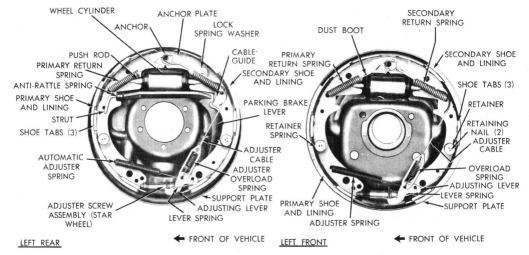

Drum brake assembly—eleven in. diameter (Courtesy of Chrysler Corp.)

0.060 inches over its standard diameter.

2. Check the drum for large cracks and scores. Replace the drum if necessary.

3. If the brake linings are wearing more on one edge than the other then the drum may be "bell" shaped and will have to be replaced or resurfaced.

BRAKE SHOES

Removal and Installation

Remove the wheel and brake drum and proceed as follows:

1. Remove the shoe return springs. Detach the adjusting cable eye from the anchor and unhook the other end from the lever. Withdraw the cable, overload spring, and anchor plate.

2. Detach the adjusting lever from the spring, and separate the spring from the pivot. Remove the spring completely from the secondary shoe web and unfasten it from the primary shoe web.

3. Remove the retainer springs and nails from the shoe. Extract both shoes from the pushrods, and lift them out. Withdraw the star wheel assembly from the shoes.

Install the brakes in the following order:

1. Lightly lubricate the six shoe tab contact areas on the support plate with Lubriplate. Match both the primary and secondary brake shoes with each other.

2. Before installation in the car, fit the star wheel assembly between the shoes with the star wheel next to the secondary shoe. The left star wheel is plated and its adjustment stud is stamped with an "L."

3. Place the assembly on the support plate while attaching the shoe ends to the pushrods.

4. Install the shoe retaining nails, springs, and retainers. Place the anchor plate over the anchor.

5. Place the adjustment cable eye over the anchor, so that it rests against the anchor plate. Attach the primary shoe return spring to the shoe web and fit the other end over the anchor.

6. Place the cable guide in the secondary shoe web and fit the end over the anchor. Hold this in position while engaging the secondary shoe return spring, through the guide and into the web. Put its other end over the anchor. Make sure the cable guide stays flat against the web and that the secondary shoe return spring overlaps the primary shoe return spring.

7. Squeeze the ends of the spring loops until they are parallel and around the anchor.

8. The adjustment cable should be threaded over the guide and the end of the overload spring should be hooked in to the lever. The eye of the adjuster cable must be tight against the anchor.

9. Install the brake drum, wheel bearing, and wheel and tire. Adjust the brakes.

WHEEL CYLINDERS

Removal and Installation

1. Jack up the car and remove the wheel and tire.

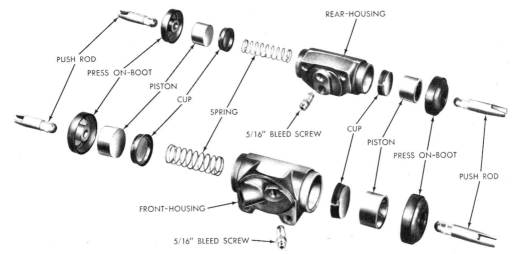

Front or rear wheel cylinder assemblies, 10 and 11 in. diameter brake drums (Courtesy of Chrysler Corp.)

2. Remove the brake drum and brake shoes.

3. Remove the brake line from the cylinder.

4. Unfasten the wheel cylinder attaching bolts and remove the cylinder from its support.

5. Pry the boots off either end of the cylinder 'and remove the pushrods. Push in on one of the pistons to force out the other piston, its cup, the spring, and the piston itself.

6. Wash the pistons, the wheel cylinder housing, and the spring in fresh brake fluid. Dry them with compressed air.

7. Inspect the cylinder bore wall for signs of wear. If it is badly scored or pitted, the entire cylinder should be replaced. Light scratches or corrosion can be removed with crocus cloth or a hone.

8. If the cylinder is to be overhauled, proceed to the overhaul section before continuing further.

9. To install the cylinder, postion the cylinder in its support, and tighten the mounting bolts.

10. Install the brake hose.

11. Install the brake shoes, brake drum, and bleed the brakes. Install the wheel and tire. If necessary, adjust the brakes.

Overhaul

1. Disassemble the wheel cylinder.

2. Dip the pistons and new cups in clean brake fluid. Coat the cylinder wall with brake fluid.

3. Place the spring in the cylinder bore.

Position the cups in either end of the cylinder with the open end of the cups facing inward (toward each other).

4. Place the pistons in either end of the cylinder bore with the recessed ends facing outward. Slide the pistons into the bore until the ends are flush with the end of the bore. Open the bleeder to relieve any pressure.

5. Fit the boots over the ends of the cylinder and push down until each boot is seated. Install the cylinder and bleed the brakes.

WHEEL BEARINGS

Removal and Installation

1. Remove the wheel, tire, and brake drum.

2. To remove and install the bearings use steps 4 through 7 given in the disc brake wheel bearings section.

Adjustment

Adjustment is the same as in the disc brake wheel bearing adjustment section.

Rear Drum Brakes

BRAKE DRUMS

Removal and Installation

1. Remove the rear plug from the brake adjusting access hole.

2. Slide a thin screwdriver through the hole and position the adjusting lever away from the adjusting notches on the star wheel.

3. Insert an adjusting tool into the brake adjusting hole and engage the star wheel. Pry downward with the tool to back off the brake adjustment.

4. Remove the rear wheel and tire. Remove the clips (if so equipped) from the wheel studs and discard the clips.

5. Remove the drum from the axle. The drum simply slips from the axle leaving the wheel studs in place in the axle. However, the drum will sometimes be rusted in place. To break the rust, strike the drum sharply several times with a heavy hammer on the corner of the drum. Strike the drum in several places around its circumference. Do not strike the drum on the edge of the open side as this will crack the drum.

6. Installation is the reverse of the above procedures.

Inspection

Inspection procedures are the same as the front drum inspection procedures.

BRAKE SHOES

Removal and Installation

Except for the following steps, rear brake shoe removal is identical to that for the front brake shoes.

1. With the anchor ends of both shoes spread apart, remove the parking brake lever strut, as well as the anti-rattle spring.

2. Detach the parking brake cable from the parking brake lever.

The installation procedure for the rear brake shoes is different than that for the front shoes.

1. Put a thin film of lubricant at the six shoe tab contact areas on the support plate.

2. Lubricate the pivot on the inner side of the secondary shoe web, and install the parking brake lever on it. Fasten the lever with its washer and horseshoe clip.

3. Connect the parking brake cable to the lever. Slip the secondary shoe next to the support plate, while engaging the shoe web with the pushrod, and push it against the anchor.

4. Position the parking brake strut behind the hub and slide it into the slot in

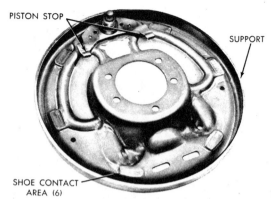

Lubrication points on backing plate (Courtesy of Chrysler Corp.)

the lever. Fit the anti-rattle spring over the free end of the strut.

5. Position the primary shoe, engage it in the pushrod and with the free end of the parking brake strut. Place the anchor plate over the anchor and fit the eye of the adjustment cable over the anchor. Connect the primary shoe return spring to its web and fit its other end over the anchor.

6. Place the cable guide in the secondary shoe web. Hold it in this position while engaging the secondary shoe return spring, wich goes through the guide and into the web. Put its other end over the anchor.

NOTE: *See that the cable guide stays flat against the web, and that the secondary shoe return spring overlaps that of the primary.*

Squeeze the spring loops around the anchor, with pliers, until they are parallel.

7. Place the star wheel assembly between the shoes, with the star wheel assembly adjacent to the secondary shoe. The left rear star wheel is plated and marked with an "L."

8. Place the adjustment lever spring over the pivot pin on the shoe web and fit the lever under the spring, but over the pin. To lock the lever, push it toward the rear.

9. Install the shoe retaining nails, retainers, and spring. Thread the adjusting cable over the guide. Hook the end of the overload spring in the adjustment lever, making sure that the cable remains tight against the anchor and is aligned with the guide.

10. Install the brake drum and adjust the brakes. Adjustment is the same as front drum brakes.

WHEEL CYLINDERS

Removal and Installation

1. Jack up the car and remove the wheel and tire.

2. Remove the brake drum and brake shoes.

3. Remove the brake line from the cylinder.

4. Unfasten the wheel cylinder attaching bolts and remove the cylinder from its support.

5. Installation is the reverse of removal. Bleed the brakes after installing the cylinder.

Overhaul

Rear wheel cylinder overhaul is the same as for front drum brakes.

Handbrake

CABLE

Removal and Installation

1. Jack up the car and remove the rear wheels.

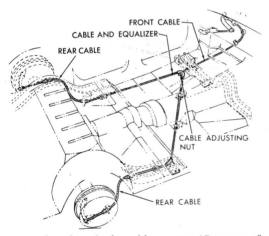

Typical parking brake cable routing (Courtesy of Chrysler Corp.)

2. Disconnect the brake cable from the equalizer.

3. Remove the retaining clip from the brake cable bracket.

4. Remove the brake drum from the rear axle.

5. Remove the brake shoe retaining springs and return springs.

6. Remove the brake shoe strut and spring from the brake support and disconnect the brake cable from the operating arm.

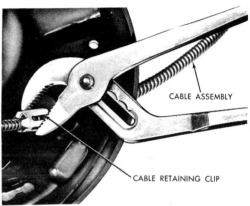

Removing parking brake cable from support (Courtesy of Chrysler Corp.)

7. Compress the retainers on the end of the brake cable housing and remove the cable from the support.

8. Installation is the reverse of removal.

Adjustment

The brakes must be properly adjusted before the parking brake is adjusted.

1. Release the parking brake lever and loosen the cable adjusting nut.

2. Tighten the cable adjusting nut until a light drag is felt while rotating the wheel. Loosen the cable adjusting nut until both rear wheels can be rotated freely, then back off the cable adjusting nut two full turns.

3. Apply the parking brake several times and test to see that the rear wheels rotate freely.

Brake Specifications

(All measurements are given in in.)

| Year | Model | MASTER CYLINDER | | WHEEL CYLINDER | | | BRAKE DISC OR DRUM DIAMETER | | |
		Disc	Drum	Front Disc	Front Drum	Rear	Front Disc	Front Drum	Rear
'68–'69	Belvedere, Satellite	——	1.0	——	1.125	0.9375	——	10.0④	10.0④
	Belvedere, Satellite	1.125	——	2.00	——	0.9375	11.75	——	10.0
'70	Belvedere, Satellite	——	1.0	——	1.125	0.9375	——	10.0⑥	10.0⑥
	Belvedere, Satellite models with disc brakes	1.125	——	2.750	——	0.9375	10.72	——	11.0
'71–'72	Satellite	——	1.0	——	1.187	0.9375	——	10.0④	10.0④
	All with disc brakes	1.00⑦	——	2.750	——	0.9375	11.75	——	11.0
'73	Satellite	1.00⑧	——	2.750	——	0.9375	10.84	——	10.0⑨

① Budd type disc brakes—1.125 in.
② Budd type disc brakes—2.375 in., Kelsey Hayes, 1.638 in., Bendix, 2.00 in.
③ When car is equipped with front disc—0.875 in.
④ 11 in. standard on some models, optional on all others

⑤ 1969—2.750 in.
⑥ 11 in. brakes optional
⑦ 1⅛ in. with Hemi engine
⑧ 1.03 with power brakes
⑨ 11 in. on station wagons
—— Not applicable

10 · Body

Doors

Removal and Installation

1. On vehicles with electric windows, disconnect the wires from the window regulator motor and remove them from the door assembly.

2. With the door in the wide open position, place a jack and block of wood as near the hinge as possible to hold the weight of the door while the hinge bolts are loosened.

3. Remove the door interior trim and hardware.

4. Scribe a line around the upper and lower hinge plates on the door panel.

5. Remove the hinge attaching screws from the door and remove the door from the car.

6. To begin installing the door, place the door in position, supported by the padded jack.

7. On electric window equipped doors, install the wiring in the doors.

8. Locate the door hinge plates on the door panel and install hinge attaching screws finger tight only.

9. Adjust the jack to align the hinge plate scribe marks and tighten the attaching screws.

10. Complete the door aligning procedure, then install the door interior trim and hardware.

DOOR PANELS

Removal and Installation

1. Remove the inside handles and arm rests.

2. Remove the screws that attach the trim panel to the door inner panel.

3. Insert a wide-bladed screwdriver between the trim panel and door frame next to the retaining clips and snap the retaining clips out of the door panel. Remove the trim panel.

4. Before installing the door trim panel, inspect the condition of the watershield.

5. Be certain the escutcheon spring is placed on the regulator shafts.

6. Align the trim panel retaining clips with the holes of the door frame and bump into place with the heel of your hand.

7. Install the trim panel-to-door screws.

8. Install escutcheon washer, handles, and arm rest.

WINDOWS

1. Loosen the division channel lower bracket screw and lower the window half way.

2. Tighten the division channel lower bracket screw.

3. Lower the window so the top of the

175

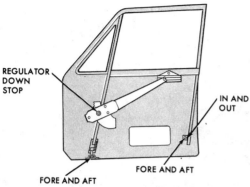

Sedan window glass adjustments (Courtesy of Chrysler Corp.)

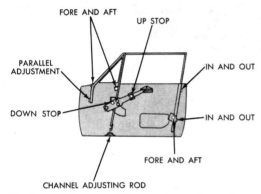

Hardtop and convertible window glass adjustments (Courtesy of Chrysler Corp.)

glass is even with or slightly below the belt line of the outer panel.

4. Position the regulator stop against the regulator sector stop and tighten the nut.

Hood

Alignment

1. Inspect the alignment at the cowl for tightness, looseness, uneven gap, and high or low elevation at the corners.

2. Scribe the hinge position on the hood.

3. Loosen the hood attaching bolts and move the hood to the desired position to correct alignment.

4. Tighten the attaching bolts.

5. After step 4, if the rest of the hood and fender are not flush, reset the fender to align with the cowl and hood.

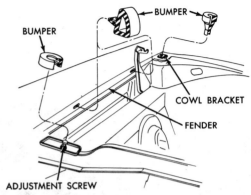

Adjustment points for leveling hood (Courtesy of Chrysler Corp.)

6. The clearance between the hood and fender is adjusted by removing the hood bumper and turning the adjusting screw in or out. It may also be necessary to loosen the fender attaching bolts and move the fender up or down to the desired position.

Trunk Lid

Alignment

1. The deck lid hinges permit only a very slight adjustment at the deck lid-to-hinge attaching points.

2. If the trunk latch fails to catch adjust the lock instead of the hood.

Fuel Tank

Removal and Installation

1968–70

Be sure the ignition switch is off and the battery is disconnected.

1. Drain the tank and disconnect the fuel line and the wire to the fuel gauge.

2. Disconnect the vent tubes.

3. Remove the screw that attaches the filler tube bracket.

4. Remove the nuts that hold the ends of the fuel tank hold-down straps to the frame. Lower the front end of the tank far enough to disengage the filler tube from the rear panel and slide the tank out from under the car.

5. Reverse the above steps to install.

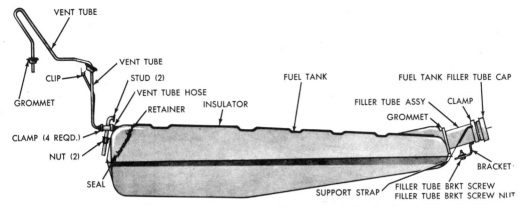

Fuel tank assembly—1969 illustrated (Courtesy of Chrysler Corp.)

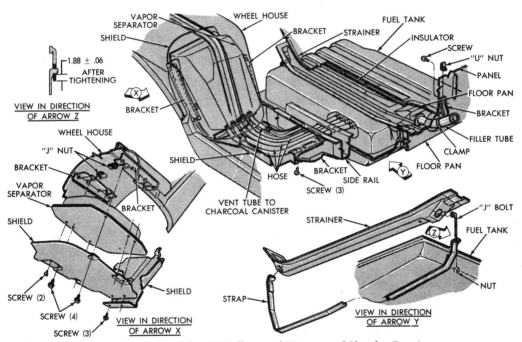

Fuel tank assembly—1972 illustrated (Courtesy of Chrysler Corp.)

1971–72

1. Disconnect the battery.

2. Drain the fuel tank.

3. Disconnect the fuel ground strap and the wire for the fuel gauge.

4. On models equipped with dual exhaust, lower the tail pipe to remove the heat shield and vapor separator hoses.

5. Remove the heat shield.

6. Remove the four clamps and hoses from the fuel tank.

7. Remove the clamp and bracket from the filler tube.

8. Grasp the filler tube with both hands and twist, working it carefully out of the tank.

9. Remove the nuts that hold the tank retaining straps to the J-bolt. Allow the straps to drop, then lower the front end of the tank and slide the tank out from under the car.

10. Reverse the above steps to install.

1973

1. Disconnect the battery cable to ground.

2. Remove the fuel tank cap and disconnect the fuel lines.

3. Remove the two vapor separator mounting screws, then disconnect the vapor hose from the top of the separator.

4. Remove the screw from the filler tube mounting bracket.

5. Grasp the filler tube with both hands and twist, working it carefully out of the rubber grommet.

6. Loosen the nuts that hold the tank retaining straps to the J-bolts and remove the J-bolts from the bracket.

7. Lower the tank until the fuel line ground strap and gauge wire can be removed from the tank gauge unit.

8. Remove the tank and vapor separator assembly from under the car.

9. Installation is the reverse of removal.

Front Fender

Removal and Installation

1. Disconnect the battery ground strap.

2. Tape the leading edge of the front door and cowl-to-fender area to avoid damaging the paint.

3. Remove the front bumper assembly.

4. Disconnect the headlamp wires and remove the nuts which attach the grille extension to the fender.

5. Remove the nuts and screws which attach the fender to the cowl. Remove the floor sill, wheelhouse, splash shield, and radiator yoke.

6. Remove the fender assembly and, if necessary, remove fender mouldings, ornamentation and headlight assemblies.

7. Installation is the reverse of removal.

Appendix

General Conversion Table

Multiply by	To convert	To	
2.54	Inches	Centimeters	.3937
30.48	Feet	Centimeters	.0328
.914	Yards	Meters	1.094
1.609	Miles	Kilometers	.621
6.45	Square inches	Square cm.	.155
.836	Square yards	Square meters	1.196
16.39	Cubic inches	Cubic cm.	.061
28.3	Cubic feet	Liters	.0353
.4536	Pounds	Kilograms	2.2045
3.785	Gallons	Liters	.264
.068	Lbs./sq. in. (psi)	Atmospheres	14.7
.138	Foot pounds	Kg. m.	7.23
1.014	H.P. (DIN)	H.P. (SAE)	.9861
—	To obtain	From	Multiply by

Note: 1 cm. equals 10 mm.; 1 mm. equals .0394".

Conversion—Common Fractions to Decimals and Millimeters

Common Fractions	Decimal Fractions	Millimeters (approx.)	Common Fractions	Decimal Fractions	Millimeters (approx.)	Common Fractions	Decimal Fractions	Millimeters (approx.)
1/128	.008	0.20	11/32	.344	8.73	43/64	.672	17.07
1/64	.016	0.40	23/64	.359	9.13	11/16	.688	17.46
1/32	.031	0.79	3/8	.375	9.53	45/64	.703	17.86
3/64	.047	1.19	25/64	.391	9.92	23/32	.719	18.26
1/16	.063	1.59	13/32	.406	10.32	47/64	.734	18.65
5/64	.078	1.98	27/64	.422	10.72	3/4	.750	19.05
3/32	.094	2.38	7/16	.438	11.11	49/64	.766	19.45
7/64	.109	2.78	29/64	.453	11.51	25/32	.781	19.84
1/8	.125	3.18	15/32	.469	11.91	51/64	.797	20.24
9/64	.141	3.57	31/64	.484	12.30	13/16	.813	20.64
5/32	.156	3.97	1/2	.500	12.70	53/64	.828	21.03
11/64	.172	4.37	33/64	.516	13.10	27/32	.844	21.43
3/16	.188	4.76	17/32	.531	13.49	55/64	.859	21.83
13/64	.203	5.16	35/64	.547	13.89	7/8	.875	22.23
7/32	.219	5.56	9/16	.563	14.29	57/64	.891	22.62
15/64	.234	5.95	37/64	.578	14.68	29/32	.906	23.02
1/4	.250	6.35	19/32	.594	15.08	59/64	.922	23.42
17/64	.266	6.75	39/64	.609	15.48	15/16	.938	23.81
9/32	.281	7.14	5/8	.625	15.88	61/64	.953	24.21
19/64	.297	7.54	41/64	.641	16.27	31/32	.969	24.61
5/16	.313	7.94	21/32	.656	16.67	63/64	.984	25.00
21/64	.328	8.33						

Conversion—Millimeters to Decimal Inches

mm	inches	mm	inches	mm	inches	mm	inches	mm	inches
1	.039 370	31	1.220 470	61	2.401 570	91	3.582 670	210	8.267 700
2	.078 740	32	1.259 840	62	2.440 940	92	3.622 040	220	8.661 400
3	.118 110	33	1.299 210	63	2.480 310	93	3.661 410	230	9.055 100
4	.157 480	34	1.338 580	64	2.519 680	94	3.700 780	240	9.448 800
5	.196 850	35	1.377 949	65	2.559 050	95	3.740 150	250	9.842 500
6	.236 220	36	1.417 319	66	2.598 420	96	3.779 520	260	10.236 200
7	.275 590	37	1.456 689	67	2.637 790	97	3.818 890	270	10.629 900
8	.314 960	38	1.496 050	68	2.677 160	98	3.858 260	280	11.032 600
9	.354 330	39	1.535 430	69	2.716 530	99	3.897 630	290	11.417 300
10	.393 700	40	1.574 800	70	2.755 900	100	3.937 000	300	11.811 000
11	.433 070	41	1.614 170	71	2.795 270	105	4.133 848	310	12.204 700
12	.472 440	42	1.653 540	72	2.834 640	110	4.330 700	320	12.598 400
13	.511 810	43	1.692 910	73	2.874 010	115	4.527 550	330	12.992 100
14	.551 180	44	1.732 280	74	2.913 380	120	4.724 400	340	13.385 800
15	.590 550	45	1.771 650	75	2.952 750	125	4.921 250	350	13.779 500
16	.629 920	46	1.811 020	76	2.992 120	130	5.118 100	360	14.173 200
17	.669 290	47	1.850 390	77	3.031 490	135	5.314 950	370	14.566 900
18	.708 660	48	1.889 760	78	3.070 860	140	5.511 800	380	14.960 600
19	.748 030	49	1.929 130	79	3.110 230	145	5.708 650	390	15.354 300
20	.787 400	50	1.968 500	80	3.149 600	150	5.905 500	400	15.748 000
21	.826 770	51	2.007 870	81	3.188 970	155	6.102 350	500	19.685 000
22	.866 140	52	2.047 240	82	3.228 340	160	6.299 200	600	23.622 000
23	.905 510	53	2.086 610	83	3.267 710	165	6.496 050	700	27.559 000
24	.944 880	54	2.125 980	84	3.307 080	170	6.692 900	800	31.496 000
25	.984 250	55	2.165 350	85	3.346 450	175	6.889 750	900	35.433 000
26	1.023 620	56	2.204 720	86	3.385 820	180	7.086 600	1000	39.370 000
27	1.062 990	57	2.244 090	87	3.425 190	185	7.283 450	2000	78.740 000
28	1.102 360	58	2.283 460	88	3.464 560	190	7.480 300	3000	118.110 000
29	1.141 730	59	2.322 830	89	3.503 903	195	7.677 150	4000	157.480 000
30	1.181 100	60	2.362 200	90	3.543 300	200	7.874 000	5000	196.850 000

To change decimal millimeters to decimal inches, position the decimal point where desired on either side of the millimeter measurement shown and reset the inches decimal by the same number of digits in the same direction. For example, to convert .001 mm into decimal inches, reset the decimal behind the 1 mm (shown on the chart) to .001; change the decimal inch equivalent (.039" shown) to .00039").

Tap Drill Sizes

National Fine or S.A.E.				National Coarse or U.S.S.		
Screw & Tap Size	Threads Per Inch	Use Drill Number		Screw & Tap Size	Threads Per Inch	Use Drill Number
No. 5	44	37		No. 5	40	39
No. 6	40	33		No. 6	32	36
No. 8	36	29		No. 8	32	29
No. 10	32	21		No. 10	24	25
No. 12	28	15		No. 12	24	17
1/4	28	3		1/4	20	8
5/16	24	1		5/16	18	F
3/8	24	Q		3/8	16	5/16
7/16	20	W		7/16	14	U
1/2	20	29/64		1/2	13	27/64
9/16	18	33/64		9/16	12	31/64
5/8	18	37/64		5/8	11	17/32
3/4	16	11/16		3/4	10	21/32
7/8	14	13/16		7/8	9	49/64
1 1/8	12	1 3/64		1	8	7/8
1 1/4	12	1 11/64		1 1/8	7	63/64
1 1/2	12	1 27/64		1 1/4	7	1 7/64
				1 1/2	6	1 11/32

Decimal Equivalent Size of the Number Drills

Drill No.	Decimal Equivalent	Drill No.	Decimal Equivalent	Drill No.	Decimal Equivalent
80	.0135	53	.0595	26	.1470
79	.0145	52	.0635	25	.1495
78	.0160	51	.0670	24	.1520
77	.0180	50	.0700	23	.1540
76	.0200	49	.0730	22	.1570
75	.0210	48	.0760	21	.1590
74	.0225	47	.0785	20	.1610
73	.0240	46	.0810	19	.1660
72	.0250	45	.0820	18	.1695
71	.0260	44	.0860	17	.1730
70	.0280	43	.0890	16	.1770
69	.0292	42	.0935	15	.1800
68	.0310	41	.0960	14	.1820
67	.0320	40	.0980	13	.1850
66	.0330	39	.0995	12	.1890
65	.0350	38	.1015	11	.1910
64	.0360	37	.1040	10	.1935
63	.0370	36	.1065	9	.1960
62	.0380	35	.1100	8	.1990
61	.0390	34	.1110	7	.2010
60	.0400	33	.1130	6	.2040
59	.0410	32	.1160	5	.2055
58	.0420	31	.1200	4	.2090
57	.0430	30	.1285	3	.2130
56	.0465	29	.1360	2	.2210
55	.0520	28	.1405	1	.2280
54	.0550	27	.1440		

Decimal Equivalent Size of the Letter Drills

Letter Drill	Decimal Equivalent	Letter Drill	Decimal Equivalent	Letter Drill	Decimal Equivalent
A	.234	J	.277	S	.348
B	.238	K	.281	T	.358
C	.242	L	.290	U	.368
D	.246	M	.295	V	.377
E	.250	N	.302	W	.386
F	.257	O	.316	X	.397
G	.261	P	.323	Y	.404
H	.266	Q	.332	Z	.413
I	.272	R	.339		

ANTI-FREEZE INFORMATION

Freezing and Boiling Points of Solutions
According to Percentage of Alcohol or Ethylene Glycol

Freezing Point of Solution	Alcohol Volume %	Alcohol Solution Boils at	Ethylene Glycol Volume %	Ethylene Glycol Solution Boils at
20°F.	12	196°F.	16	216°F.
10°F.	20	189°F.	25	218°F.
0°F.	27	184°F.	33	220°F.
−10°F.	32	181°F.	39	222°F.
−20°F.	38	178°F.	44	224°F.
−30°F.	42	176°F.	48	225°F.

Note: above boiling points are at sea level. For every 1,000 feet of altitude, boiling points are approximately 2°F. lower than those shown. For every pound of pressure exerted by the pressure cap, the boiling points are approximately 3°F. higher than those shown.

ANTI-FREEZE CHART

Temperatures Shown in Degrees Fahrenheit
+32 is Freezing

Cooling System Capacity Quarts	Quarts of ETHYLENE GLYCOL Needed for Protection to Temperatures Shown Below													
	1	2	3	4	5	6	7	8	9	10	11	12	13	14
10	+24°	+16°	+ 4°	−12°	−34°	−62°								
11	+25	+18	+ 8	− 6	−23	−47								
12	+26	+19	+10	0	−15	−34	−57°							
13	+27	+21	+13	+ 3	− 9	−25	−45							
14			+15	+ 6	− 5	−18	−34							
15			+16	+ 8	0	−12	−26							
16			+17	+10	+ 2	− 8	−19	−34	−52°					
17			+18	+12	+ 5	− 4	−14	−27	−42					
18			+19	+14	+ 7	0	−10	−21	−34	−50°				
19			+20	+15	+ 9	+ 2	− 7	−16	−28	−42				
20				+16	+10	+ 4	− 3	−12	−22	−34	−48°			
21				+17	+12	+ 6	0	− 9	−17	−28	−41			
22				+18	+13	+ 8	+ 2	− 6	−14	−23	−34	−47°		
23				+19	+14	+ 9	+ 4	− 3	−10	−19	−29	−40		
24				+19	+15	+10	+ 5	0	− 8	−15	−23	−34	−46°	
25				+20	+16	+12	+ 7	+ 1	− 5	−12	−20	−29	−40	−50°
26					+17	+13	+ 8	+ 3	− 3	− 9	−16	−25	−34	−44
27					+18	+14	+ 9	+ 5	− 1	− 7	−13	−21	−29	−39
28					+18	+15	+10	+ 6	+ 1	− 5	−11	−18	−25	−34
29					+19	+16	+12	+ 7	+ 2	− 3	− 8	−15	−22	−29
30					+20	+17	+13	+ 8	+ 4	− 1	− 6	−12	−18	−25

For capacities over 30 quarts vide true capacity by 3. Find qua Anti-Freeze for the ⅓ and multi by 3 for quarts to add.

For capacities under 10 quarts multiply true capacity by 3. Find quarts Anti-Freeze for the tripled volume and divide by 3 for quarts to add.

To Increase the Freezing Protection of Anti-Freeze Solutions Already Installed

Cooling System Capacity Quarts	Number of Quarts of ETHYLENE GLYCOL Anti-Freeze Required to Increase Protection													
	From +20°F. to					From +10°F. to					From 0°F. to			
	0°	−10°	−20°	−30°	−40°	0°	−10°	−20°	−30°	−40°	−10°	−20°	−30°	−40°
10	1¾	2¼	3	3½	3¾	¾	1½	2¼	2¾	3¼	¾	1½	2	2½
12	2	2¾	3½	4	4½	1	1¾	2½	3¼	3¾	1	1¾	2½	3¼
14	2¼	3¼	4	4¾	5½	1¼	2	3	3¾	4½	1	2	3	3½
16	2½	3½	4½	5¼	6	1¼	2½	3½	4¼	5¼	1¼	2¼	3¼	4
18	3	4	5	6	7	1½	2¾	4	5	5¾	1½	2½	3¾	4¾
20	3¼	4½	5¾	6¾	7½	1¾	3	4¼	5½	6½	1½	2¾	4¼	5¼
22	3½	5	6¼	7¼	8¼	1¾	3¼	4¾	6	7¼	1¾	3¼	4½	5½
24	4	5½	7	8	9	2	3½	5	6½	7½	1¾	3½	5	6
26	4¼	6	7½	8¾	10	2	4	5½	7	8¼	2	3¾	5½	6¾
28	4½	6¼	8	9½	10½	2¼	4¼	6	7½	9	2	4	5¾	7¼
30	5	6¾	8½	10	11½	2½	4½	6½	8	9½	2¼	4¼	6¼	7¾

Test radiator solution with proper hydrometer. Determine from the table the number of quarts of solution to be drawn off from a full cooling system and replace with undiluted anti-freeze, to give the desired increased protection. For example, to increase protection of a 22-quart cooling system containing Ethylene Glycol (permanent type) anti-freeze, from +20°F. to −20°F. will require the replacement of 6¼ quarts of solution with undiluted anti-freeze.

Chilton's Repair & Tune-Up Guides

The complete line covers domestic cars, imports, trucks, vans, RV's and 4-wheel drive vehicles.

CODE	TITLE	CODE	TITLE
#7199	AMC 75-82; all models	#6935	GM Sub-compact 71-81 inc. Vega, Monza, Astre, Sunbird, Starfire & Skyhawk
#7165	Alliance 1983		
#7323	Aries 81-82	#6937	Granada 75-80
#7032	Arrow Pick-Up 79-81	#5905	GTO 68-73
#7193	Aspen 76-80	#5821	GTX 68-73
#5902	Audi 70-73	#7204	Honda 73-82
#7028	Audi 4000/5000 77-81	#7191	Horizon 78-82
#6337	Audi Fox 73-75	#5912	International Scout 67-73
#5807	Barracuda 65-72	#7136	Jeep CJ 1945-81
#7203	Blazer 69-82	#6739	Jeep Wagoneer, Commando, Cherokee 66-79
#5576	BMW 59-70	#6962	Jetta 1980
#6844	BMW 70-79	#7203	Jimmy 69-82
#7027	Bobcat	#7059	J-2000 1982
#7307	Buick Century/Regal 75-83	#7165	Le Car 76-83
#7045	Camaro 67-81	#7323	Le Baron 1982
#6695	Capri 70-77	#5905	Le Mans 68-73
#7195	Capri 79-82	#7055	Lynx 81-82 inc. EXP & LN-7
#7059	Cavalier 1982	#6634	Maverick 70-77
#5807	Challenger 65-72	#7198	Mazda 71-82
#7037	Challenger (Import) 71-81	#7031	Mazda RX-7 79-81
#7041	Champ 78-81	#6065	Mercedes-Benz 59-70
#6316	Charger/Coronet 71-75	#5907	Mercedes-Benz 68-73
#7162	Chevette 76-82 inc. diesel	#6809	Mercedes-Benz 74-79
#7313	Chevrolet 68-83 all full size models	#7128	Mercury 68-71 all full sized models
#7167	Chevrolet/GMC Pick-Ups 70-82	#7194	Mercury Mid-Size 71-82 inc. Continental, Cougar, XR-7 & Montego
#7169	Chevrolet/GMC Vans 67-82		
#7310	Chevrolet S-10/GMC S-15 Pick-Ups 82-83	#7173	MG 61-80
#7051	Chevy Luv 72-81 inc. 4wd	#6973	Monarch 75-80
#7056	Chevy Mid-Size 64-82 inc. El Camino, Chevelle, Laguna, Malibu & Monte Carlo	#6542	Mustang 65-73
		#6812	Mustang II 74-78
#6841	Chevy II 62-79	#7195	Mustang 79-82
#7059	Cimarron 1982	#6841	Nova 69-79
#7049	Citation 80-81	#7049	Omega 81-82
#7037	Colt 71-81	#7191	Omni 78-82
#6634	Comet 70-77	#6575	Opel 71-75
#7194	Continental 1982	#5982	Peugeot 70-74
#6691	Corvair 60-69 inc. Turbo	#7049	Phoenix 81-82
#6576	Corvette 53-62	#7027	Pinto 71-80
#7192	Corvette 63-82	#8552	Plymouth 68-76 full sized models
#7190	Cutlass 70-82	#7168	Plymouth Vans 67-82
#6324	Dart 68-76	#5822	Porsche 69-73
#6962	Dasher 74-80	#7048	Porsche 924 & 928 77-81 inc. Turbo
#5790	Datsun 61-72	#6962	Rabbit 75-80
#7196	Datsun F10, 310, Nissan Stanza 77-82	#7323	Reliant 81-82
#7170	Datsun 200SX, 510, 610, 710, 810 73-82	#7165	Renault 75-83
#7197	Datsun 1200, 210/Nissan Sentra 73-82	#5821	Roadrunner 68-73
#7172	Datsun Z & ZX 70-82	#5988	Saab 69-75
#7050	Datsun Pick-Ups 70-81 inc. 4wd	#7041	Sapporo 78-81
#6324	Demon 68-76	#5821	Satellite 68-73
#6554	Dodge 68-77 all full sized models	#6962	Scirocco 75-80
#7323	Dodge 400 1982	#7059	Skyhawk 1982
#6486	Dodge Charger 67-70	#7049	Skylark 80-81
#7168	Dodge Vans 67-82	#7208	Subaru 70-82
#6326	Duster 68-76	#5905	Tempest 68-73
#7055	Escort 81-82 inc. EXP & LN-7	#6320	Torino 62-75
#6320	Fairlane 62-75	#5795	Toyota 66-70
#7312	Fairmont 78-83	#7043	Toyota Celica & Supra 71-81
#7042	Fiat 69-81	#7036	Toyota Corolla, Carina, Tercel, Starlet 70-81
#6846	Fiesta 78-80	#7044	Toyota Corona, Cressida, Crown, Mark II 70-81
#7046	Firebird 67-81	#7035	Toyota Pick-Ups 70-81
#7059	Firenza 1982	#5910	Triumph 69-73
#7128	Ford 68-81 all full sized models	#7162	T-1000 1982
#7140	Ford Bronco 66-81	#6326	Valiant 68-76
#6983	Ford Courier 72-80	#5796	Volkswagen 49-71
#7194	Ford Mid-Size 71-82 inc. Torino, Gran Torino, Ranchero, Elite, LTD II & Thunderbird	#6837	Volkswagen 70-81
		#7193	Volaré 76-80
		#6529	Volvo 56-69
#7166	Ford Pick-Ups 65-82 inc. 4wd	#7040	Volvo 70-80
#7171	Ford Vans 61-82	#7312	Zephyr 78-83
#7165	Fuego 82-83		

Chilton's Repair & Tune-Up Guides are available at your local retailer or by mailing a check or money order for **$10.95** plus **$1.00** to cover postage and handling to:

Chilton Book Company
Dept. DM
Radnor, PA 19089

NOTE: When ordering be sure to include your name & address, book code & title.

Tai Chi
for ARTHRITIS
HANDBOOK

NOTE ON THE AUTHOR

Dr Paul Lam, a family physician in Sydney, Australia, is a world leader in the field of tai chi for health improvement. To make tai chi easy and effective to many people, Dr Lam has created the programs Tai Chi for Arthritis, Tai Chi for Back Pain and Tai Chi for Diabetes. These programs have helped people improve their health and well-being. He is also a past international competition gold medalist (Beijing 1993) and an author of several books on health and tai chi.

First published January 2001
Reprinted June 2001
Revised and reprinted May 2002
Revised and reprinted July 2004

ISBN 0-9578605-0-1

Published by East Acton Publishing Pty Ltd
(A subsidiary of Tai Chi Productions)
6 Fisher Place, Narwee NSW 2209 Australia
Telephone: 9533 6511 ; 9533 6150
Facsimile: 9534 4311

Email: service@taichiproductions.com
Web Site: www.taichiproductions.com

Cover design by Matthew Lam
Editing and text design by Valerie Sayce
Printed by AQ Colour Printing

ACKNOWLEDGEMENTS

The idea of a special Tai Chi program for arthritis struck me like a thunderbolt. I soon found a team of Tai Chi and medical experts to work with me on it.

I was fortunate to have a group of talented Tai Chi instructors, familiar with different styles. I am grateful for the expertise of Julie King, Michael Ngai, Robyn Nicholls and Ian Etcell. The medical team consisted of Professor John Edmonds, conjoint professor of Rheumatology at the University of NSW and head of the Rheumatology Department at St. George Hospital; prominent rheumatologist, Dr. Ian Portek and Guni Hinchy, a senior rheumatology physiotherapist at St. George Hospital. We worked hard to produce a simple, safe and effective program.

I am grateful to the various Arthritis Foundations and Societies and the National Association for Gentle Exercise that have supported the program, promoting it widely to people with arthritis.

The editing of the Handbook was done by Valerie Sayce. Without her tireless efforts, this book would never have eventuated. Her wonderful knack of turning many sophisticated concepts into simple and easy-to-understand pieces, without losing any of their essential meaning, is simply magical. I especially thank Valerie for making this Handbook possible.

My appreciation also goes to the many others - instructors, students, friends and family - whose enthusiasm for the Program contributed to the production of this publication. In particular, Anna Bennett, for her administrative support and ability to transcribe my words into print; Jana Solovka and Sally Swan, enthusiastic instructors at Knox Community Health Service, for providing very useful feedback; my friend Tony Coyle for his vision and encouragement and my sister Celia Lam Liu for her support in developing the Program.

Finally, I thank my family for their ongoing support in numerous ways especially with my Tai Chi projects.

~ Dr. Paul Lam

DISCLAIMER

Readers should consult their physicians before engaging in the activities described in this book. The authors, publisher, distributors and anyone involved in the production and distribution of the book will not be held responsible in any way whatsoever for any injury which may arise as a result of following the instructions given in this book. Readers who engage in these activities do so at their own risk.

NOTE

This publication is intended for use in conjunction with the Tai Chi for Arthritis Program classes or the Tai Chi for Arthritis self-teaching video. It is not recommended that it be used by itself to learn the Program. The video is available through many Arthritis Foundations or from Dr. Lam.

Tai Chi for Arthritis Part 2 is now available, see page 59

CONTENTS

TAI CHI & ARTHRITIS

Many thousands of people with arthritis have discovered Dr. Paul Lam's Tai Chi for Arthritis Program. There are classes led by trained instructors, and the self-teaching video, Tai Chi for Arthritis, for use at home. By learning the specially designed movements and practising them regularly, many have found significant relief from symptoms of arthritis within a short time. Reports of benefits include:

- reduced pain and stiffness
- uplifting of the spirit
- increasing sense of tranquillity
- improved muscle strength and joint flexibility
- continuing enjoyment of practice

The Tai Chi for Arthritis Handbook assumes you are learning the complete Tai Chi for Arthritis Program from an instructor in a class, or by studying Dr. Paul Lam's Tai Chi for Arthritis instructional video. It is designed to assist you with your practice and provides a summary of the 6 Basic Movements and the 6 Advanced Movements with photographs and brief instructions. The Warm Up and Wind Down Exercises and the Qigong Exercise are also included. It would be very difficult to learn the Tai Chi for Arthritis Program correctly from this Handbook alone.

You may also be interested in the additional information about Tai Chi, Qigong, arthritis, how to improve your practice, and the Tai Chi for Arthritis Program itself. Towards the back of the Handbook you can learn more about the deeper principles of Tai Chi and where to find out more about arthritis and its management.

Always be aware that arthritis is different for everyone who has it. If you are experiencing any difficulties with the movements in the Tai Chi for Arthritis Program, discuss them with your instructor, medical practitioner or other health practitioner.

Tai Chi for Arthritis Instructor's Workshop conducted by Dr. Lam (San Francisco, April 2001)

About Tai Chi

Originating in ancient China, Tai Chi is an eminent form of martial art. Nowadays, over 300 million people throughout the world practise it as an effective exercise for healthy mind and body. Although an art with great depth of knowledge and skill, the basics are easy to learn and it soon delivers its health benefits. For many it continues as a lifetime journey.

Tai Chi is gentle, focusing on fluid, circular movements that are relaxed and slow in tempo. Breathing is deep and slow, aiding concentration, relaxing the body, and allowing the life force, or Qi, to flow unimpeded throughout the body. Total harmony of the inner and outer self comes from the integration of mind and body through the ongoing practice of Tai Chi.

Anyone can learn Tai Chi. It is inexpensive and can be practised almost anywhere. The movements are slow and gentle and the degree of exertion can be easily adjusted, making it suitable for people of all levels of ability.

The health benefits of Tai Chi include:
- increased flexibility and muscle strength
- greater fitness
- correct body posture
- integration of body, mind and spirit
- improved flow of Qi

Tai Chi encompasses a wide range of styles and forms, each with their own characteristics, strengths and principles. The Sun (pronounced Soong) style, on which the *Tai Chi for Arthritis Program* is based, is the most recent of the four major styles, being created early in the 20th century by Sun Lu-tang (1861-1932). In 1912, Sun happened to meet Hao Weizheng, a famous Tai Chi master, although Sun did not know this at the time. Hao was ill and Sun kindly found him a doctor and a place to stay. After he recovered, Hao taught Tai Chi to Sun, who was already a well-known exponent of two other internal martial art styles, Xingyiquan and Baguaquan. Sun incorporated his expertise of these styles with that of Tai Chi to create his own style.

About Qigong

Qigong is another ancient Chinese practice that enhances health and relaxation. Qi is the life energy within you, flowing through specific channels, called meridians. It is a combination of the innate Qi you are born with, the Qi absorbed through your digestive system from food and water, and the Qi acquired from the air you breathe. Qi circulates through the body, performing many functions to maintain good health. The storage house of Qi is the *Dan-tian*, a small area situated three finger-breadths below the belly button.

The concept of Qi is fundamental to traditional Chinese medicine. Practitioners claim that good health comes when your Qi is strong and harmonious.

There are a number of different forms of Qigong but, in essence, it is the studied practice of cultivating Qi and consists of special breathing exercises, often integrated with movement and meditation. Tai Chi has incorporated Qigong as an integral part of its practice.

When you practise Qigong, you can focus on your inner self, without having to think about moving your arms and legs. This concentration on mental imaging and relaxation will also improve your Tai Chi.

About Arthritis

The word arthritis means, literally, inflammation of the joint but, in general, refers to a range of conditions affecting joints, muscles, bone and connective tissue. Sometimes the overall term *musculoskeletal condition* is used. Over 100 different forms of arthritis and other musculoskeletal conditions affect about 25% of the Australian population. Although there is a considerable range of variation in different people's experience of arthritis, the most common feature is pain. People with arthritis usually have to modify, to a greater or lesser extent, their normal lifestyles because of pain, limited mobility, reduced joint function and the unpredictability of the condition. Many forms of arthritis are long-term, chronic conditions. Good treatment is aimed at developing an effective management program.

Osteoarthritis is the most common type of arthritis. It is a degenerative condition of the cartilage that covers the ends of the bones and becomes more prevalent with age.

Rheumatoid Arthritis can develop at any age, most often in the 25-50 year old age group, and is three times more common in females than males. It affects the whole body with painful inflammation and swelling of the joints.

An arthritis management program will vary from one person to another. Your medical practitioner, other health professionals and the Arthritis Foundation are all helpful sources of information and support. The more you learn about your arthritis and the various forms of therapy available, the better you are able to work with your health practitioners to develop an effective management plan. Some of things you might need to consider are exercise, medication, pain management techniques, complementary medicine, nutrition, aids for daily living, joint protection and surgery.

How Tai Chi Helps Arthritis

Exercise is known to benefit most aspects of health and is recognised as an essential part of the management of arthritis. Pain, stiffness, and fear of further damage can deter people with arthritis from exercising. However, without regular exercise, joints become stiffer and more painful, muscles lose strength, bones weaken, stamina diminishes, blood circulation slows, and the risk of heart disease, high blood pressure and diabetes increases.

The answer is to develop an exercise program that is safe and effective for your own condition and capabilities. Tai Chi is an ideal choice since it involves a variety of movements that work on all aspects of your fitness and well-being.

Flexibility exercises work on how far you can move your joints (range-of-motion) and how easily they move. Stiff joints are difficult and painful to move. Tai Chi gently moves all the joints, muscles and tendons of the body.

Strengthening exercises maintain and increase muscle strength. With strong muscles to support them, your joints are more stable and protected from injury. The slow, controlled movements of Tai Chi build up muscle strength in your legs, arms and trunk.

Stamina or **cardiovascular** exercises increase the work of your heart and lungs, thereby improving the blood and oxygen supply circulating through your body. Regular practice of Tai Chi improves cardiovascular fitness.

Posture exercises correctly align your spine and open your lungs. Tai Chi focuses on an upright posture throughout.

Coordination and **balance** exercises help integrate the way your body moves in everyday activities. With good balance and coordination, you can perform tasks more efficiently and are less likely to fall. Tai Chi incorporates simultaneous arm and leg movements to challenge your coordination and balance.

Mind-body techniques show how the power of the mind can help heal the body. Feelings of stress and depression are common with arthritis. Tai Chi integrates mind and body, using the conscious mind to direct the internal force that, in turn, directs each movement. When practising Tai Chi, you focus on the performance of each movement. The mental training of Tai Chi enhances the clarity of your mind, releases stress and uplifts your mood.

According to Chinese medicine, arthritis is the result of the weak and sluggish flow of Qi through the meridians. The slow and gentle movements of Tai Chi open up your energy channels and the rhythmic movements of the muscles, joints and spine pump energy through the whole body. Tai Chi is one of the most effective exercises for cultivating Qi.

In a randomized controlled study published by the Journal of Rheumatology Sept 2003, a group of women with osteoarthritis (OA) practised tai chi for 12 weeks. Compared to a control group, who received only standard treatment, the tai chi group reported significantly less pain and fewer difficulties in carrying out their daily activities, as well as improved balance. The researchers from the Korean National University concluded that Tai Chi for Arthritis is a safe and effective form of exercise for older people with OA.

About the Tai Chi for Arthritis Program

Nearly 30 years ago, Dr. Paul Lam, then a young medical graduate, realised he was experiencing the early signs of osteoarthritis. He decided to take up Tai Chi, a traditional Chinese therapy recognised for its many health benefits, including the improvement of arthritis. Dr. Lam has since become so proficient at Tai Chi that he won a gold medal in an international competition (Beijing, China, 1993).

In 1997, Dr. Lam realised he wanted to share his experience of the benefits of Tai Chi with other people with arthritis. Working with a group of Tai Chi and medical experts, he developed the Twelve-Movement *Tai Chi for Arthritis Program.*

The *Sun style* (pronounced Soong), one of the four major recognised styles, was chosen by Dr Lam as being particularly effective for people with arthritis since it features:

- agile steps, with many forward and backward movements. This

improves flexibility.
- powerful Qigong exercises to improve relaxation and facilitate healing.
- higher stances, making it easier for beginners and older people to learn and practise.

The program is easy, safe and effectively relieves pain and improves quality of life. It is supported by the Arthritis Foundation of Australia, Arthritis Care of UK and adapted by the Arthritis Foundation of USA.

Dr. Lam is a family physician in Sydney, Australia and regularly travels worldwide to teach the program.

Tai Chi Practice

The benefits of Tai Chi come with ongoing practice. By establishing good habits, each practice session will be an enjoyable, relaxing and satisfying experience. Exercising with arthritis is not always easy and you need to find a balance between doing too much and giving up too easily. The following guidelines will help you decide when and where, how much, how to progress, and how to avoid problems with your arthritis.

1. Set up a regular practice time, so your Tai Chi practice becomes a part of your daily routine.
2. Avoid practising in a place that is too hot, too cold or is windy.
3. Practise in an area that is clear of obstacles, has a non-slippery surface and no loose mats.
4. Wear loose, comfortable clothing and flat, well-fitting shoes.
5. Do not practise when you are very hungry, immediately after a meal, or when you are very upset.
6. Begin your session with the Warm Up Exercises and end with the Wind Down Exercises. These help prevent pain and stiffness.
7. Continue your session only for as long as you feel comfortable. Listen to your body and rest when you start feeling tired, in pain, or lose concentration.
8. Gradually build up the length and number of practice sessions, aiming for about 10-20 minutes on most days. A simple indication of how long to practise initially is the length of time you can walk comfortably at a steady pace. If you can practise for just 10 minutes in one session, you can do another 10 minutes after you have rested.

9. Arrange to practise with someone else, especially when you are feeling unmotivated.

10. Be gentle with yourself and stay within your comfort range for level of exertion and length of practice session. Some days you will be able to do more than others.

11. Don't continue doing any movement that is painful or causes you discomfort. If you experience chest pains, shortness of breath or dizziness, or if additional pain in your joints persists, contact your doctor.

12. Take extra care to move with awareness and caution when you are having a flare up.

13. Talk to your instructor about any movements you are finding difficult or uncomfortable.

14. Do all movements slowly, continuously and smoothly. As you become more familiar with the movements, they will start to flow more easily and feel more graceful.

15. Stand up between movements if your knees become stiff or painful in the bent position. As your muscles become stronger you will be able to stay comfortably in the squatting position for longer.

16. Breathe slowly, naturally and easily. As you become more familiar with the movements, try to coordinate them with your breathing, as instructed. Return to your natural breathing, if you find this feel too forced.

17. Use the minimum effort necessary to do the movements. This will help you cultivate Qi and to relax.

18. Imagine the air around you is slightly dense and you are gently pressing against this resistance as you move. This helps cultivate Qi.

19. Practise the Qigong exercise at any time to help you relax.

Following the Instructions

It is assumed you are learning all the movements of the *Tai Chi for Arthritis Program* from an instructor in a class, or by studying Dr. Paul Lam's *Tai Chi for Arthritis* instructional video. This *Tai Chi for Arthritis Handbook* gives you an outline of the complete *Tai Chi for Arthritis Program* to assist you in your practice. It is not intended to provide detail instructions. If you are unclear about a movement, speak with your instructor.

The easiest way to learn a complete movement is to first divide it into smaller sections, corresponding to the stages shown in the photographs. Practise the first section until you feel confident then add the next one. Start again from the beginning, practising section one plus section two. When you are ready, gradually add the next section. Always return to the constant starting point.

The description of the *Tai Chi for Arthritis Program* is divided into two sections: the *6 Basic Movements* and the *6 Advanced Movements*. At the beginning of each section, the names of each of the movements are listed. This may be enough to remind you of what comes next. If you need further guidance, the movements are shown more fully in the following pages.

Each movement is shown with photographs of Dr. Paul Lam in key positions with accompanying brief instructions. When you look at the photographs, imagine you are looking at Dr. Lam as though he is your instructor facing you in class and showing you a mirror image of what you are doing. The written instructions tell you whether you are using your right or left arm or leg for the movement.

Tai Chi in the Park organised by Arthritis Foundation of Victoria as a part of the year 2000 Arthritis Week activities.

WARM UP EXERCISES

These gentle Warm Up Exercises help prepare your body and focus your mind before you begin your Tai Chi practice. The Wind Down Exercises help release muscle tension and prevent stiffness.

- Move through the exercises slowly and gently, with attention to how your body is responding. Ease off if you feel any pain.
- Respect your comfort range and adapt each exercise to your individual situation. If you have any discomfort or doubt about a movement, consult your instructor, doctor or physiotherapist.
- Hold each stretch for 10-15 seconds to allow time for your muscles to relax.
- Repeat each stretch 3-5 times.
- Stretch to about 80% of your full range for the first stretch, gradually increasing the amount of stretch each time.

The Warm Up

Begin your Tai Chi practice session by walking around for a minute or two, letting go of everyday thoughts and starting to think about your Tai Chi movements.

1. **The Right Stance**
   Stand upright but relaxed. Imagine your body is aligned along an invisible string passing in a line with your ears, shoulders, hips and heels. Your chin is tucked in slightly and your eyes are focused straight ahead.
2. **Beginning Breath**
   Breathe in slowly and fully, lifting both arms up gently. Breathe out, slowly lowering arms.
3. **Head Tuck**
   With your chin tucked in, bend your head forwards. Slowly lift it to look straight ahead.

4. **Head Side Bend**
   With your chin tucked in, bend your head over sideways, ear towards your shoulder. Repeat on the other side.

5. **Head Turn**
   With your chin tucked in, turn gently to look over each shoulder.

6. **Spinal Stretch**
   Push one palm upwards to the ceiling, the other downwards to the floor. Change.

7. **Leg Back**
   With your weight on one leg, gently push the other foot backwards until your toes rest on the floor, 10-20 cm. behind the front foot.

8. **Leg Side Lift**
   Lift one leg out sideways, hold and lower. Repeat on the other side. Hold on to some support if necessary.

9. **Knee Stretch**
   Stand on one leg with the other leg lifted in front. Slowly straighten the knee, bringing the lower leg forwards, then bend the knee, bringing the lower leg backwards. Alternatively, you can touch forwards with the heel and backwards with the toe. Hold on to some support if necessary.

10. **Walk Around**
    • clenching and stretching fingers
    • with palms facing each other, bend at the wrists upward gently and then let them drop naturally downward.

11. **Shake Out**
    Gently shake both hands and each foot.

REVISED WARM UP EXERCISES

The revised warm up exercises are based on my later program, Tai Chi for Beginners.

Both sets of warm up exercises are similar and you can chose to do either. However, the revised warm up exercises are more systematic, easier to remember and incorporate more tai chi principles,

Step 1. One Warm Up Exercise

These special Tai Chi warm up and stretching exercises are designed to prepare you to practice Tai Chi by tuning up your muscles and helping you focus.

Shake your feet and hands between every few movements.

Always do the easy alternative first. Do the more difficult movements only when you're comfortable with them. Use a chair or wall to give yourself support whenever you need it.

Warm Up Exercise:
Walk around slowly, clenching and unclenching your hands for 1-2 minutes.

Step 2. Two Stretching Exercises

We will do two stretches for each part of the body, starting from the top, down.

Do each stretch 3-5 times, ensuring that you stretch both left and right sides. It doesn't matter which side you stretch first.

Use a chair or the wall for support if you have any difficulty balancing.

Neck

1a. **Head down** - Bring hands up slowly, breathing in.

2a. **Turn Head** - Left hand up, right hand down, looking at your palm.

1b. Bring palms towards your chest and push chin gently in.

2b. Move left hand to the left, turn head to the left.

1c. Push hands out and then bring hands down, bending neck slowly.

Shoulders

1. **Shoulder Roll** - Roll shoulders gently forward and then backward.

2a. **Gathering Qi** - Bring hands up in a curve, breathing in

2b. Press down gently, breathing out.

Spine

1a. **Spine Stretch** - Hands in front, as though you are carrying a large beach ball.

1b. Stretch one hand up, push the other hand down, breathing out when stretched.

Hip

2a. **Spine Turn** - Hands in front, as though you are carrying a large beach ball.

1a. **Forward Stretch** - Step forward on left heel, push both hands back to help balance.

1b. Step back on toes, stretch hands forward.

2b. Knees slightly bent, turn waist gently to one side and then change hands to turn to the other side.

2. **Side Stretch** - Push hands to the side as though you are pushing a wall and stretch the opposite foot sideways.

Knees

2a. **Step Forward** - Bend knees and step forward on the heel.

1a. **Kick** - Fists resting at both sides of the hip with palms side up.

2b. Move forward and punch out with opposite fist. Step back and do the other side.

1b. Kick out gently. Punch out the opposite fist. Step down and do the other side.

Ankles

1a. **Tapping** - Tap foot with heel.

1b. Tap foot with toes

2. **Rotation** - Lift up the heel and gently rotate foot in one direction three times and then the other direction three times.

6 BASIC MOVEMENTS

1. Commencing Movement

2. Opening & Closing Hands

3. Single Whip

4. Waving Hands in the Clouds

5. Opening & Closing Hands

6. Closing Movement

Starting Position

Stand with your body upright but relaxed: feet slightly apart, knees loose, eyes looking forward, chin tucked in, shoulders relaxed.

Cleanse your mind.

1. Commencing Movement

Positions are represented as a mirror image

a) Breathing in, lift both arms.

b) Breathing out, lower arms and bend knees slightly.

c) Lift arms, elbows bent. Step forward with left heel.

d) Pushing hands forward, bring right foot in line with left.

2. Opening & Closing Hands

a) Bring hands in to front of chest.

b) Breathing in, open hands.

c) Breathing out, push hands in towards each other.

3. **Single Whip**

Positions are represented as a mirror
image

a) Step to right and slightly forward
with right heel.

b) Shifting weight onto right leg, push
palms forward.

c) Turn palms to face forward and extend arms outwards, watching left hand.

4. Waving Hands in the Cloud

Positions are represented as a mirror image

a) Bring right hand toward left elbow, right foot in line with the left.

b) Stepping sideways with right foot, move right hand upwards, left downwards.

d) Move right hand down, left hand up.

c) Bringing left foot closer, turn upper body and arms to right.

e) Turn upper body and arms to the left.

Second Waving Hands

Positions are represented as a mirror image

c) Move right hand down, left hand up.

a) Stepping out with right foot, move right hand upwards, left downwards.

d) Turn upper body and arms to the left.

b) Bring left foot in, and turn upper body and arms to the right.

Third Waving Hands

c) Move right hand down, left hand up.

a) Stepping out with right foot, move right hand upwards, left downwards.

d) Turn upper body and arms to the left.

b) Bring left foot in, and turn upper body and arms to the right.

5. Opening & Closing Hands

b) Breathing in, open hands.

a) Bring hands to front of chest.

c) Breathing out, push hands towards each other.

6. Closing Movement

a) Stretch both hands forward.

b) Straightening knees and breathing out, slowly lower arms.

6 ADVANCED MOVEMENTS

Follow-on Position

Follow-on Position
Follow on from the Basic Movement 5,
Opening & Closing Hands.

6. **Brush Knee**

Positions are represented as a mirror image

a) Watch right hand stretch out, and bring left hand towards right elbow.

b) Stepping left foot to side, stretch up with right hand, push down with left.

c) Shifting weight onto left foot, turn body to left, moving left hand across knee and right towards the ear.

d) Pushing forward with right hand, move right foot in.

7. Playing the Lute

Positions are represented as a mirror
image

a) Turning both palms inwards, stretch
forward with right hand and step
backwards with right foot.

b) With weight on right foot and
drawing left foot back, move right
hand back, left hand forward.

8. Parry & Punch

Positions are represented as a mirror image

a) Placing left foot out, turn right palm upwards, left palm down.

b) Transferring weight forwards to left foot, push right palm forward and bring left palm back.

8. **Parry & Punch** *(continued)*

Positions are represented as a mirror
image

c) Stepping forward with right foot,
turn palms over, right down, left up.

d) Transferring weight forward, move
hands, right backwards, left forwards.

e) Stepping forward with left foot, make fists and bring right hand toward hip.

f) Bringing right foot in slightly, punch forward with right fist over left wrist.

9. **Block & Close**

Positions are represented as a mirror image

a) Stepping back with right foot, stretch both hands forward.

b) Transferring weight to back foot, draw both hands backward.

10. **Pushing the Mountain**

Stepping forwards onto left foot, push
both palms forward, stepping right
foot forward.

11. Opening & Closing Hands

b) Breathing in, open hands.

a) Moving right heel and ball of left foot inward, turn to face front. Bring hands to front of chest.

c) Breathing out, press hands closer

12. **Closing Movement**

a) Stretch both hands forward.

b) Straightening knees and breathing out, slowly lower arms.

QIGONG EXERCISE

a) Stand with your body upright but relaxed: feet slightly apart, knees relaxed, eyes looking forward, chin tucked in, shoulders relaxed.

Cleanse your mind.

b) Bending knees, bring hands to front of chest.

c) Breathing in, open hands, air travelling gently through your nose and windpipe and filling your lungs and abdomen. Imagine a gentle magnetic force between your palms. Gently straighten your knees if necessary

d) Breathing out, push hands towards each other, air being expelled from abdomen and lungs, through windpipe and nose.

Imagine pushing against a gentle resistance.

Bend your knees slightly if you have straightened them at the previous movement.

e) Continue opening and closing hands several times, starting with three repeats (for three weeks), increasing to six, then nine times.

Complete the exercise by stretching hands forward.

f) Return to original position, lowering arms and staightening knees.

Yin and **Yang** are polar opposites of each other. There is a bit of yin inside yang and a bit of yang inside yin; both sides complement each other and together form a perfect whole. Yin and yang are found in all things in life and those which are perfectly balanced and in harmony will be at peace. Thus, a perfectly harmonised person will show this balance and completeness through tranquillity and peacefulness of mind.

WIND DOWN EXERCISES

1. **Thigh Punch**
   Lift one knee and gently punch the top of the thigh. This exercise can be done sitting.
2. **Walk with Hands**
   Walk around the room clenching and stretching your fingers.
3. **Clench and Release**
   Stand on your toes (if this is comfortable) with fists clenched and body tight. Drop down off your toes, relaxing your fists and body.
4. **Arm Circles**
   Breathe in, lifting both arms in a curve upwards. Breathe out, as you press both arms in a curve outward and down.
5. **Shake Out**
   Gently shake both hands and each foot.

MORE ABOUT TAI CHI

Six Tai Chi Principles for Beginners

Tai chi contains essential principles, all of which are fundamental and similar in the different styles. When you concentrate on the essential, you speed up your progress, and you improve, no matter what style you are practising. Don't worry about the minor details, focus your practise on these principles.

In my workshops and videos, I mention these essential principles. Here, I have converted them into simple, easy to understand terms.

1. Make your movements slow, even and continuous, maintaining the same speed throughout. In other words, control your movements.

2. Move as though there is a gentle resistance. Imagine that the air around you is dense and you have to move against this dense air. This will help you to cultivate your inner force.

3. Be aware of your weight transference. First, centre yourself, then control your balance, keeping your body alignment, and when you move backwards, forwards or sideways, touch down first, then gradually and consciously transfer your weight forward or backward.

4. Body alignment. Be sure you keep your body in an upright position.

5. Loosening the joints. It is important to do Tai Chi movements in a relaxed manner but relaxation does not mean that your muscles go floppy, you should be stretching and loosening. Try to consciously gently stretch most joints from within, almost like an internal expansion of the joints.

6. Mental focus. Be sure not to let your mind distract you from what you are doing and focus on your movements so that your internal and external are well integrated.

The Ten Essential Points

The lifelong journey into the full extent of the art of Tai Chi starts as you begin to incorporate its essential principles for body, posture and mind into your practice. The following Ten Essential Points are based on the writings of Yang Cheng-Fu, a prominent figure in the 1930s, and now known as the father of modern Tai Chi. These principles provide a focus that will keep your Tai Chi practice fresh, interesting and challenging. Some of the concepts may be difficult to understand at first but, as you think about them when you practise, they will become clearer and you will attain a higher level of Tai Chi. The classics say Tai Chi is "like a river, rolling on unceasingly"; it looks smooth and tranquil on the outside but there is immense power within.

1. **Keep the head upright**
    Imagine your head is suspended from above by a string. Stiffness in the neck will impede the free flow of Qi. Tuck your chin in slightly and visualise the Qi reaching the top of your head.

2. **Depress (relax) the chest and raise the upper back**
    Relaxing the chest muscles allows the Qi to sink to the Dan-tian. By raising your upper back (without hunching or stiffening) and suspending your head from an imaginary string, your lower body settles toward the ground and your upper body is stretched upwards; Qi is able to reach your back.

3. **Loosen (relax) the waist**
    The waist is the commander of the body, controlling the change from substantial to insubstantial (solid to empty). When your waist is loose, your legs will have power and your body will be firm and stable. To loosen your waist, gently stretch your hips outward and concentrate on relaxing the area of the Dan-tian, directing the Qi downwards with your out-breath.

4. **Distinguish between substantial and insubstantial**
    When you are able to distinguish between substantial and insubstantial (solid and empty) your movements become light and nimble. Touch your foot down lightly, like a cat. Touch down with your heel first as you go forward and your toe as you go backward, then consciously and gradually transfer your weight.

5. **Sink (relax) the shoulders and elbows**
    If your shoulders are tense, the Qi moving towards your shoulders will not flow through to the Dan-tian. Your movements will show a deficiency of inner strength and lack of continuity. To relax the shoulders and elbows, imagine elongating your shoulder joints and stretch the points of your elbows downwards.

6. **Use your will (mind) and not your force**
   By relaxing the body and focusing just on the movement, your movements will be light and nimble, exactly as your mind directs.

7. **Coordinate the upper and lower body movements**
   The Tai Chi classics say, "motion should be rooted in the feet, released through the legs, controlled by the waist, and manifested by the hands through the shoulders and arms". The whole body acts as an integrated unit. When there is lack of coordination, the movement appears disjointed and lacks strength. Focus on coordinating your arm and leg movements so they reach their designated positions at the same time.

8. **Unify (coordinate) internal and external movements**
   The internal is the inner force, mind and spirit; the external includes the movements, posture and body. When you are in total focus, your mind and spirit will unite with the external movements. This is difficult to achieve all the time but with committed practice you will take small steps towards it.

9. **Maintain absolute continuity of movement**
   The movements of Tai Chi are continuous and without interruption. In Tai Chi every movement is a curve or circle, with no beginning or end. When you practise, think of this circular path and control the movements so that they are slow, even and continuous. Gradually your inner force will develop and will become unceasing.

10. **Seek stillness (serenity in movement)**
    Though active externally, the Tai Chi practitioner is calm internally. Cleanse your mind and concentrate on the slowness and evenness of your movements with your breathing long and deep, thus enabling the Qi to sink to the Dan-tian.

Reverse Direction

Once you are familiar with the 12 movements of Tai Chi for Arthritis, you can extend your practice by adding the reverse direction of the set. As well as giving you an extra challenge, it helps balance right and left.

The reverse of the 12 movements follows on from the 6 Basic and the 6 Advanced Movements.

6 Basic Movements
1. Commencing Movement
2. Opening and Closing Hands
3. Single Whip *(right)*
4. Waving Hands in the Cloud *(right)*
5. Opening and Closing Hands
6. Closing Movement

6 Advanced Movements
6. Brush Knee *(left)*
7. Playing the Lute *(left hand in front)*
8. Parry and Punch
9. Block and Close
10. Pushing the Mountain
11. Opening and Closing Hands
12. Closing Movement

To do the reverse, follow on from Movement 11.
12. Single Whip *(left)*
13. Waving Hands in the Cloud *(left)*
14. Opening and Closing Hands
15. Brush Knee *(right)*
16. Playing the Lute *(right hand in front)*
17. Parry and Punch
18. Block and Close
19. Pushing the Mountain
20. Opening and Closing Hands
21. Closing Movement

Tai Chi for Arthritis Part 2 is now available. See page 55 for details

MORE ABOUT ARTHRITIS

Your local Arthritis Foundation can provide more information about arthritis and its management (much of the information is provided free-of-charge) and put you in contact with their many services (membership, seminars, courses, classes and support groups)

Australia

Arthritis Foundation of Australia
GPO Box 121, Sydney, NSW 2001
Ph: (02) 9552 6085
Fax: (02) 9552 6078
www.arthritisfoundation.com.au

Arthritis Foundation of New South Wales
Locked Bag 16,
North Parramatta, NSW 2151
Ph: (02) 9683 1622
Fax: (02) 9683 1633
www.arthritisnsw.org.au

Arthritis Foundation of Victoria
PO Box 130, Caulfield South, VIC 3162
Ph: (03) 8531 8000; 1800 011 141
Fax: (03) 9530 0228
www.arthritisvic.org.au

Arthritis Foundation of Queensland
PO Box 2121, Windsor, QLD 4030
Ph: (07) 3857 4200
Fax: (07) 3857 4099
www.arthritis.org.au

Arthritis Foundation of South Australia
Unit 1, 202 Glen Osmond Rd,
Fullerton, SA 5063
Ph: (08) 8379 5711
Fax: (08) 8379 5707

Arthritis Foundation of Western Australia
PO Box 34, Wembley, WA 6014
Ph: (08) 9388 2199
Fax: (08) 9388 4488
www.arthritiswa.org.au/

Arthritis Foundation of the ACT
PO Box 4017, Weston Creek, ACT 2611
Ph: (02) 6288 4244
Fax: (02) 6288 4277

Arthritis Foundation of Tasmania
Box 30 McDougall Building, Ellerslie
Rd, Battery Point, TAS 7004
Ph: (03) 6224 4755
Fax: (03) 6223 7318
www.arthritistasmania.com.au

Arthritis Foundation of the NT
PO Box 452, Nightcliff, NT 0814
Ph: (08) 8948 5232
Fax: (08) 8948 5234
www.aont.org.au

U.S.A.

Arthritis Foundation (USA)
PO Box 7669
Atlanta, GA 30357-0669 USA
Ph: 1800 283 7800
www.arthritis.org

Canada

Arthritis Society
393 University Avenue, Suite 1700
Toronto, Ontario, M5G 1E6 CANADA
Ph: 416 979 7228
Fax: 416 979 8366
www.arthritis.ca

New Zealand

Arthritis Foundation of New Zealand
PO Box 10020,
Wellington NEW ZEALAND
Ph: 4721 427
Fax: 4727 066
www.arthritis.org.nz

United Kingdom

Arthritis Care
18 Stephenson Way
London NW1 2HD ENGLAND
Ph: 020 7380 6500
Fax: 020 7380 6505
www.arthritiscare.org.uk

Tai Chi videos , DVD's & other products

Dr Paul Lam's team of experts has produced several series of Tai Chi videos for students of varying interests and levels. The Self-Teaching Beginner Series is designed to improve your health and lifestyle. The Advanced, Self-Defence and Demonstration Series enable you to expand your skills.

Self-Teaching Beginner Series

- *Tai Chi for Arthritis* - *80 mins.*
- *Also in DVD with a choice of 4 languages*
- *Handbook (60 pages)*
- *Talking CD*

Tai Chi has been known in China for centuries as an effective therapy for arthritis. Dr. Lam's team of Tai Chi and medical experts created this simple and safe program especially for people with arthritis. You can learn from the video or a class.

The handbook is light, stays open in one position and is complementary to the video or a class. The program is supported by the Arthritis Foundation of Australia.

The Talking CD is an invaluable assistant to instructors or learners and contains 10 soundtracks at learning and practicing paces.

- *Tai Chi for Arthritis - Part 2 - 65 mins*
  - Also in DVD

This more challenging sequel is designed for people who have completed the original *12-Movement*. It starts with updated warm-up and wind-down exercises, continues with the reverse side of the *12-Movement* and concludes with the step-by-step instructions of the *9-Movement*. You will learn new perspective and gain deeper understanding in Tai Chi.

- *Overcoming Arthritis Book*
  - 144 pages & 165 photos

A practical guide for a more active, pain-free life, this book features Dr Paul Lam's innovative Tai Chi for Arthritis program to relieve symptoms and promote better health. It includes descriptions of various types of arthritis and outlines both conventional and alternative treatment from the latest drug to dietary supplements and meditation.

- *Tai Chi for Beginners - 90 mins*
  - Also in DVD
  - Handbook (60 pages)

Tai Chi is one of the most effective ways to improve health, fitness and relaxation. Dr. Lam has developed an innovative *Step 1-2-3* method to make learning easy and enjoyable for beginners. You will learn a simple set of Yang style Tai Chi for better health and acquire a solid foundation for progression.

The handbook is designed to make learning and practicing easier when used together with the video or class instructions.

- **Tai Chi for Older Adults (Tai Chi for Over 55)** - *110 mins*
This easy-to-follow authentic Yang style Tai Chi form is specifically designed for older adults to improve fitness, flexibility, relaxation and mental concentration. It includes a sitting Qigong for relaxation.

- **Qigong for Health** - *60 mins*
  - *Also in DVD*
Qigong uses gentle breathing and movement to balance the flow of Qi (the vital life energy inside the body), promoting mental and physical health. The *5 Element Qigong* is easy to learn and a part of Tai Chi. The video includes a demonstration of the *Sun Style 73* Tai Chi Forms by Dr Lam.

- **Tai Chi for Young People** - *70 mins*
This challenging, faster-paced program, based on the *42 International Competition Forms*, is designed for young people to improve concentration and fitness and is complementary to other sporting activities.

- **Tai Chi for Diabetes** - *90 mins*
  - *Also in DVD*
Designed to help prevent and improve the control of diabetes by gently increasing physical activities, cellular uptake of glucose and relaxation. It also enhances Qi (life energy), which helps to control diabetes according to traditional Chinese medicine. The program includes a general introduction, warm up and cooling down exercises, Qigong, basic and advanced sets. It is supported by Diabetes Australia and is also suitable to improve health and wellbeing for almost anyone.

- **Tai Chi for Back Pain** - *90 mins*
  - *Also in DVD*
Based on the 12-movement Tai Chi for Arthritis, this program is designed to relieve back pain, restore your ability to work and play, improve health and quality of life, also suitable for people in wheelchairs and with other chronic conditions.

- **Tai Chi for Health - The 6 Forms**
  - *Also in DVD*
  - *100 mins*
  - *English & Chinese (Cantonese) versions available*
Based on the 24 Forms, this program is designed for beginners wanting to gain maximum health benefits in minimum time. It also includes the 3-in-1 Qigong exercise for relaxation.

- **Tai Chi Anywhere** - *80 mins*

This adaptable program can improve health and relaxation almost anywhere, anytime. Based on Sun Style, it is designed for busy people to practise for varying time periods. It can be practiced sitting or standing and in limited space.

Intermediate Series

- **24 Forms** - *120 mins*
  - *Also in DVD*
  - *English & Chinese (Cantonese) versions available*

This is a detailed instructional video of the world's most popular Tai Chi Forms. Based on Yang Style, it is suitable for people of almost any level of physical fitness and age. It includes instructions for an additional 6 Qigong exercises and 7 single movements.

- **Tai Chi Sword - The 32 Forms**
  - *95 mins*

The sword is an extension of the essential principles of Tai Chi. This detailed instructional video is the best-known Sword Forms based on Yang Style and includes a demonstration of the Combined 48 Forms.

- **Sun Style 73 Forms** - *95 mins*
  - *Also in DVD*

This detailed instructional video includes a demonstration of the set by its creator, Professor Men Hui Feng. Sun Style is characterised by its powerful Qigong elements, agile steps and flowing movements.

Advanced Series

- **The Combined 42 Forms** - *75 mins*

Containing the essential principles of the four major Tai Chi Styles, these are the official Forms used in major international competitions. The set is divided into two volumes, they can be studied independently or as a whole. The creator of the 42 Forms, Professor Men Hui Feng, provided technical advice for the video.

- **The Combined 42 Sword Forms**
  - *95 mins*

Created to complement the Combined 42 Forms, the Sword is a beautiful extension of the essential principles of Tai Chi. This video teaches the official Forms for major competitions, with its creator, Professor Kan Gui Xiang, providing technical advice.

- **The 36 Forms Video & Book**
  - *100 mins (video) ; 189 pages (book)*
  Created by Prof. Kan Gui Xiang, the 36 Forms is the best known expression of the more vigorous Chen Style with its emphasis on combat techniques. It features a demonstration of the set by the creator herself. The book, written by Prof. Kan and Dr Lam, contains 400 photos of Prof. Kan performing the set.

- **The 56 Chen Style Competition Forms** - *90 mins*
  Created by Prof. Kan Gui Xiang, the 56 Forms represents the essential principles from the Chen Style's two classical routines. This difficult set is recommended for advanced practitioners. The video features a demonstration of the set by the creator herself.

- **Chen Style Self-Defense Applications**
  - *Part I 60 mins, Part II 95 mins*
  Part I contains the first 10 of the Chen Style 32 Forms, including instructions, analysis and demonstration of its self-defense applications at different angles and varying speeds. Part II contains the last 22 Forms and a demonstration of the 32 Forms Cannon Fist.

Demonstrational Series

- **The 3 Most Popular Forms** - *50 mins*
  This video contains the 3 most popular sets of Forms in the world today - the 24 Forms, the 32 Sword Forms and the Combined 42 Competition Forms. Dr Lam demonstrates them in the front on and back on views.

- **The Chen Style Collection**
  - *4 Outstanding Sets - 60 mins*
  Each set has its own individual characteristics and points of interest. The most popular, the official competition and the specialised self-defense Forms of Chen Style are shown. The video features the creators of these Forms, Prof Kan and Master Wu.

Other Products

- **Tai Chi Music CD**
  The four beautiful and relaxing pieces of music are especially composed to enhance Tai Chi practise and performance, also suitable for relaxation. Each piece correlates to a major Tai Chi style.

- **Exercise Danger Book**
  30 exercises to avoid and 100 safer and more effective alternatives illustrated with pictures. A must-read book for all Tai Chi and exercise instructors.

As we are continually updating our range of products please check our website for the latest additions www.taichiproductions.com

Tai Chi Workshops

Dr Lam and his team conduct workshops which are designed to be positive, enjoyable and interactive.

1. The two-day *Tai Chi for Arthritis* **Instructors' Training Workshop.**
You will learn how to teach this program safely and at the same time learn or improve your level of Tai Chi. Many arthritis foundations support this program, which is shown by medical studies to be safe and effective.

2. The two-day *Tai Chi for Diabetes* **Instructors' Training Workshop.**
Based on Sun and Yang style tai chi, Tai Chi for Diabetes is designed to prevent and improve the management of diabetes. With a knowledge of this program you will be able to help those who have diabetes.

3. The two-day *Tai Chi for Back Pain* **Instructors' Training Workshop.**
This program, based on modern medical findings and the Tai Chi for Arthritis program, is designed to relieve back pain and improve health. It is suitable for people in wheelchairs and with cronic illnesses. To attend this workshop, Participants must be certified Tai Chi for Arthritis Instructors.

4. The Annual January One-Week Workshop in Sydney
This workshop offers an extensive choice of classes with optional live-in accommodation.

N.B.

For any enquiries regarding workshops or products please contact:

East Acton Publishing
6 Fisher Place, Narwee NSW 2209
Australia
Telephone: 9533 6511
                          9533 6150
Facsimile: 9534 4311

Email:
service@taichiproductions.com
Web Site:
www.taichiproductions.com